NELL GWYN

NELL GWYN

by

Roy MacGregor-Hastie

ROBERT HALE · LONDON

ISBN 0 7090 3099 1

Robert Hale Limited
Clerkenwell House
Clerkenwell Green
London EC1R 0HT

British Library Cataloguing in Publication Data

MacGregor-Hastie, Roy
  Nell Gwyn.
  1. Gwyn, Nell   2. Actors—Great Britain
  —Biography   3. Great Britain—Kings
  and rulers—Mistresses—Biography
  I. Title
  941.06'6'0924   DA447.G9

Photoset in North Wales in Ehrhardt by
Derek Doyle & Associates, Mold, Clwyd.
Printed in Great Britain by
St Edmundsbury Press Ltd, Bury St Edmunds, Suffolk.
Bound by WBC Bookbinders Limited.

Contents

Illustrations

Picture credits

The National Portrait Gallery: 1 4, 5, 7. The Queen: 2. Bodleian Library, Oxford: 3. The Army & Navy Club: 6, 9. The Denys Eyre Bowes Bequest, Chiddingstone Castle, Kent: 8. Victoria & Albert Museum: 10.

Mistress followed mistress, and the guilt of a troop of profligate women was blazoned to the world by the gift of titles and estates. The royal bastards were set among English nobles. The ducal house of Grafton springs from the King's adultery with Barbara Palmer, whom he created Duchess of Cleveland. The Dukes of St Albans owe their origin to his intrigue with Nell Gwynn, a player and courtesan. Louise de Quérouaille, a mistress sent by France to win him its interests, became Duchess of Portsmouth and ancestress of the house of Richmond. An earlier mistress, Lucy Walters, was mother of a boy he raised to the Dukedom of Monmouth and to whom the Dukes of Buccleuch trace their line.

A Short History of the English People, Green, 1895

This book is dedicated to all royal bastards, especially Nelly's.

Acknowledgements

I am grateful to many people for their help and encouragement, and especially to: M. Georges Dethan, Chef de la Division Historique, Archives et Documentation at the French Foreign Ministry, Paris; Dr Sonia Finzi Pasquali, Director of the Biblioteca Civica, Venice; Prof. Scilla Abbiati Sivazhyan of the University of Venice; the staff of the Biblioteca Civica, Florence; Mr George Hoare, Archivist and Historian, Theatre Royal, Drury Lane (Stoll Moss Archives); Canon Peter May, Newmarket; Mr Alan Bell and the Bodleian Library, Oxford; Miss D.A. Betts of Forest Heath District Council, Mildenhall; the Chelsea Libraries and Arts Service (Mr Curle); the Archives and Local History Department, Victoria Library, Westminster; the churchwardens of St Martin-in-the-Fields; Mr Stephen Nelson and the Nonsuch Antiquarian Society; Miss J. Williams, Librarian at Lincoln Cathedral; Colonel D.O. O'Reilly, Secretary of the Army and Navy Club (the Rag) which holds the priceless collection of bills, prints, warrants and Exchequer papers collected by Peter Cunningham; local history librarians at Hereford, Epsom and Tunbridge Wells, and Megan Tafner. The Duke of St Albans and the 'family historian' have been helpful in correspondence.

Restoration orthography: there was no generally received spelling at this time, so I have used as many variants as I could find, to help in cross reference; where I have chosen one, it has usually been Aubrey's.

Preface

A place known for its 'exquisite bottled beers', as the Medici heir, Prince Cosimo, recorded in his Diary. His more down-to-earth secretary, Count Magalotti, noted in his that it was possible to buy a girl, in reasonable condition, for half a crown. The food was marvellous — oysters, shrimps, cockles, mussels, lobster, gudgeon, herrings at give-away prices, beef, mutton, venison, pheasant and partridge. There were splendid parks in the capital, a green and pleasant hinterland.

There were some negative points to be made. The countryside was pleasantly furnished by Nature, not too well by Man; the monarch had a place at Newmarket 'which does not deserve to be called a king's residence'. Even in the capital, most of the houses, set close together, were insanitary. The air and the waters stank. A bubonic plague was soon to wipe out a substantial part of the population of the capital, and the timber-framed houses there would be destroyed by fire.

Nevertheless, it was a place in which to have a good time, and not expensive at that. It was Restoration England, exploding in joy after the death of Oliver Cromwell and the flight of his son and successor. The great gossips of the age, Aubrey, Pepys and Evelyn, were convinced at first of direct Divine Intervention, though they had their doubts later. A reinvigorated theatre employed Dryden, Wycherley, Etherege, Shadwell, Otway; women took women's parts on stage (and provoked a mixed reaction). The King's House (Theatre Royal, Drury Lane) and the Duke's House (Duke of York's) were places of pilgrimage for European playgoers, and accredited training schools for high-class whores. Vice was both plain and polished in an age when the Queen was barren and the King had fourteen children.

Restoration politics was an activity for the greedy and corrupt; Andrew Marvell, poet and MP for Hull, bought Members for the Dutch; the woman playwright Aphra Benn was a spy for the King in Holland; the King of France, Louis XIV, sent over an ambitious Breton noblewoman to put his point of view in the King of England's bed — she had intense competition from whores sent to promote the Irish interest, the Country Party and other associations licit and illicit. It was a time of moral relaxation and religious bigotry.

If it were possible to find a single person who summed up the age, the good and the bad, in her own person and actions, public and private, it is the real Queen of Restoration England, Nell Gwyn.

She is one of the best-loved, if not the most respectable, women in British history. Paradoxically, little is generally known about her. What was her name? Nell, Eleanor, Ellen? Gwyn, Gwine, Gwynne, Gwinn? Where was she born? London, Hereford, Oxford? All three cities have claimed her. Who was her father? Her mother? If we are sure of the date of her birth it is because, at the height of her fame, astrologers vied with each other to cast her horoscope (which is strikingly similar to that of today's actress Vanessa Redgrave). We also know when she died, though few people know that her funeral sermon was preached by a future Archbishop of Canterbury. The last upsurge of literary interest in her was fifty years ago, and as the tercentenary of her death approached, it was astonishing to find there was no biography of her in print.

Nell Gwyn was a whore. Euphemisms were found for the word in Victorian and Georgian biographies, but she would have disdained them. Shortly after she had been set up by Charles II at 79 Pall Mall, she looked out of the first-floor window and saw her coachman fighting a neighbour's footman.

'Ho,' she cried, 'what are you at?'

'He called you a whore, Mrs Nelly!'

'Well, I am a whore. Find something better to fight about.'

The reply came: 'You may not take it ill to be called a whore, but I will not be called a whore's coachman.'

She was a member of a crowded profession. Several of today's dukedoms date from skirmishes of pleasure; there were also thousands of common whores, and foreigners came to London to admire their 'black eyes, abundance of light-coloured hair and neatness'. Even the French thought things had gone a bit far in sexual licence, though John Bunyan managed to live through it and write *Pilgrim's Progress*.

Nell Gwyn was probably the most professional whore of her day. She had to be to survive as the King's favourite for eighteen years. She is an early example of total job-satisfaction and never pretended to be anyone other than a girl from Coal Yard Alley who had whored herself onto the stage, into the history of the House of Stewart, and of England. She kept herself spotlessly clean. A French ambassador was shown the underwear of which she was very proud, and was struck by its 'cleanliness, neatness and sumptuousness' in a none-too-particular age. Like all the best whores, she kept a good table and entertained lavishly. Details of this entertainment are few and far between in accounts of her life, but they are to be found in English country houses, even in the Army and Navy Club (which has one of the best portraits of her, and some of her silver). Her cellar contained fine wines from France, Italy, Portugal and Spain as well as whiskies, the gift of the first President of the Royal Society, Sir Robert Moray.

She was also vicious at times in defence of what she thought her rights, poisoning a rival, encouraging the writing of lampoons and ballads to ridicule others (I have used what I consider the best of them).

The archives of the French Foreign Ministry, the Venetian State Archives and those of the Grand Duchy of Tuscany are full of reports of the doings of what Evelyn called 'Misses, the curse of the nation'. A foreign government without an ear on important pillows had no idea what was going on in English politics, for a quarter of a century. French, Tuscan, Venetian and German diplomats eagerly sought invitations to 79 Pall Mall, where much State business was discussed at candle-lit suppers. Four French ambassadors and two Venetian chronicled Nell's life as a political hostess; one was replaced because he did virtually nothing else. She was immensely powerful and custodian of many secrets, with which the King would never have trusted her rivals. She was able to free the Duke of Buckingham from the Tower when he rashly joined Shaftesbury in an attempt to limit the King's power. The Duke of Monmouth, the King's favourite bastard, asked for her help when he fell from favour. She even procured the release of Samuel Pepys, wrongly accused of being involved in the 'Popish Plot'. The coded reports by French ambassadors in particular list the intrigues at whose centre she spun her many webs.

Before she became a political hostess and full time royal whore, she had played many other roles, in the theatre. It is difficult to over-stress her importance here. She was anything but just a light comedienne who used the theatre to launch herself on a meretricious career. She was one of the first generation of women on the stage and rose to fame thanks to a natural talent and hard work. She was a professional actress, virtually illiterate (she had to have her parts read over to her again and again) but quick to learn and loyal to the King's House. She had a great personal following. All the most important playwrights of the day created roles for her. She was by all accounts one of the great comic actresses of all time, but she also played many serious roles.

What was the secret of her success, on and off stage? The best portrait of her in London (by Verelst) shows her to be petite, her breasts finely raised but not full, her waist well defined but not too narrow, her belly and thighs well rounded. There are portraits of other royal whores in the National Portrait Gallery and elsewhere which suggest she was not the most beautiful; Hortense Mancini Mazarin, Louise de Quérouaille, Jane Middleton, Moll Davis – all were more strikingly attractive. The secret of her survival was her wit, her unpretentiousness and lack of greed. She also shared with the King a love of horse-racing (they were always together at Newmarket, spring and autumn) and is in part responsible for the launching of Epsom and Newmarket as centres of a national sport. She was at the end, like Montespan and Pompadour in France, the monarch's best friend, and he treated her as such.

The men and women of the Town liked her because she never gave herself airs, and so never threatened the position of the well born; she was still a commoner when she died, though she would have liked to have been a countess, but she mothered a duke. The Queen liked her and she was on friendly terms with the Duke of York ('Dismal Jimmie', she called him). The Duke of Ormonde and the Earls of Rochester were devoted to her.

Her natural behaviour also endeared her to the mob. She loved to be surrounded by the common people and exchange coarse jokes and insults with them. At the height of her political fame and power she was 'the Protestant Whore', as important to those who would exclude the Catholic Duke of York from the succession as 'the Protestant Bastard', Monmouth. She had the vocabulary of a girl who had grown up to hawk fish and serve strong drink in brothels, and it was difficult to best her. Nell's former neighbours liked her because when she became famous she did not cast off her mother, who was a drunk, or her sister, who had married a criminal.

For one who was a friend of the most distinguished poets and playwrights of the day, she has been somewhat scurvily treated by English literature. Histories of Restoration drama, if they mention her at all, do so as a little light relief, though she created or re-created most of the important roles these histories appraise. Rochester's poem is unworthy of her, as are the anonymous ballads. There have been some full-length biographies, but very few for a subject who was at the centre of Court and cultural life for sixteen years. Most foreign State Archives do not seem to have been explored, and the largest collection of memorabilia is kept locked in a safe in Pall Mall. The Ashmolean and Bodleian Libraries have not been much consulted, and the Greater London Council Record Office as was, which has the deeds to her properties in London, seemed, in its Communist heyday, to be faintly ashamed of this daughter of the people.

Nell has always been remembered with affection, but many people do not seem sure just why they should do so. This book tries to explain.

Overture and Beginners, 1650-62

The pious mother of this flaming whore –
Maid, Punk and Bawd full sixty years and more
Dy'd drunk with Brandy in a common shore –
No matter that, nor what we were does shame us,
'Tis what we last arrive to that must Fame us,
Fam'd be the cellar then wherein this Babe
Was first brought forth to be a Monarch's Drab.

Hopgarden, Cellar to the Throne – The Life of Nelly: Anon.

One of Aubrey's many eccentric friends, Elias Ashmole – exciseman, collector of curiosities, Windsor Herald and amateur astrologer – has fixed the birth of Nell Gwyn at 6 a.m. on Saturday, 2 February 1650. During the nineteenth century, two editors of Cunningham's manuscript suggested that, as the year began officially on 25 March until 1751 (the year of the new Calendar), her birth date should be in the year 1651, but almanacs and the like did not recognize the 'official' beginning of the year, marking as it did the Christian Feast of the Annunciation. Ashmole's master in astrology, Lilly, used the present-day convention, and in his *Almanack for 1650* 2 February (Candlemas) is recorded as falling on a Saturday, and that is the year now generally accepted as the 'dawn of Nelly',

> ... a frail young sprite
> Look'd kindly when I met her;
> I shook my head perhaps, – but quite
> forgot to quite forget her
>
> (Locker-Lampson)

She was, then, an Aquarius subject, born just after the new moon, with the Sun, Mercury, Mars and the Moon all in Aquarius.

Capricorn and Venus are on the Ascendant. Venus and Neptune are prominent, and both the Sun and the Moon are well aspected to Saturn. Professional and amateur astrologers have gone on casting her horoscope, using Ashmole's chart (now moved from the Ashmolean to the Bodleian

Library). They all agree that the chart suggests sexual attractiveness, quick wit and charm, a delight in entertaining, and long-lasting popularity. (The horoscope for the same hour on 2 February 1651 paints an entirely different portrait.)

What is less certain than her birth date is where she was born (Ashmole's chart leaves a blank after '*Nata*'), who her parents and grandparents were and, indeed, how her surname should be spelt. Anthony á Wood, another of Aubrey's friends (who later fell out with him, dubbing him 'a shiftless person, roving and magotie-headed, and sometimes little better than crazed') mentions Nell Gwyn in his life of Oxford worthies. According to Wood, she was the grand-daughter of Dr Edward Gwyne or Gwynne (installed Canon of the fourth stall in Christ Church, Oxford, on 11 May 1615). His son Thomas (or James Thomas) married a Miss Eleanour [*sic*] Smith of the parish of St Thomas, Oxford, and had two daughters, Rose and Eleanour (Nell); his other son, Henry, had two sons, Matthew and Henry by a Susan (?) of Reuley. Rochester, in his *Paneygyrick On Nelly* says that Thomas died in Oxford, thus explaining why she was such a frequent visitor in later life, and why her elder son took his first titles (Baron Burford and Earl of Headington) from the county:

> From Oxford prison many did she free,
> There dy'd her father, and there glory'd she.

Frederick van Bossen, writing in 1688, confuses the issue a little by stating that Nell's father was 'Thomas Gwine, a captain of ane antient family in Wales', but Thomas's brother was doubly an Oxford man. Aubrey writes of him: 'A better instance of a squeamish, slighting, insolent fellow can't be found than in Gwin, the earl of Oxford's secretary. No reason satisfies him, but he overweenes, and cuttes some sower faces that would turn the milke in a fair ladie's breast.'

Gwyn, Gwine and Gwin are only three forms of the surname used by Nell (Ellin, Eleanor, Ellen) in dealings with her bankers, Child & Rogers (now Glyn Mills & Co., of No. 1 Fleet Street, London); she also used Gwynne and Gwinne.

Oxford historians have claimed that Nell and her father were born in Oxford, St Frideswide's, perhaps in the parish of St Clement, but there is no evidence to support this. A history of Surrey even suggests that she was born there as Margaret Symcott – 'King Charles's Eleanor Gwyn' – who left money for the distribution of '65 penny loaves every eight weeks; paid by the Chamberlain, £2 0s 0d'. John Fairburn (who edited the *Life, Amours and Exploits of Nell Gwinn*) refers to her 'retirement from public life and the stage (as Lady Simcock)'. There is no other mention of a Surrey connection.

The Dictionary of National Biography (W.P. Courtney) says simply: 'Historians of Hereford accept the tradition that she was born in a house in

Pipe Well Lane, Hereford, since called Gwyn Street. This account is said to be confirmed by a slab in the cathedral, of which James Beauclerk, her descendant, was bishop from 1746 to 1787.' David Garrick, who certainly was born in Hereford and was a contemporary of Nell's grandson, the bishop, believed in the story, retold in the *Handbook to Hereford* (1856): 'Branching eastward, at the lowest point of Bridge Street, is a narrow thoroughfare, formally called Pipewell Street and afterwards Pipewell Lane, and now designated Gwynne Street, from the circumstance of its being the birthplace of the celebrated Nell Gwynne. There seems to be some doubt as to whether the exact house was not taken down some years ago; but a building at the rear of the Royal Oak Inn is usually pointed out as the place.' The building, a cottage of brick and timber, was on land now part of the bishop's palace garden. It was pulled down in 1859 (Cunningham has a foggy photograph), and in 1883 a plaque was fixed to the garden wall (with the permission of the then bishop, Dr James Atlay) to indicate the site. The 'hopgarden' in the scurrilous anonymous ballad (preserved in the British Library's Harleian MSS) would make sense here – hops have long been grown along the Wye at Hereford.

When a coat of arms was found for her in later life, the Herald chose a device (Per pale argent and or, a lion azure) which is common in the Marches among the Gwynnes. Again, Charles II certainly paid for the restoration of the organ at Hereford Cathedral, from all accounts at Nell Gwyn's bidding.

London has made a weak claim to be the birthplace of the woman who added lustre to the place. Her mother's monument, erected by her daughter in the south aisle of St Martin-in-the-Fields (and pulled down in 1721) bore the inscription: 'Here lies the body of Helena Gwynn, born in this parish, who departed this life ye 20th July, MDCLXXIX, in the LXI yeare of her age'. In Captain Alexander Smith's *The Lives of the Court Beauties* (1715), Nell's birthplace is given as Coal Yard Alley, Drury Lane, and this is repeated in William Oldys' short history of the English stage, but Hanoverian writers are not to be trusted when writing of the Stewarts and their friends. There is no mention of any Gwyn in the records of St Martin-in-the-Fields, other than a David Gwyn (a petitioner on 24 January 1653) until Nell and her mother in later life, nor do Overseers' and Poor Collectors' accounts for St Mary le Strand or St Paul's, Covent Garden (all kept in Westminster City Public Library), offer anything to support Smith, Oldys and those who have followed them. As there were no baptismal registers kept at St Thomas's, Oxford, at the cathedral in Hereford or at St Martin's, the matter will never be resolved. Perhaps Nell never knew where she was born, or had reasons to keep quiet about it.

The genealogical probabilities are that Dr Edward Gwyn was a Hereford man (the name is common enough there) who made good, settled in Oxford but left his poor parents in Pipewell Lane. Between Wales and the Marches there had been much coming and going since the rise of the Tudors, so the Gwyns, Gwynnes or Gwines could well have been an 'antient family in Wales', fallen on evil times. Thomas, born in Royalist Oxford, would surely have rallied to Charles I's standard; the fact that his father was an Anglican clergyman of some note there would have made this allegiance virtually instinctive, and the rank of captain suggests some sort of recommendation for preferment. Perhaps Miss Eleanour or Helena Smith of St Martin-in-the-Fields chose this man among the rude soldiers who hastened the death of Dr Kettle, the second President of Trinity College, which was 'turned into a Daphne for the ladies and their gallants to walk in'.

There was certainly a lively Court in the town in 1642, as the Civil War began. King Charles I tried to set a good example, attending Divine Service regularly in Christ Church, walking with sober and righteous men in college gardens, 'as good as any Puritan in that house,' but his example was not followed. There were concerts, dances, duels and bouts of drunkenness (eventually the sale of strong drink after nine o'clock in the evening was prohibited). A wartime newspaper, *Mercurius Aulicus*, chronicled the misdeeds of the Cavaliers and their women, among whom was the wife of John Milton. ('She was a royalist, and went with her mother to the king's quarters neer Oxford. I have perhaps so much charity to her that she might not wrong his bed: but what man, especially contemplative, would like to have a young wife environ'd and storm'd by the sons of Mars?') Lady Isabella Thynne and her friend Mrs Fanshawe went to chapel 'half dressed like angells'.

What could girls of humbler origin, like Miss Eleanour Smith, do but dress or undress like their social superiors? As in all garrison towns in wartime, there were many liaisons, official and unofficial, some brought to the altar, many not. There is no record of Captain Gwyn's marriage to Miss Smith. Probably, 'As Tacitus sayd of Agrippina, *Cuncta illi adfuere, praeter animum honestum* – she was most beautifull, most humble, charitable, etc but she could not subdue one thing.' Somehow she avoided an early pregnancy.

The early optimism which suffused the royal camp, encouraged by the victory of Edgehill (23 October 1642) soon vanished. There were other victories, a few, but by the end of April 1646 the King had surrendered to the Scots, who sold him to the English Parliamentarians for £400,000 only half of which was ever paid. On 20 January 1649, after a show trial, he woke early, put on an extra shirt so that he should not shiver on the scaffold and be accused of fear, gave a watch to each of his gaolers and went to his death.

Like most of his brother officers, Captain Gwyn had a choice – flight to the Court of the new king, Charles II, in Paris, or self-effacement at home. Lacking money and influential friends, he probably returned to the birthplace of his father, Hereford, and hoped he would not be noticed. It is said that, like his friend Colonel Popham, he became a brewer and sold ale, perhaps to the local inn, later renamed the Royal Oak. Whatever he did in Hereford, he was left in peace, and his daughters Rose and Nell were born in 1648 and 1650; it has been suggested that Rose was born somewhere else, while he was on the run after 1646, but he may already have sought refuge in Hereford before the regicide.

In 1657 Oliver Cromwell, the Lord Protector, died of a quartan ague and, like many optimistic Cavaliers, Popham and Gwyn expected almost hourly a restoration of the monarchy. Gwyn, it is thought, went back to Oxford, where he was promptly gaoled. His wife, or the mother of his children, fled to her place of origin, to a cellar in Coal Alley Yard, Drury Lane, in the parish of St Martin-in-the-Fields, then in the County of Middlesex. Some biographers have suggested that Gwyn went to London, too, before Oxford, and sold fruit and vegetables there, but there was no organized market in Covent Garden at that time, and anyway he would have sold ale and not fruit and vegetables. It is more likely that he never saw his family again and died in Oxford gaol in 1658 or 1659, as Rochester suggests.

The London area in which Mrs Gwyn and the two girls settled was not as Puritanical as some of the late Oliver Cromwell's cronies would have liked. Richard Cromwell, who succeeded his father, was less given to prayer and good works, though he had the same dreary worthiness. The City merchants, grateful for stable government and prosperity in trade, were tired of exhortations to do good works; in private they ate and drank heartily – one of them fell down drunk at the Lord Protector's funeral. Though, as Ronald Hutton has suggested in his recent *Political and Religious History of England and Wales, 1658-67,* Richard Cromwell's regime seems to have enjoyed a considerable body of support even in 1659, all social classes found their own ways to circumvent the dreariness. Christmas, which the Puritans had tried to abolish as a public feast (Gladstone in 1832 was afraid the Reform Bill would do the same), was an occasion for gargantuan eating; the plum pudding seems to have taken its place on the Christmas table at this time, perhaps in unspoken commemoration of the fact that the last spasm of the Civil War was begun by a group of people carrying one in procession down Canterbury High Street. Banned maypoles, stored away against the return of the King, were carefully tended. Many sports and entertainments had gone in the first flush of Puritan enthusiasm after the execution of Charles I. Ireton had sent troopers to the Bear Garden to shoot the unfortunate animals kept there for baiting. Cockfights were illegal but took place in secret. The Spring Gardens at Vauxhall, a pleasant place of assignation where tarts, cheesecakes and reputations were bought and sold, were closed but business was merely transferred to the villages of Chelsea and Kensington or to the gardens at Charing Cross or Lambeth. Some attempt had been made to control drinking to excess, and from 1652 coffee-houses had been encouraged; the first was opened in St Michael's Alley in Cornhill by 'one Bowman, coachman to Mr Hodges a Turkey merchant, who putt him upon it' (Aubrey). However, numerous taverns and thinly disguised brothels flourished in the hamlets of Paddington, Wandsworth and Islington, and around the markets.

One category of person Oliver Cromwell really hated all his life was the actor. On 11 February 1648, even before the regicide, all actors had been made liable to punishment – whipping at the tail of a cart or imprisonment but they were not discouraged and went on performing at the Cockpit and other 'theatres', though a few, like Charles Hart, great-nephew of William Shakespeare, joined the army. In spite of the oppression, in 1654 there seems to have been an illicit theatrical boom and a law was passed for the suppression of 'a wicked sort of people called Hectors, and Playes, and other wicked disorders', but the 'playes' went on in taverns like the Red Bull. Sir William Davenant, who like Hart was to figure prominently in Nell Gwyn's life, found a way round this proscription. Captured by the Parliament fleet while on his way to America with thirty-six French convicts (to set up a weaving industry), he was saved from death as an unrepentant Cavalier by his old friend 'Sir' Harry Martyn with a speech in the House: 'In sacrifices they always offered pure and without blemish: now yee talke of making a sacrifice of an old rotten rascall.' Then, as Aubrey notes: 'Being freed from imprisonment, because playes, scil. Tragedies and Comoedies were in those Presbyterian times scandalous, he contrives to set-up an Opera *stylo recitativo*, wherein serjeant Maynard and severall citizens were engagers [backers]. It began at Rutland-house in Charter-house-yard; next at the Cockpitt in Drury Lane, where were acted very well *stylo recitativo Sir Francis Drake's* and *The Siege of Rhodes*. It did affect the eie and eare extremely. This brought scenes into fashion in England; before at playes, was only a hanging.' A Mrs Coleman was probably the first woman to appear on an English stage, in *The Siege of Rhodes*; until then men had always played women's roles.

For some reason the Puritans did not find Opera wicked; perhaps they confused the singing with their hymns. Evelyn was surprised. On 5 May 1659 he records in his Diary: 'I went to visit my Bro, and next day to see a new Opera after the Italian way in Recitative Music and Scenes, much inferior to the Italian composure and magnificence [he had seen Opera in Paris in 1651 and before that in Venice in 1645]: but what was prodigious, that in a time of such publique consternation, such a Vanity should be kept up or permitted.' In December 1658, in fact, as the *Public Intelligencer* had reported, a court had been ordered to 'take into consideration the Opera', but Davenant seems to have been, as usual, convincing about his purity of motive.

Nell Gwyn was only eight or nine when she went to live in Coal Yard Alley, Drury Lane. It was a noisy place; there were fish, fruit and vegetables cried everywhere, sheep as well as sedan chairs in the streets, taverns and brothels and illegal establishments of all kinds. The smells were very strong, especially on the City side of Drury Lane; lavender and other fragrant herbs were sold everywhere, in little muslin bags, to be held to sensitive noses. It was a strangely mixed area, in persons as well as perfumes. The Earl of Bedford's garden wall lined the south side of Inigo Jones's Covent Garden piazza, and he was forever complaining about the movable stalls set up against it. There were slum tenements like Nell's home, but the Earls of Craven and Salisbury and Lord Howard lived there in noble mansions. The Rose Tavern in Russell Street was a haunt of actors and writers, and several of them slept there for days at a time in a sort of drunks' dormitory. There were coffee-houses, the most famous of them being Will's and Farr's; John Dryden had his own chair by the fireplace at Will's in winter, and on a balcony in summer.

Rose Gwyn started to earn money selling oysters. Her mother drew ale at the Rose Tavern and drank a good deal herself; eventually she was dismissed when she moved on to drink a bottle of brandy a day and became a part-time procuress. Nell is said to have run errands for her mother for a time before joining Rose on the street with a barrow. Etherege has her selling vegetables:

> You that have seen me in my youthful age,
> Preferred from stall of turnips to the stage.

Rochester said that her

> ... first employment was with open throat
> To cry fresh herrings even ten a groat.

Whatever she was doing, her pitch was in Lewkenor's Lane (Macklin Street), named after Sir Louis Lewkenor, Master of Ceremonies and reputedly the meanest man at the Court of James VI and I.

Nell already had a talent for mimicry and repartee. Rose had her barrow nearby, and, as in later life, they exchanged witty and affectionate insults, decrying each other's wares to the delight of actors, writers and loiterers alike. At the end of the day they would help their mother at the Rose, until she lost her job, then procure for the brothels. In the evenings they bartered witticisms with the linkboys who carried torches for gentlemen as they moved from establishment to establishment in the unlit streets. According to Basil Montagu, she never forgot 'poor Dick' who had the heart of a gentleman. She is said to have recalled: 'I shall never forget when he came flushing and stammering, and drew out of his pocket a pair of worsted stockings which he had bought for my naked feet. It was bitter cold weather and I had chillblains which made me hobble about till I cried. My mother bade him put them on; and so he did, and his warm tears fell on my chillblains, and he said he should be the happiest Lord on earth if the stockings did me any good.'

When she was not engaging the affections of her linkboy, she seems to have done the housework before she set off for the streets. Etherege writes:

> He that hath seen her muddling in the Street,
> Her face all Pot-lid black, unshod her Feet,
> And in a Cloud of Dust her Cinders shaking,
> Could he have thought her fit for Monarch's taking?

Nell was in her tenth year when the dynastic succession of Richard to Oliver Cromwell ended in farce and restoration. The Commonwealth, which had begun as a dream for some, ended in a nightmare for all. After the failure of a rising by some Royalists (the Sealed Knot) on 1 August 1659, it was obvious that only the Army could get rid of the Army, which had the kingdoms in its power, and the only general who seemed likely to make a move was George Monck, with whom Charles II was in secret correspondence about 'the seasonable opportunity ... which may be offered sooner than you expect.'

Monck was known to be greedy and ambitious. Born in Devon, second son of an old and wealthy family, 'he was a strong, lusty well-sett young fellow; and in his youth happened to slay a man, which was the occasion of his flying into the Low Countries where he learned to be a soldier. He was first an ensign and after a captain ... and for making false musters was like to have been cashiered.' When the Civil War began, he rallied to Charles I and was captured and imprisoned in the Tower ('where his seamstress, Nan Clarges, was kind to him in a double capacity. Here she was gott with child'). He was released and given a command at sea by Parliament – 'the sea-men would laugh, that instead of crying *Tack about* he would say *Wheel to the right (or left)*'. He was then appointed military governor of Scotland, where he quickly created a wide personal powerbase, rivalling that of Oliver Cromwell in England. When Oliver died, Monck was unsure what to do. The Scots had drafted a Bill for Union with England, which he sent to Westminster (where thirty-three Scots sat in Parliament), and he may well have seen himself as Head of the new State. On the other hand, the failure of the attempt to get all Oliver's supporters to sign the Address (to pledge their lives and fortunes to his son) may have made him think again. As Aubrey says, 'Had not Dick Cromwell sneak't away, then it is certain that the Rump [Parliament] would have cutt-off his head.'

Monck hesitated until the beginning of 1660, then sent Sir John Grenville to advise the King to move to Breda to await developments. On 10 February 1660, after discussing 'realities' with Fairfax on the way, Monck arrived in London with 10,000 men, at Parliament's invitation (ostensibly to disband a rebel army under General Lambert). At Breda, Charles celebrated this turn of events by taking a new mistress, Barbara Palmer, née Villiers, who had been launched in society by the Earl of Chesterfield. She was a beautiful, greedy, ambitious girl who was to promote her family's interests and her own, between the royal sheets, for many years to come.

On 11 February Monck narrowly escaped an attempt to assassinate him, an attempt he rightly ascribed to Parliament fanatics. 'Thredneedle Street was all day long, and late at night, crammed with multitudes, crying out *A Free Parliament, a Free Parliament*, that the aire rang with their clamours. One evening he comeing out on horseback, they were so violent he said *'Pray be quiet, ye shall have a free Parliament'*. This about 7, or rather 8, as I remember, at night. Immediately a loud holla ... all the bells in the city ringing ... Bonfires prodigiously great and frequent ... roasted rumps of mutton – nay I saw some good rumps of beef. Healths to the King, Charles II, were drunk in the streets by the bonfires, even on their knees' (Aubrey).

Thus convinced, Monck called 'a free Parliament'. Sir Harbottle Grimston was chosen Speaker. When Parliament met, the first thing he put to the question was: 'Whether Charles Steward should be sent for or not? It was *nemine contradicente*, and Sir John Grenville was sent to Breda to advise the King.' Monck, having now committed himself and his career to the King, thoughtfully sent a warship, with a treasure chest containing £25,000 (the French Ambassador in London reported £50,000), to the port of The Hague at Schevenigen. For the next few days, tailors and seamstresses worked round the clock to dress the King and his Court as if they were dressing a new play for the theatre (which, in a way, they were). When he was satisfied with the effect, Charles II, with Barbara Palmer, Rochester and other cronies, went on board the *Royal Charles* (the *Naseby*, hurriedly renamed) and, to the sound of Dutch salvoes, sailed to regain his kingdoms.

As the *Royal Charles* hove to at Dover, as many people crowding on board as possible, Pepys noticed a lot of 'ruffians and placemen' trying to get near the King. Many were distressed officers who had lost everything, like Nell's father, in the service of the Stewarts; they hoped for the return of confiscated property and a place at Court for their children. There were men like Tom Killigrew, for Pepys 'a merry droll, but a gentlemen of great esteem with the King'. And as the May breezes blew gently over the docks, fluttering the flags, the Mayor of Dover and other worthies came bringing formal homage and gifts. The Mayor, after a lengthy address, gave the King a Bible, the English edition commissioned by his grandfather; the Mayor was not to know that Charles and his brothers were under constant pressure to be received into the Roman Church. The King thanked the Mayor and said the Bible would be a treasured possession, that it was the book he loved best in the world. Then the triumphal march to London began, Monck by his monarch's side, Barbara Palmer and the 'ruffians and placemen' in the ranks.

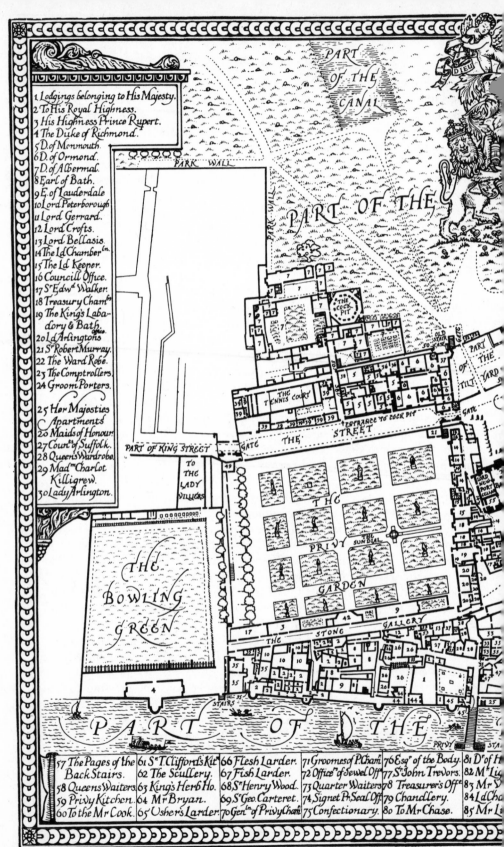

DIEU

PART OF THE CANAL

PART OF THE

PARK WALL

1. Lodgings belonging to His Majesty.
2. To His Royal Highness.
3. His Highness Prince Rupert.
4. The Duke of Richmond.
5. D. of Monmouth.
6. D. of Ormond.
7. D. of Albermal.
8. Earl of Bath.
9. E. of Lauderdale.
10. Lord Peterborough.
11. Lord Gerrard.
12. Lord Crofts.
13. Lord Bellasis.
14. The Ld Chamberᶠⁿ.
15. The Ld Keeper.
16. Councill Office.
17. Sʳ Edwᵈ Walker.
18. Treasury Chamᵇˢ.
19. The King's Laba-
    dory & Bath.
20. Ld Arlingtons opᶜˢ.
21. Sʳ Robert Murray.
22. The Ward Robe.
23. The Comptrollers.
24. Groom Porters.

25. Her Majesties
    Apartments.
26. Maids of Honour.
27. Court of Suffolk.
28. Queens Wardrobe.
29. Madᵐ Charlot
    Killigrew.
30. Lady Arlington.

PART OF KING STREET

TO THE LADY VILLIERS

GATE   THE   STREET   ENTRANCE TO COCK PIT

THE COCK PIT

OLD STAIR CASE   PART OF THE TILT YARD

THE TENNIS COURT

THE
BOWLING
GREEN

THE
PRIVY
THE SUN DIAL

GARDEN

THE STONE GALLERY

STAIRS

PART   OF   THE

PRIVY

Joan Kingsford del

57. The Pages of the Back Stairs.
58. Queens Waiters.
59. Privy Kitchen.
60. To the Mr Cook.

61. Sʳ T. Clifford's Kitᶜ
62. The Scullery.
63. King's Herb Ho.
64. Mr Bryan.
65. Usher's Larder.

66. Flesh Larder.
67. Fish Larder.
68. Sʳ Henry Wood.
69. Sʳ Geo. Carteret.
70. Genᵗⁿ of Privy Chamᵇ

71. Groomes of P.Chamᵇ
72. Office of Jewel Off
73. Quarter Waiters
74. Signet Pᵗ Seal Off
75. Confectionary.

76. Esqʳ of the Body.
77. Sʳ John Trevors.
78. Treasurer's Offᶜᵉ
79. Chandlery.
80. To Mr Chase.

81. Dʳ of H...
82. Mʳ Lig...
83. Mʳ ...
84. Ld Cha...
85. Mʳ L...

Plan of the Palace of WHITEHALL

from a survey taken in 1668

DROIT

N. NORTH S. SOUTH

THE SPRING GARDENS

PARK

PARK GATE

STABLES

STABLES

THE HORSE GUARD HOUSE

HALL

THE PASSAGE INTO THE PARK TO

GATE

S: JOHN DENHAMS BUILDINGS

NEW BUILDINGS

THE CLOCK HOUSE

STABLES

CORN COTTAGE HALL

D: WRENS COACH HO:

SCOTLAND YARD

SCOTLAND YARD

COURT

THE SPICERY

THE COURT

CHARCOAL HOUSE

DUKE OF YORKS WOOD YARD

SAND PIT

THE DEALE YARD

COURT

THE GREAT HALL

THE PANTRY

THE PASTRY

THE KITCHEN

THE PAULTRY

OUTWARD VESTRY

THE CHAPPELL

VESTRY

THE COMPTING CELLAR

THE WOOD YARD

QUEENS BAKER

KINGS COAL YARD

THE DRY OFFICE

THE SMALL BEER BUTTERY 97

GREAT BAKE HO:

SCOTLAND DOCK

THE WHARFE

THAMES

E R

Emery Walker Ltd. Sculp.

The towns of Kent were decorated overall, the free beer flowed in the taverns. The Mayors of Canterbury and Rochester brought their homage, no Bibles but, realistically, gifts of money and a gold tankard; they were anxious to see the soldiers move on, their thirsts slaked, and they had locked up their daughters. As the procession reached the outskirts of the City of London, Evelyn recorded that they rode 'along ways strewed with flowers ... streets hung with tapestry, fountains running with wine; the Mayor, Aldermen and all companies in their liveries, chains of gold and banners, lords and nobles clad in cloth of silver, gold and velvet; the windows and balconies well sett with ladies; trumpets and myriads of people flocking even so far as from Rochester, so they were seven hours in passing the city even from two in the afternoon till nine at night. ... It was the Lord's doing, for such a restoration was never mentioned in any history, ancient or modern, since the return of the Jews from the Babylonian captivity.'

Bells rang from every steeple. Aubrey noted that the bonfires were still burning in the streets and had set light to some of the balconies, causing the ladies to scream and run. Not often poetical, he wrote: 'Now as the morne growes lighter, and more glorious, till it is perfect day, so it was with the joy of the people. Maypoles, which in the hypocriticall times 't'was forbidden to sett-up, now were sett-up in every crossway; and at the Strand near Drury Lane was sett-up the most prodigious one for height that perhaps ever was seen; they were faine to have the assistance of the sea-mens art to elevate it.' Since 1642, as Professor Conrad Russell observed (*London Review of Books*, 5 September 1985), the maypole had been an aggressive symbol, a rallying point for opposition to Puritanism, and soldiers had wasted weeks searching barns and attics for those involved in 'the defence of maypoles'; Professor Russell does not hesitate to describe their failure as one of the main failures of the Interregnum regimes. For Nell and her sister, more so for their mother, that giant near their home meant liberation.

The whole nation, excepting the Puritans, suffered almost an indigestion of joy. Mature ladies of quality shook out gowns not worn for a decade. Younger ladies hurriedly learned etiquette. Seamstresses worked night and day to copy the new French fashions which had come over with the Court (though most of the Cavaliers and their ladies had been impoverished during the exile). New refinements were invented every day. There was a buttoned smock for easy sexual access, devised by a genteel whore, Bess Broughton and taken up by Barbara Palmer (Aubrey's seamstress helped to work it). Nothing was worn under the petticoats, nor would be for many years to come.

Poor girls were quick to emulate their social superiors. Tens of thousands of them flocked in from the provinces to find places, most of them in the hundreds of brothels which opened that glorious summer. Experienced madames made a fortune, improving the quality of the food and wine served to their clientele. Nell Gwyn and her sister Rose found places in one of the most notorious brothels, kept by a Madame Ross; this establishment achieved immortality in poems by Rochester, who patronized it, and Pepys got drunk there on one occasion. Nell always maintained that she was never one of Madame Ross's whores (they cost from half a crown up, according to youth, beauty and style), but 'only served strong waters to the gentlemen'; Rochester had his doubts and wrote that she

> Then was by Madame Ross exposed to town,
> I mean to those who will give half-a-crown.

The author of the anonymous *Memoirs* (1752), an unreliable biography, suggests that Nell's mother resolved to protect her daughter's virtue by sending her to relatives in Yorkshire, but: 'Nell heard this proposal with ineffable contempt, not wanting to be sent to the country to live in obscurity and contract rustic habits, by which she would lose all power of pleasing for ever.' But the idea of old Mrs Gwyn even entertaining such thoughts is preposterous. She put Rose to work straightaway entertaining the gentlemen in the original premises in Lewkenor's Lane, and at an annexe which soon became necessary. The girls brought home money and 'strong waters'.

By the end of the summer what Pepys called the 'lewdness and beggary of the Court' were matched by the 'lewdness and beggary of the Town'. Foreigners heard the news and flocked to London to enjoy the girls, though Samuel Butler wrote that there were more varieties of venereal disease there than anywhere in Europe. The Countess of Sussex, recently widowed, 'sends for one, formerly her footman and makes him groom of the chamber. He had the pox and shee knew it ... his nostrils were stufft and burne out with corks in which were quills to breathe through ... a sad example of the power of lust'. Sir Henry Blount was 'called to the barre for spreading abroad that abominable and dangerous doctrine that it was far safer to lye with common wenches than with ladies of quality'.

Common wenches like Nell and Rose did their best to become uncommon. Their ambition was always to leave the brothels when they had had their basic training and set up or be set up on their own; the supply of girls from the provinces was steady enough for madames to make no objection when the girls bought themselves out. Rose Gwyn seems to have found powerful protectors quickly, and this is perhaps not surprising.

The Whitehall Palace complex quickly became the focal point of social, political and cultural life, the Strand the thoroughfare along which City merchants and dignitaries travelled to and from Court. The whole area from Charing Cross to Aldwych became an entertainment centre, as it were. On one of his excursions, Harry Killigrew, son of the King's favourite, went to

Madame Ross's and met Rose; he seems to have set her up later that year or early in 1661.

Nell recalled that life was like a fair all day as the nation went on celebrating the Restoration. Access to the King was easy and he was kindness itself to his enemies. There were, of course, old scores to be settled. In Scotland, Argyll was executed and his head spiked. Warriston and Guthrie, leaders of the Covenanting extremists and collaborators with Cromwell, were hanged. The bodies of Oliver Cromwell, Ireton and Bradshaw were dug up before an invited audience (they had been buried in Westminster Abbey) and their remains were put in a cage hanging from Tyburn Tree. The surviving Major-Generals were hanged, drawn and quartered (Pepys noted of one of them that he looked as cheerful as any man could do in that condition), but many of the King's enemies were spared. Fairfax was saved, partly at Monk's intercession, and because he was 'a lover of learning ... [and] had set a good guard of soldiers to preserve the Bodleian Library'. The poet Waller was received very kindly, notwithstanding his poems in praise of the Lord Protector. John Wilkins, who had married Oliver Cromwell's sister (and had been made first Warden of Wadham College, Oxford, then Master of Trinity College, Cambridge), was removed tactfully to Ripon as Dean. John Milton and Andrew Marvell (who was to become a sworn enemy of Nell) were left undisturbed; Marvell remained MP for Hull until his death. Even Sir William Petty, who had made a fortune in Ireland as one of Parliament's Surveyors, was received into good grace.

Friends were rewarded for their fidelity, but not all claims were met for desequestration of property. Thomas Hobbes, the great philospher, who had been the King's tutor in Paris, was urged to come to Court from Derbyshire (where he had fled from the wrath of the Anglican bishops) so that in London 'he could have convenience of books and learned conversation'; the King always 'delighted in his wit and smart repartees'. This attention to stimulating cultural life, which was to be a haphazard characteristic of the reign, was already noticeable; Charles himself had made a point of referring to it in a letter to his cousin Louis XIV in June 1660.

Charles' day began before dawn. He exercised on horseback in fine weather and walked in the Privy Gardens or St James's Park before breakfast; this early rising persisted no matter whose bed he had got into the night before, nor at what time he had got into it. Nell, who seems to have had her mornings free at Madame Ross's, often saw him in the park, or playing tennis or pall mall – the street is named after the game (a variant of croquet). Later she spoke lovingly of her first sight of the 'Two Yards of King'. She was so small that he must have seemed even taller than he was, but 'in spite of his height, he was so easy and graceful that they do very much commend his person'. His hands were especially beautiful, with long, strong, spatulate fingers. His complexion was dark – he was still the 'Black Boy' of Cromwell's Wanted posters and innumerable pub signs – and his hair was long, curled in ringlets, and fell down to his shoulders 'which was very handsome to see'. His eyes were sharp, missing nothing. Family tragedy and scandal etched further lines into his face at the outset of his return (but these did not make him any the less attractive): his sister Mary and brother Henry died of smallpox that year, and his brother James got the Lord Chancellor's daughter Anne with child. (Charles forced his brother to marry her, and she turned out to be a good wife and the mother of two queens.) There was still his favourite sister, Henrietta Anne ('Minette'); she had been forced to marry the homosexual Duke of Orleans at the age of fifteen, but found excuses to visit her brother, and other consolations in the 'new London'.

Life revolved around the King. On most of those morning when Nell saw him in the Park, he would be collected at about ten o'clock by Lord Chancellor Hyde, and after a brisk rub down would receive foreign dignitaries. At midday he had lunch in the Banqueting Hall at Whitehall, and this was rather like a Mad Hatter's Tea Party on a royal scale. Courtiers and official visitors came and went. Some were received by the King and ate a course or two with him, then moved on. Some took only a glass of wine, presented a petition, then ate elsewhere. Guards and Gentlemen Pensioners stood behind his chair; his food and wine were always tasted by a page. Women were seldom invited to sit down and eat, though they were to be seen lurking everywhere in the Great Hall, making assignations and ruining reputations. It was not unusual for the meal to go on for three or four hours. Ten courses were served. There would be several meats, always roast leg of mutton, rib of beef, rump of beef and venison in season. The King fell upon this with the enthusiasm which had horrified an heiress he had hoped to marry in Paris – 'La Grande Mademoiselle' was put off by his bad table-manners and the fact that he did not play billiards, for which she had a passion. The King did not like fowl, though there were always spits full for visitors. After the meats came the syllabubs and sweetmeats. Canary wine and claret were drunk throughout the meal; after it, Charles would walk in the Privy Gardens for an hour and then look for some gentle entertainment.

Sir William Davenant had hoped to be appointed Master of the King's Playhouse after the Restoration; he had had several years of running his Opera, after all, and had a company ready. Unfortunately for Davenant, Tom Killigrew was not only the son of one of the King's most respected courtiers, he was also one of the King's closest friends; Killigrew had been resident in Venice and Mantua and had acquired a passion for the theatre there – he had also written several plays waiting to be acted. Unfortunately for them both, Sir Henry Herbert, Master of the Revels (appointed by James VI and I), thought he ought to rule all players and dispose of theatrical licences. The King, who had acquired a taste for the theatre in France, tried to reconcile the three men but failed. In the end he issued Royal Patents to both Davenant and Killigrew and pensioned off the old Master. He, Charles, would be patron of Killigrew's company, and his brother James would lend his name to Davenant's. Killigrew's King's Servants (as he liked to call them) opened on 8 November 1660 at a theatre improvised in Vere Street, Clare Market, and the Duke's players a week later at Salisbury Court. Theatres opened in the afternoon (they had not solved the problems of lighting in a public place of entertainment), and the two royal establishments soon had their cliques and claques.

In the evening there were no formal dinners as such: ladies gave intimate suppers to their lovers in their private apartments. The King always had to wait until Barbara Palmer could get rid of her husband, so he often went into Town to eat at the Pallsgraves Head, returning about nine o'clock. He would then pretend to retire, pass through his 'guardian' Chiffinch's adjacent appartment, down a staircase to the Thames and away. When Palmer was indisposed, he would go to one of the better-known brothels, Madame Ross's, 'Lady' Bennet's, Madame Cresswell's, 'Mother' Temple's or Damaris Page's, all of whose customers would pretend they did not recognize him.

Louis XIV was always puzzled by the attitude of the Church of England to this sudden transformation of the country. Was there no danger of the Army bringing back the Puritans? The French Ambassador reported that a special tax, gladly paid, had been levied to pay off most of the troops and (11 October 1660) had commented that 'Monck has no more credit with his troops, he does not like the Chancellor, and his wife is very rough.' Though it was desirable to find the King a Catholic wife as soon as possible, the answer was that the Church of England was glad to be Established again; for the upper clergy morals were a matter for the private conscience (the Dean of St Paul's wife 'could scarce deny anyone'). The lower clergy were ignorant and complaisant as ever; Hobbes' father had only been able to read 'the prayers of the church and the homilies and disesteemed learning'. Nell Gwyn and her mother went regularly to services at St Martin-in-the-Fields, and even when she was notorious she was on friendly terms with at least two bishops. The drunks and whores left their marks on that church: the *London Spy* reported that, 'The malt duty is nowhere better promoted than in this parish' and 'There are rails erected round the altar to prevent persons sitting on it, throwing hats on it, writing on it and abusing it to other profane uses.'

There were two great, nominally ecclesiastical events to come which Nell always spoke of when taken with nostalgia for the happy moments of her childhood. On 23 April 1661 the King's Coronation took place. She was outside the Abbey when the great procession arrived. At Charles' wish the service was liberally seasoned with music, played by his own musicians in their red-and-white livery. Bishops, lords and ladies were in splendid robes, refurbished after years of disuse. After the ceremony, the Treasurer of the Royal Household threw silver coins into the crowd, and Nell always swore she had one of them. The show eventually moved to Westminster Hall, followed by the crowd. A banquet of forty courses was served. Hyde, the Lord Chancellor, raised to an earldom (Clarendon) for being omnipresent in good times and bad, was in tears. Barbara Palmer's husband, raised to an earldom (Castlemaine and Baron Limerick) for being absent at the right times, was drunk. The Savilian Professor of Astronomy composed bawdy verses. The King's Champion rode into the Hall, threw down his gauntlet and challenged anyone to doubt the right to succession of 'the pattern of piety and patience, the most righteous and justest of Kings, the most knowing and experienced of princes, the holiest and best of men, the severest of judges and punishers of vice, the strictest rewarder of virtue, the constantest preserver of religion and the truest lover of his subjects'. It was a St George's Day to remember and, like Samuel Pepys, many drank till they could drink no more. At about nine o'clock the strictest rewarder of virtue slipped away into the arms of the new Lady Castlemaine.

The man who did best out of the Coronation, in terms of hard cash, was a Scotsman, John Ogilby, who not only arranged the ceremonial but published an account of it in folio with woodcuts; he had made a small fortune the previous year, 'as if by a prophetic spirit, forseeing the restoration of King Charles II and also the want there might be of [Anglican] Church Bibles, he printed the fairest impression, and the most correct of English Bibles, in royal and imperial paper'.

The next show was the Royal Wedding. Charles had, it is estimated, five illegitimate children already, four boys and a girl. He would not have been averse to legitimizing James Scott, Duke of Monmouth, now that his mother Lucy Walters was dead, but the Queen Mother had not recovered from the forced marriage of her son James to a pregnant commoner. Several French and even German princesses were suggested as prospective brides, but Charles thought they looked 'dull and foggy'. There was even a suggestion that he should marry the daughter of the Tsar, but this was thought too exotic. Then Samuel Cooper, 'the prince of limners', brought a painting of the daughter of the King of Portugal. Princess Catherine of Braganza was well into her twenties and not startlingly beautiful, but her father was ready to give her a large dowry (£300,000 in cash), plus the cities of Tangiers and Bombay and the right to British merchants to set up trading stations in Portuguese Brasil. It was a very tempting package and, while Charles was not short of young, beautiful girls, he was always short of money. The marriage contract was signed that autumn of 1661.

There was an unseemly rush by poets, balladeers and playwrights to celebrate the coming event. Davenant, who had stolen a march on Killigrew by moving out of the temporary accommodation in Salisbury Court to a new theatre in Portugal Row, Lincoln's Inn Fields (June 1661), put on an early winter season of royal slush. He was brought up sharp by one of Killigrew's lawyers who pointed out that Sir William had not yet surrendered the Patent he had been granted by the King's father on 26 March 1639, so probably the new Patent granted by Charles was not valid. While legal quibbling went on, Killigrew hurriedly completed the foundations of his theatre (the first stone had been laid on 2 March, according to Rugge's *Mercurius Britannicus*) 'on the back side of Brydges Street' and, even more important, on 25 April 1662 received a separate Patent granting him extra privileges as the manager of the King's House. Meanwhile the wedding preparations went on. Hearing the royal bride was given to taking the waters, Dudley, Lord North, who had discovered a medicinal spring on Lord Abergavenny's estate, hastened to promote his new resort of Tunbridge Wells.

On 20 May 1662 the bride arrived at Portsmouth. The bridegroom had mistaken the date of her arrival and had to ride hard to the coast to meet her. He was exhausted on arrival, but fortunately she was indisposed. As Charles wrote to his sister: 'It was happy for the honour of the nation that I was not put to the consummation of the marriage, for I was so sleepy, by having slept but two hours in my journey, that I fear matters would have gone very sleepily.'

Nell Gwyn confided in her friends that 'her heart was broke' seeing the King with his bride. She was so heartbroken that though only twelve years old she sold or surrendered her virginity to a young City merchant, a regular visitor to Madame Ross's. The 1752 memorialist suggests: 'She had now observed how gaily many ladies lived who had no other means of supporting their grandeur but by making such concessions to men of fortune, and stipulating such terms as both of them could afford to comply with.' Oldys confirms that: 'One Mr Duncan, a merchant, taking a fancy to her smart wit, fine shape and foot, the least of any woman's in England, kept her about two years.' Etherege suggests that he paid her for his exclusive enjoyment, set her up at the Cock & Pie and remained her friend all their lives; when she was able to patronize him, she procured for him a commission in the Guards.

Whatever the truth of this, Nell certainly moved out of the cellar to the Cock & Pie and watched with interest the growth of the new theatre on her doorstep. Killigrew, in partnership with Charles Hart, Michael Mohun and Nicholas Burt, had bought from the Earl of Bedford a forty-one-year lease on Rideing Yard, Brydges Street, half in the parish of St Martin-in-the-Fields and half in St Paul's, Covent Garden. The lease specified that the building was to be substantial (112 feet by 59 feet) and that at least £1,500 should be spent on it. To make sure that the standard of acting was high, a drama school was opened in the Barbican (visited approvingly by Pepys).

Tom Killigrew and his partners supervised every detail of the construction of the theatre, down to the arrangements for the refreshment of the playgoers. 'Strong waters' were not to be sold for fear they would inflame tempers, but some way had to be found to slake the thirsts of those who would spend hot afternoons there. It was decided to grant a licence to one Mary Meggs, 'with full, free and sole liberty, license, power and authority to vend, utter and sell oranges, lemons, fruit, sweetmeats and all manner of fruiterers and confectioner's wares'. The licence was granted on 10 February 1663, and Meggs agreed to pay 6s. 8d, every day the theatre was open, as a sort of royalty; she was given £100 as working capital. Now it so happened that Meggs, or 'Orange Moll' as she was known, was an intimate of Madam Gwyn (she is referred to thus in 1663, so may have become a fulltime bawd and procuress). The opening of such a theatre, the largest in London; Court patronage assured by its nearness to Whitehall; the King himself expected to grace performances and seen already on the site – it was all a prospect to excite more ambitious mothers than the ageing Eleanour. Rose was still being visited by Harry Killigrew, the son of one of the theatre's owners; now here was Orange Moll with access to the very pit where the bucks and gallants would stroll. Madam Gwyn saw it all clearly. Both girls were to be taken on as 'orange girls'; who knew where it would lead?

Orange Moll had a sharp eye for promising girls and agreed to take on Rose and Nell. She had them uniformed provocatively and rehearsed. They were to bring her 5d. an orange and could keep whatever they could get above that figure. They would have to put up with a good deal of ribaldry from the customers, but these would be mostly courtiers and potential customers for other, not so forbidden fruits. It was an opportunity for work experience coveted by any young girl hoping to go on the Town.

The girls would hardly wait as the last nails were hammered in, and the last licks of paint applied. On 7 May 1663 the King's playhouse opened, with *The Humorous Lieutenant* by Beaumont and Fletcher, always a crowd-puller. Nell and Rose were in the pit with their oranges. As Rochester wrote later:

> But first the Basket her fair arm did suit,
> Laden with Pippins and Hesperian Fruit.
> This first step rais'd, to the wond'ring Pit she sold,
> The lovely Fruit, smiling with streaks of Gold.

It was to be a very important first step.

Stagestruck, 1662-5

Next in the Playhouse she took her degree
As men commence at University.
No doctors, till they've masters been before;
So she no player was till first a whore.

A Paneygryric on Nelly, Rochester

Then enter Nelly on the public stage
Harlot of harlots, Lais of the age.

Hopgarden, Cellar to the Throne – The Life of Nelly, Anon.

The *beau monde* filled the taverns, including the Cock & Pie, before and after the opening of the new theatre. The Town could talk of nothing else. For one thing, the Patent given exclusively to Killigrew had contained permission for women's parts to be performed by women, which would add to 'the harmless delights [and] useful and instructive representations of human life to such of our good subjects as shall resort to the same'. Colley Cibber wrote that the King insisted on this departure from previous custom because, in 1660, 'coming a little before his usual time to a Tragedy, [he] found the actors not yet ready to begin, when His Majesty not chusing to have as much patience as his good subjects, sent to know the meaning of it; upon which the master of the company came to the Box, and rightly judging that the best excuse for their default would be the true one, fairly told His Majesty that the Queen was not shaved yet'. The unshaven Queen was Edward Kynaston; after this contretemps, Charles decided that his Queens at least should be female.

Then there was the building itself, not a converted tennis-court or cockpit but a purpose-built theatre. It was still built largely of wood, like its neighbours, but it owed a great deal to the houses at which Cavaliers in exile had seen plays in Paris, Venice and Mantua. The ground floor or pit had both benches to sit on and a large area in which playgoers could walk about and exchange witticisms with the actors and actresses; it was in the pit that the orange-wenches sold their fruit and sweetmeats. The price of admission to this part of the theatre was half a crown, the price of an acceptable whore at Madame Ross's. Round the pit on three sides there were boxes, slightly raised above the floor; admission to these was 4 shillings, and they were popular with Court ladies and distinguished foreigners who did not want to risk mixing with the rakes and gallants. There were two galleries above the boxes, one accessible for only 1s. 6d. and the other free to servants waiting for their masters.

The roof over the stage and boxes was tiled, and the pit area covered by a glass dome, not very well made, which sometimes was to let in the rain. The orchestra (another innovation) was sheltered by the stage itself and was squeezed into a narrow space beneath the boards. Also beneath the stage was a honeycomb of dressing-rooms. The less important actors and actresses shared what were called 'the Men's Shift' and 'the Women's Shift'. The 'stars' had rooms of their own, furnished with one or two chairs, occasionally a divan, mirrors, candles, chamberpots and commodes. It was all very luxurious when compared with the spartan amenities of Shakespeare's Globe or Ben Jonson's Mermaid.

Spies from the Duke's House were at the King's on opening day, heralding years of intense rivalry and partisanship on behalf of actors and audiences alike. The King had tried to avoid this by persuading Sir William Davenant and Tom Killigrew to share out between them the best plays in the national repertoire. Killigrew, who had the best actresses, got hold of nearly all Ben Jonson's plays (including *Bartholomew Fair, Every Man in His Humour, Volpone* and *The Alchemist)*, all Beaumont and Fletcher's works and a share of Shakespeare's, including *A Midsummer Night's Dream, The Merry Wives of Windsor* and *Othello*. Davenant, who had the best actor, Thomas Betterton, got *Lear, Macbeth, Hamlet, Henry VIII* and other plays with strong roles for men. Both managers tried to recruit from among the new generation of playwrights: John Dryden was snapped up by Killigrew, as were the Howards, popular not-withstanding Evelyn's sneers ('At night saw acted *The Committee*, a ridiculous play of Sir R. Howard'). Davenant was less successful with the new writers but had the best scenic designers, and the Duke's House quickly became known for the sumptuousness of its stage settings.

The King's House was said to be better managed. Killigrew always spoke of himself as 'born to the theatre' and spread a tale that even as a boy he had had a walk-on part as a devil at the Red Bull. He was certainly very close to the King and adept at getting extra privileges for his company, though he was an unsuccessful playwright:

> Had Cowley neer spoke nor Th Killigrew writ
> They'd both have had a good witt.
>
> (Sir John Denham)

Killigrew's partner, the actor Michael Mohun, was known not only for his resonant voice but also for his organizing ability: he had been a supply officer in the army and was always known as Major Mohun or 'the Major'. Another partner, Charles Hart, had also served in the army (in Prince Rupert's Horse) and was not only well connected but a fine actor (he had specialized in women's roles in the pre-Commonwealth theatre). They had the advice of a longtime enemy of Davenant, John Ogilby, who after his *coup* with the Bibles and the Coronation went to Ireland and built a large theatre in Dublin, replacing the one in St Warburgh Street.

The rival manager, Sir William Davenant, was a selfmade man, son of the keeper of the Crown Inn at Oxford. As Shakespeare found himself edged out of favour by Ben Jonson in Jacobean times; he used to go home to Stratford at least once a year, and Davenant built on this circumstance, during drinking bouts with his friend Samuel Butler, boasting that he was Shakespeare's illegitimate son, which was why he wrote so well; he was always envious of Hart, whose father William really was the son of Shakespeare's sister Joan. Davenant did, in fact, write well (*Madagascar*, *Gondibert*) but not as well as he thought. He had fought bravely in the war and had been knighted on the field, but he was less famous for that than for his whoring. Aubrey records: 'He got a terrible clap of a black handsome wench that lay in Axe-Yard, Westminster, whom he thought of when he speaks of Dalga in *Gondibert*, which cost him his nose.'

The great gossips of the age, Aubrey, Pepys and Evelyn, divided their allegiance. Aubrey was a patron of the Duke's House and only mentions Killigrew disparagingly. Pepys favoured the King's House because he liked pretty women, though after Davenant's death in 1668 he went often enough to the Duke's. Evelyn, always pretending to be dragged reluctantly to the play, made sharp remarks about both companies.

There are various theories about how Nell Gwyn made the transition from pit to stage.

The 1752 memorialist suggests that she plotted her own rise: 'She cast her eyes on the stage, and as her person was admirably calculated to inspire passion, she imagined that if she was arrayed in the pomp of tragedy heroines, her figure alone, without any theatrical requisites, would make her pass upon the Town; or at least, if she could not wear the buskin with success, she could see no objection to her appearing as a Lady-in-waiting or one of the Maids-of-the-Bedchamber to the Queen of the Stage.' Who the reigning Queen was is not specified, but it could have been Mrs Corey, Mrs Eastland, Mrs Knapp or Knipp, Mrs Anne or Mrs Rebecca Marshall, even Mrs Uphill or Mrs Weaver, all paid from 20 to 50 shillings a week (which seemed an unreal sum to Nell), dressed in splendid clothes and lavishly entertained after the show.

'The thought filled her with rapture,' the memorialist goes on. 'After living a month or two in this manner, she wrote a letter to Mr Betterton, inviting him to her lodgings, to whom she disclosed the scheme of coming on the stage, and desired he might give his opinion of her powers of recitation. He told her plainly that she was not then fit for the stage, though she seemed to have a genius that was, and advised her to prosecute some other scheme of livelihood.' Later he seems to have relented and 'appointed one of his subalterns to pay her frequent visits and initiate her in the principle of playing. This subaltern was himself a promising genius, he had made a rapid progress on the stage, and was held in esteem. ... He was of a constitution sanguine and amorous ... so it is not to be doubted but he made some advances to Nell. ... '

There are some difficulties to be faced here. There is no evidence that she could read or write, so it would be almost impossible to recite anything other than a snatch or two of a play memorized in the pit. Then, why should she approach an actor from the Duke's House, when the King's House was on her doorstep and her sister Rose had been kept by Killigrew's son? Again, what was Duncan, supposedly still keeping Nell, doing while the 'subaltern' visited her at her lodgings? Etherege says that Duncan was tiring of her, and recommended her himself to Killigrew. Duncan was 'Nell-sick' – 'with the Expense of Purse or Love', but

> How're he would not leave her as he found her,
> That had been base, since he had got the Plunder,
> Besides, he knew that she had both Wit and Sence,
> Beauty and such a stock of Impudence
> As to the Play-house well might recommend her,
> And therefor thither was resolv'd to send her.

Duncan seems to have resented the expense of keeping her at the Cock & Pie, or perhaps discovered that he was being cuckolded. During the summer of 1663 Nell moved to the Cat & Fiddle in Lewkenor's Lane, which was an annexe to Madame Ross's main establishment. In Dryden's play *The Wild Gallant*, Madame Ross appears as Lady du Lake 'of St Lucknor's Lane at the Cat & Fiddle; Samuel Butler commemorates it:

> The nymphs of chaste Diana's train,
> The same with those of Lewkenor's Lane.

And in *The Beggar's Opera* a man was sent for whores 'as far as Hockley-in-the-Hole for three of the ladies, for one in Vinegar Yard, and for the rest of them somewhere about Lewkenor's Lane'. Whether or not Duncan recommended her to the theatre, Nell was soon to-ing and fro-ing between the Cat & Fiddle and Tom Killigrew's lodgings in the Piazza, Covent Garden. Rose Gwyn seems to have been cast off that summer without the usual gratuity, though there is no record of a quarrel with Harry Killigrew. She looked about for another 'cully' but the competition since the opening of the new theatre was very fierce, and she was neither as attractive nor as intelligent as her sister. For some reason, perhaps just loneliness, she married a petty criminal, John Cassells. (Gordon Goodwin, who edited Cunningham in 1903, suggests that Cassells was the highwayman and burglar 'Captain' John Cassells who certainly frequented the brothels and taverns in Drury Lane.) Ingenuous and inexpert as she was, Rose seems to have combined business with pleasure on her honeymoon; she was arrested for burglary at the house of a customer and clapped into Newgate gaol in December.

Nell and her mother were desperate. It was not difficult to get into Newgate but it was extremely difficult to get out. Nell, being (to understate it) the more attractive of the two, was sent to Harry Killigrew to plead with him to intervene; Rose's former keeper, known as 'Harry the Liar' or 'Lying Harry', washed his hands of the affair, not wanting to tarnish what was left of his reputation. The Gwyns then tried a two-pronged attack. Rose herself wrote from Newgate to Harry Browne, the Duke of York's Cupbearer 'begging him to obtain her release from this woeful place of torment until a pardon is pleaded'. Her father, she adds, 'lost all he had in the service of the King and it is hard she should perish in a gaol'. From this note it seems that she had already been convicted. As the letter left Newgate on 26 December, Nell besieged Thomas Killigrew in the Piazza, and said it was a shabby way to treat a poor girl who had given her all to his son. However, it was Browne who acted and had Rose reprieved and, on the last day of the year, pardoned. Lewis Melville came across 'a foul draught entry book' of Charles II with the entry:

> Whereas we are given to understand that Rose Gwynne having been convicted ... at the late sessions held at the Old Bailey, was yet reprieved by ye bench before judgement and reserved as an object of our princely compassion and mercy, upon humble suite made to us in favour of ye said Rose, we have thought good hereby to signify our Royal pleasure unto you, that you forthwith grant her liberty and discharge upon good bail first taken in order to ye sueing out her pardon, and rendering our gracious mercy and compassion to be effectual. for which &c., dated Decr, 1663.
>
> By His Matys Command,
HB

This meeting with Thomas Killigrew in unfortunate circumstances was probably the occasion of Nell's rise. What struck him about the girl as she pleaded for her sister was that she did not whine. She complained about his son's behaviour, it is true, but then she was not the only one. More important, she did it wittily, observing that it was really a waste of a promising career to leave a young whore, neither poxed nor clapped, in gaol for the free use of the gaolers. Almost certainly she raised the matter of her own theatrical ambitions and, if she did not 'recite', played on her own fiddle of jokes and mimicry. Killigrew, it is said, liked her, believed she deserved a chance of promotion from the pit and referred her to Hart and Lacy.

John Lacy and Charles Hart used to drink at the Cock & Pie, so might well have met her even before she became an orange-girl. Everybody in the company was always on the look-out for new talent, as well as amusement, and scrutinized the girls in the taverns and brothels to see if they promised any more than they were paid to give. It was one of Lacy's hobbies to try out attractive girls by teaching them a few lines from a prologue, and trying to improve the way they spoke and held themselves; as he was by then middle-aged, this may well have been a useful device for attracting them and engaging their interest. Hart's methods were more simple and direct: he would put a girl on stage during a play just to see how she reacted. The author of *Hopgarden, Cellar to the Throne* says that Nell obliged them both:

> ... what Lacy's fumbling age abus'd
> Hart's sprightly vigour more robustly us'd.

Fumbling or not, Lacy taught Nell how to dance. He had been a pupil of the ubiquitous Ogilby when this artistic entrepreneur first arrived in London from Scotland and opened a dancing school (he had sprained his foot and had to give up a promising beginning as a dancer at masques).

Nell's first appearance on stage may well have been in Lacy's own play, *The Old Trooper*, a parody of Ogilby's verses *The Description of a Trouper* (written in Ireland while he was in Lord Strafford's troop of horse guards). Lacy was given to parodying other people's plays and verses and also upset people with his mimicry, which was brilliant and a gift he shared with Nell Gwyn. *The Old Trooper* is a satirical work about the behaviour of Cavalier soldiers billeted on unsuspecting peasants during the Civil War – Nell and Rose always boasted that their father had served in Sir Thomas Dallison's troop with Lacy and that this was the reason for Lacy's interest in the younger sister. Whatever this interest, John Lacy and Nell Gwyn enjoyed a tender friendship, more like that of a father and daughter than lovers. Lacy was very patient, not only teaching her how to dance but urging her to listen to parts recited on stage and learn them by heart. They would sit outside the Cat & Fiddle and go through what she had learnt, correcting here and there, although a certain amount of inventiveness and impromptu authorship was encouraged in the Restoration theatre; Nell is said to have inserted into the play some lines instructing virgins how to masturbate and open the orifice without damaging the saleable hymen.

After her début in *The Old Trooper* Nell was taken into the company and passed on to Hart as student and whore. Colley Cibber disagrees: 'Hart introduced Mrs Gwyn upon the dramatic boards, and has acquired the distinction of being ranked among that lady's first felicitous lovers, by having succeeded to Lacy in the possession of her charms.'

During 1664 she also attracted the attention of John Dryden. He had married the eldest daughter of the Earl of Berkshire, Lady Elizabeth Howard, and was a favourite at Court as poet, playwright and wit; his brothers-in-law were also playwrights and friends of the Killigrews, and it was this connection which brought him into the orbit of the King's House. He was to be very important in Nell's rise to fame on the stage, and was at first struck by her presence and the way her voice carried even over the noise in the pit; it was said that only Betterton at the Duke's House and Nell at the King's could make themselves heard at all times. Some chroniclers have suggested that Nell worked for a time at Will's and met Dryden first there; there is no proof of this, but they certainly became great friends, as it were, overnight. He did not see *The Old Trooper* but watched her first on stage in *Thomaso, or The Wanderer*, one of Thomas Killigrew's bad plays; in the cast list she appears as 'Nelly – Paulina, a courtesan of the first rank'. The play ran for one performance in late November 1664 and never surfaced again.

Though he was often teased by Dryden and others, Killigrew was never put out by the universally bad reception he had as playwright. Sir Charles Bulstrode relates that on one occasion the King was being shaved while Tom stood at the window reading a book of his plays he had published at his own expense. 'Tom,' said the King, 'what account will you give at the Day of Judgement of all the idle words in that book?' Tom's riposte was: 'I shall give a better acount than Your Majesty shall do of all your idle promises and more idle patents which have undone many, but my idle words in this book have undone nobody.'

Nell deserved better, and Dryden was determined that she should have it. He suggested that she be given some of the prologues and epilogues of his own plays to speak, that he was even prepared to write for her an important role in a piece he planned for the spring or summer of 1665. All he asked was that she be taught the craft and be given a suitable wardrobe. This latter was important because actors had to provide their own swords, feathers and gloves, and actresses dresses, petticoats, collars, neckerchiefs, silk stockings, fans, garters and shoes trimmed. The theatre supplied only the basic costumes. Perhaps Hart supplied the money for the 'extras', though William Kent, in his *London Worthies* writes of a manuscript in the British Museum according to which 'a gentleman of the law carried her from the playhouse by force (in 1665) and deflowered her and placed her safe in the house of

Mrs Croswold (Crosswell) mentioned in one of Otway's *Epilogues*. Here she continued for half a year'; this seems unlikely if only because she had already been 'deflowered', and Madame Ross would have protested about this poaching on her preserve.

As far as Nell's theatre schooling went (and that was certainly in the hands of Hart, Lacy and Mohun), it consisted of learning to be Tragic or Comic. In later life she would reduce her friends to hysterics with demonstrations of how she was taught to pout or languish, half invite and half repel a seducer, and whirl her skirts so that she showed just enough of her thighs to arouse an appetite for more; and she could parody Hart as tragedian, flinging his arms about, clapping his hands to head or heart and above all dying in a pool of pig's blood after being attacked with a collapsible sword or dagger. It was always dangerous to teach actresses how to fight: Elizabeth Barry, who had quarrelled with Anne Boutel, thrust a stage dagger so hard into Boutel's body that it went through her stays and into her flesh.

The courtiers on the rampage made more convincing teachers. Lord Buckhurst, to celebrate being pardoned for killing a tanner in a brawl, got drunk at the Cock & Pie with Sir Charles Sedley and Sir Thomas Ogle. Sedley rose from the table at five in the afternoon, stripped off his clothes and walked onto the balcony, where he gave a mock sermon and pissed on the crowd. He was accused of breaking the peace and causing an affray to the scandal of the government (the Lord Chancellor was in the crowd), but he swore he would use the incident in a play one day.

At the end of 1664 or beginning of 1665, Nell had a part in Sir William Killigrew's *The Siege of Urbino*, an Italian melodrama, which meant flashing teeth, tears, intrigue and above all poisoning, which was what Italians were said to do best after painting – Webster had established this canon and in only two of his plays Italians poison their victims in four ways, touching the leaves of a book, the horn of a saddle, the lips on a portrait and a specially prepared helmet. The heroine of this piece, Celestina, was played by Anne Marshall, a strapping woman who was dressed on stage in man's clothes (periwig, coat and breeches) and was supposed to be striding the world in search of adventure to avoid being forced into an unwelcome marriage. Nell was her maid, Melina, also dressed in men's clothes, which suited her well. Her legs were better than Marshall's, which caused bad feeling between them, and with the Boutel-Barry incident in mind there was an explicit stage direction: 'Florio [Marshall] and Pedro [Nell] must not fight on stage through the whole play.' Though *The Siege of Urbino* was very dull, the King himself came one afternoon to see it; he was fond of all the Killigrews, Sir William, Sir Philip, Tom and Harry, and gave them grace-and-favour apartments in Whitehall Palace.

Nell, at fifteen, was now a full member of the company and the subject of several doubtful anecdotes. She began to dine out with Hart and meet rakes and gallants, and members of the newly formed Royal Society. There is some difference of opinion about the ancestry of the Society. Aubrey says that, 'John Wilkins, Bishop of Chester was the principal reviver of experimentall philosophy (*secundum mentem domini Baconi*) at Oxford, where he had an experimentall philosophicall clubbe, which began 1649 and was the *incunabula* of the Royall Society. When he came to London, they mett at the Bull-head tavern in Cheapside (eg 1658, 1659, and after), till it grew to big for a clubb, and so they came to Gresham colledge parlour.' But he also suggests that James Harrington's Rota Club, which met in the Turk's Head, New Palace Yard, and Miles Coffee-house was the germ of the idea. When Harrington was gaoled for his unorthodox political views (he likened the change from Parliament rule to absolute monarchy to the evolutions of an Italian carnival horseman, dressed half in Spanish and half in French habit who twisted and turned to please the different factions in the crowd), his cronies urged Sir Robert Moray to form the Society, half scientific, half Harrington-querulous; Sir Robert, who helped the King with 'his chymicall operations' persuaded Charles II in his turn to do just this.

It was very important for Nell at the outset of her career to add a little polish to her native wit, and learn how to behave in polite society. She was lucky in that Restoration society was not very polite. Table-manners were appalling. Everyone ate too much and got drunk, even ' ... the greatest physician of his time, William Butler who kept an old mayd whose name was Nell. At nine or ten Nell comes for him [to the tavern] and says "Come home, you drunken beast." By and by Nell would stumble; then her master calls her "drunken beast"; and so they did drunken beast one another all the way until they came home.' Bad table-manners, drunkenness or no, there were great opportunities for Nell Gwyn to widen her acquaintance. Her willingness to learn, as well as her fresh young beauty, captivated many famous men; as well as Dryden, she charmed other members of the Royal Society, including Sir Robert Moray (the President), Dr Christopher Wren and Robert Hooke. Aubrey did not like her (he was a Fellow) but this was perhaps because he was too loyal to the Duke's House and Davenant,

> Since it was he, this later age,
> Who chiefly civilised the stage.

There were also more plebeian excursions, and entertainments in her new lodgings, next door to the Cock & Pie. What she had learnt of the English language was mostly unprintable even in a permissive society. Until recently, the only speech she had heard which had contained a few ideas were the sermons on Sundays at St Martin-in-the-Fields and the occasional snatch of good talk overheard in a brothel or tavern, and she found the company of brilliant men rather tiring. She used to go for relaxation to cockfights with John Pritchard, son of the owner of the Cock & Pie (he later became a Dissenting minister). There was a pit nearby in Shoe Lane, which Pepys also favoured. It had a mixed clientele – Members of Parliament, 'the poorest prentices, bakers, butchers, brewers' draymen … swearing, cursing and betting'. Nell swore with the best of them and put her money on the outcome of every match; she was to become a lifelong gambler and wagered recklessly even then, though her wages for 1665 were only £20 (the year).

She also liked public executions, of which there were many. Once the summary execution of Cromwell's surviving cronies was done, there was an endless supply of highwaymen and the occasional gentleman who had committed murders too often to be ignored by discriminating magistrates. Executions were always announced well in advance, with broadsheets and ballads recording the crimes and eccentricities of the condemned. Refreshments were available. There was always a good crowd, varying from an attendance of 20,000 for a popular highwayman to 10,000 for a less-known unfortunate. Richard Knolles, author of *The Battles of Lepanto* was just such an unfortunate. Aubrey says that Lord Burleigh 'was extremely pleased at the description of the battail … hunted after him and traced him from place to place and at last to Newgate. He was hanged but a 14 night before. He unluckily lost a good opportunity of being preferred.'

There were, too, always fights and duels to enjoy. Gentlemen brawled as did the butchers at Moorfields, 'who knocked down all for weavers that had green or blue aprons'. Notorious whores who gave the pox or the clap to married men were often set upon by irate wives, were whipped or had their pudenda shaved in public (the five women barbers of Drury Lane meted out this sort of punishment). Sir William Curtin's daughter married her footman who 'beates her, gettes her money and runs away' pursued by an enthusiastic crowd.

The coffee-houses, too, were not patronized exclusively by Puritans. Nell went often to Farres at the Inner Temple Gate and John's in Fullers Rents. Least boring of the teetotallers was Sir Henry Blount, who 'much exclaimed against drunkennesse but he allowed wenching', which must have been a comfort for Nell. It was Sir Henry who wagered with a handsome braggart 'that let the two of them go together to a bordello, he only with his handsome person and Sir Henry with a xxs piece on his bald crowne, that the wenches would choose Sir Henry. Sir Henry won the wager,' says Aubrey.

There were also blameless pursuits. In fine weather the pleasure gardens at Charing Cross were only a few minutes walk away, and the larger ones at Lambeth and Vauxhall a short drive. All sorts of jugglers and rope-dancers performed, especially at the great fairs, like St Bartholomew's on 24 August in West Smithfield. The streets themselves were a living theatre. Nell had been part of it all and still laughed at the street cries and banter between the hawkers.

But as the winter warmed towards spring, more and more time had to be spent on preparation for her first major role. Dryden had been as good as his word and had written or revised a part for her in his new play *The Indian Emperor or The Conquest of Mexico by the Spaniards*. It was very important for Dryden that this should be a success. His first play, *The Wild Gallant*, had not pleased the critical public; Pepys dismissed it as 'as poor a thing as ever I saw in my life and so little answering the name that from beginning to end I could not tell which was the Wild Gallant'. His next had been an improvement (*The Rival Ladies*) but had not run. With Sir Robert Howard he had written a verse play called *The Indian Queen* (not much of it was his) and from it had extracted the nucleus of the new play. In order to intrigue the King and make sure he attended, Dryden had dedicated the play to the wife of Charles' favourite bastard, James Scott, Duke of Monmouth, with the words: 'I have neither followed the Truth of History nor altogether left it: but have taken the liberty of a Poet, to adde or alter or diminish as I thought might best conduce to the beautifying of my work, it not being the business of a Poet to represent Truth but probability.' Historical subjects always went down well with a London audience. Dryden, as the play's title suggests, chose a series of incidents in the conquest of Mexico by Cortez as the setting for an amorous Court intrigue. Charles Hart was cast as Cortez, who falls in love with Cydaria, daughter of the Emperor Montezuma; Nell took the part of Cydaria, to the huge delight of everybody 'in the know' that she was Hart's love of the moment in real life. They also read into her reply, when commanded by her father to marry an Indian prince, Orbellan, a reference to the supposed rivalry between Hart and Lacy:

> So strong a hatred does my nature sway
> That spight of my duty I must disobey.
> Besides you warn'd me still of loving two,
> Can I love him, already loving you?

Montezuma was played by Michael Mohun, and Alibech by Elizabeth Weaver, mistress of Tom Killigrew. There were as many private intrigues on stage and off as there were dramatic incidents. Dryden turned what could have been just a melodramatic clash of wills and conflict of desires into a very fine tragedy, and his skill in the use of rhyme makes the play never stiff or laboured. It is in many respects his best tragedy, and the various prologues, epilogues and songs (many of them sung or spoken by Nell) refreshed it over the years. It all ends well, with Cydaria marrying Cortez, and Nell's rival in the company, Anne Marshall (Almeria), discomfited.

Though the critics, led by their doyen Gerard Langbaine, praised the play, they had grave doubts about Nell Gwyn's suitability for the role of Cydaria. They made allowances for the fact that she was only just fifteen and forecast a brilliant future for her, but the general opinion was that this was a very

gifted comic actress in the making, who should not be put to playing
tragedy, even well-written tragedy. Amateur experts like Samuel Pepys
agreed. He noted in his Diary: 'I was most infinitely displeased with her
being put to act the Emperor's daughter, which is a great and serious part,
which she does most basely.' However, Pepys' comment should be taken
with some reserve because he was trying to get his own doxy, Mary Knipp,
into the play, believing she would do Cydaria better; he was not pleased
when all he achieved two years later was to get Knipp into the lesser role of
Alibech.

The *Paneygyric* contradicts all the critics:

> Fate now for her did its whole force engage,
> And from the pit she's mounted to the stage,
> There, in full lustre did her glories shine,
> And, long eclipsed, spread forth their light divine.

The King did not, after all, attend the opening of *the Indian Emperor* in
March 1665. For one thing, he did not like tragedy. His taste had been
formed during his exile in Paris and he liked best the work of Molière and
Corneille, which he was always urging Tom Killigrew to have translated.
Anyway, he had two other things on his mind. The first was potentially
pleasurable. For two years he had been pursuing Frances Teresa Stewart, the
elder daughter of a doctor in his mother's service who had returned to
England in January 1663 to captivate the Court. The susceptible Pepys
noticed ' ... Mrs Stewart in this dress, with her hat cocked and a red plume
with her sweet eyes, little Roman nose, and excellent *taille* ... the greatest
beauty I ever saw, I think in my life'; she displaced Barbara Castlemaine,
about whom he had had erotic dreams, in his pantheon of beauties. But Mrs
Stewart (the style 'Miss' was accorded only to whores) was after marrying
'any gentleman of £1,500 a year that would have her in honour' and held
the King off though he 'had more in dalliance than any man should have
had'. The King's appetite was whetted by her refusal to go farther, and he
was determined to have her. He even wrote her poems:

> I pass all my hours in a shady old grove,
> But I live not the day when I see not my love ...

but they were not very good and had no effect. He had organized balls and
banquets in an effort to get her drunk or dizzy or both, and he had recruited
all the members of what Marvell called 'the Merry Gang' (the Duke of
Buckingham, the Earl of Mulgrave, Lord Buckhurst and the Earl of
Rochester) to the cause of 'getting La Belle Stewart for the King'. Even the
Queen had got to know of the chase and attended one feast herself,
unannounced, to her husband's great embarrassment. As Nell was enjoying

the applause at his playhouse, he was making yet another desperate effort to please, commissioning the famous goldsmith Jan Roettiers to engrave Frances' profile and use it on the new coinage as the face of Britannia (it is still used today on the 50p coin).

When he was not pursuing La Belle Stewart, the King was pursuing the Dutch. The origins of the Dutch War are obscure and are probably to be found in the greed of City merchants. The beginning of the decline of Spanish and Portuguese seapower in mid-century had left the Dutch and English merchant fleets the largest and most powerful in the world. They clashed frequently during local disputes in the Mediterranean (the Queen's dowry of Tangiers was a very useful naval station), in the West Indies, along the coasts of Africa and North America and in the Far East. Sometimes the clashes became more serious than 'incidents'. In the previous autumn there had been a naval battle off Cabo Verde, which had been taken by the English, who seemed to have no intention of leaving the Dutch forts. Charles had tried to shrug off protests by the Dutch Ambassador, who reminded him of the dynastic ties between the two countries and of Dutch hospitality during the Interregnum, but it was clear that King and Parliament had decided to prepare for all-out war. The question of supremacy had to be settled once and for all. War was in fact declared in March 1665, and a warship was launched on the very day Nell Gwyn was launched in *The Indian Emperor* at Drury Lane. The new warship joined over a hundred large vessels and thirty smaller, 21,000 men and 4,200 guns, a Navy of which everybody was proud; it was commanded by the Duke of York, Pepys' patron and employer. Nothing happened immediately, as both sides prepared to do battle, and Pepys had time to go to the theatre. On 3 April 1665 he records: ' ... and then with Creed, my wife and Mercer to a play at the Duke's of my Lord Orrery's, called *Mustapha*; which being not good made Betterton's part and Ianthe's part but ordinary, too, so that we were not contented with it at all. ... All the pleasure of the play was, the King and my Lady Castlemayne were there; and pretty witty Nell, at the King's House, and the younger Marshall sat next us which pleased me mightily.' In spite of his doubts about her acting, he knew the lines, already abroad:

> More cruel than the Tyger o'er his spoyl;
> And falser than the Weeping Crocodile;
> Can you adde Vanity to Guilt, and take
> A pride to hear the Conquests which you make?
> Go, publish your renown: let it be said
> You have a woman, and that lov'd, betrayed.

Nell's approach to Cortez in the play was already 'popular'. Aubrey was at the Duke's House that night, too, with some other members of the Royal Society, wondering whether or not he should take up an offer of some land in America, around the recently captured New Amsterdam, now renamed New York in the Duke's honour. The two gossips did not speak. At supper Pepys raved about the actresses and toasted a better play next time for Betterton.

Behind the façade of lusty patriotism and *joie de vivre*, Pepys was worried. He knew that the Fleet looked good and sounded impressive, but he also knew that many of the sailors were forcibly recruited, ill trained and low in morale. He knew too, that the Dutch fleet, though smaller, was better chandlered and: 'The Dutch are not to be trampled on, if you do they will kick. Their trade is their God, if you depress that by force, they will venture all for it.' And he knew that the Duke of York, his master, was thirsting for war, cost what it might. All the Stewarts seem to have been perennially short of money. Even the coronation ballad of King James VI and I goes:

> And at the arse of them marched the Scottish peers
> With lowzie shirts, and mangie wrists, pricking up their
> eares.

James, Duke of York was a typically impecunious Stewart. Like his brother, the King, he had expensive tastes in women, but he was without his brother's revenues. He had become Chairman of the Royal Africa Company and was determined to make the money he needed by trade, acquiring monopolies by fair means or foul. Already a secret convert to Roman Catholicism (the precise date is unknown), he would have had some difficulties with his Jesuit confessor had he planned to steal French, Spanish or Portuguese trade routes, but the Dutch were Protestants and so fair game. He thought he could not go far wrong. He had a fine fleet and a group of experienced commanders, including Monck, Duke of Albermarle, Prince Rupert, the Earl of Sandwich, Sir William Penn (James' Captain General, Admiral under Cromwell and father of the Quaker) and Charles Berkeley (whose wife was an occasional royal whore). His conscience was not troubled by the fact that if he broke the Dutch at sea he would inherit not only the spice trade but also the slave trade to America. The nature of the trade was of no moral concern. What mattered was that, 'The trade of the world is too little for us two, therefore one must go down.'

Throughout the month of April, James waited impatiently. As John Wilson observed in his (1952) life of Nell: 'The audience at the theatres grew daily thinner as patriotic young gentlemen volunteered for naval service and timorous old gentlemen took their families to their inland estates.' On 3 May James could wait no longer. To Pepys' horror (he knew the fleet was not properly victualled), he boarded his flagship, the *Royal Charles* and sailed for the Dutch coast. The wind was fair and the fleet made good time to the North Sea, where it took up station outside the Dutch ports. Unfortunately by the time the blockade had become effective, the beer had run out and the Lord High Admiral was told there was food left for only a week. After ten days of resolute inaction, James had to order a return to port for victualling.

As the anchors went down again in friendly home waters, the chandlers and victuallers, and Pepys, swarmed aboard. Among the shouts and clink of coin there were heard the screams of some sailors' women, caught aboard by the sudden sailing, and they detected 'legs to the hams hanging out at the end of hammocks or over the end'. The women were whipped ashore to the sound of trumpets.

On 30 May the stores were full and the hammocks empty, and the fleet set sail again. Pepys noted: 'Lord, how some poor women did cry, and in my life I never did see such natural expression of passion as I did in some women's bewailing themselves.' He himself bewailed the profiteering of naval suppliers ('I see that it is impossible for the King to have things done as cheap as other men') and the general shortage of money in the Navy, especially for maintenance and repairs.

Charles, unworried (all his life he believed that trouble, if ignored, would go away), went to the theatre that night. Dryden and the Howards at the King's House and Etherege at the Duke's wrote patriotic prologues, delivered to the dwindling audiences by Nell Gwyn, the Marshalls and the 'irreproachable Mrs Bracegirdle'. The King did not neglect his private pleasures either; when Pepys had the news that the English and Dutch fleets were about to engage off Lowestoft, he had to go to Barbara Castlemaine's house to find his monarch.

The Duke of York's officers were certainly very able, and James himself was very brave. The battle was fought in accordance with the latest English view of tactics, that war at sea was a question of accurate gunnery rather than sharp cutlasses after boarding. At dawn on 3 June James took advantage of a south-west wind to sail in line ahead at the Dutch fleet, taking the wind out of their sails; as the fleets came abreast, the English sailing north and the Dutch south, all guns were fired which could find a target. This deadly promenade was repeated, the English sailing south and the Dutch north, with more artillery duels at long distance. Then James decided he would close with the Dutch flagship and hammer it out at close quarters, if possible killing the Dutch admiral, Opdam. It was soon obvious, as each ship sought out what its captain thought was his equivalent in rank, that English gunnery was better than the Dutch, though casualties were horrifying on both sides. On the *Royal Charles*, James was distressed when his friend Berkeley had his head smashed by chain shot; later the unfortunate and unpopular sailor was commemorated rather unkindly by Sir John Denham:

His shattered head the fearless Duke disdains,
And gave the last first proof that he had brains.

Willem van der Velde, the offical war artist with the Dutch fleet, narrowly escaped death when the Dutch flagship blew up, a shot having found the magazine.

When they became aware of this disaster, the rest of the Dutch fleet sensibly ran for its home ports. Had it been hotly pursued, as James ordered, Dutch naval strength would have been nominal for years to come. Incredibly, while James rested after eighteen hours on deck, a member of his staff decided that sail should be shortened 'to give a greater calm'; when the Duke woke, he found the fleet he had defeated had escaped him.

Notwithstanding the farcical outcome of the Battle of Lowestoft, James sailed home to a hero's welcome.

That week began with celebrations in London and other towns almost as frenetic as those which followed the Restoration. Taverns and brothels worked hard to keep pace with the demand for what they had to offer. In the pleasure gardens a special cheesecake was made called 'Dutch Crust', sold to the hungry and patriotic. The streets were full of drunken sailors, who were 'treated' everywhere. The King congratulated his brother and gave him a novelty, a guitar, and urged him to find a lady who could play it; he himself worried about the late arrival of some silk waistcoats from France, and wrote a sharp letter of complaint to his sister about it.

Unfortunately for the whores and the hawkers, the King, the Court and the heroes, the celebrations did not last a week.

The first sign of trouble was a mutiny among the sailors who had remained at Lowestoft. Only a few of these were volunteers. Most of them had been pressganged during the weeks James' fleet was refitting; some of them were not even from the south-east and included the crews of some Newcastle colliers, pressed into service because at least they had some experience of sailing in the North Sea. Virtually nobody had been paid. There was, it seems, no money with which to pay off the ships. Hopefully, the naval authorities at Lowestoft had offered promissory notes, called 'tickets', to be redeemed at some future date, but no collier crew was going to leave for Newcastle in the vague hope that somebody in London would remember to send up funds with which to redeem them. Added to the discontent of the pressed men was an epidemic of scurvy which swept through the fleet. There were no doctors to look after the sick because there was no money to pay the doctors. When the wages of the dockyard workers were found to be missing, too, there was uproar and rioting and threats to let the ships rot in future, even in the middle of a war. All this was good news for the Dutch, who had their spies everywhere.

Nell Gwyn in London knew nothing of the mutiny at Lowestoft. Even had she done so, she would have put it out of her mind as being less important than her rapid rise from brothel barmaid to emerging star of the King's House; she was, of course, now a civil servant, or more properly one of the King's servants, with a number of privileges and a clearly defined social status. She was too young, as well as too taken up with her own affairs, to pay much attention to politics, something which interested men when they were not panting after young girls like her and her colleagues. Only the threat of death or, even worse, disfigurement could have shaken her out of her complacency.

It was on 7 June, the day Charles Hart told her she was to have a dressing-room of her own and gave her a necklace (not a very expensive one, his salary being only £3 a week) that she was brought face to face with the possibility of either.

On that same day, Samuel Pepys had a similar shock. It was, he recorded in his Diary, 'the hottest day that I have ever felt in my life'. He was walking in Drury Lane, probably on his way to see Knipp, when he saw a red cross painted on the doors of several houses there, 'which was a sad sight to me, being the first of that kind that, to my remembrance, I ever saw'. Before Nell and Knipp could go to the theatre for the day's rehearsal, the Lord Chamberlain had enforced the edict, signed three days before, closing all theatres and places of public entertainment indefinitely.

On 10 June Pepys' own doctor, Burnett, shut his door, a sign that he too had the Plague. It was 'spreading fast from the City to Westminster'.

On 14 June Tom Killigrew ordered all his actors and actresses out of Town. Weeping, afraid and frustrated, Nell took her mother and fled in Pritchard's cart to Oxford until the horror was over.

The Road to Tunbridge Wells, 1665-7

[The Plague] occasioned Sir John Denham's distemper of madness in 1665, which first appeared when he went from London to see the famous freestone quarries at Portland in Dorset, and when he came within a mile of it, turned back to London again and did not see it. He went to Hownslowe, and demanded rents of lands he had sold many years before; went to the king and told him he was the Holy Ghost.

Aubrey

The Great Plague of 1665 has almost a literary *genre* of its own, though the disease was virtually confined to the capital and the Home Counties. Puritans in the West Country, Cheshire and East Yorkshire kept their presses busy printing pamphlets and tracts denouncing the 'lewdness and ungodliness' which had brought down this latest instalment of God's wrath; Andrew Marvell was particularly scathing, even suggesting that the King's crony Lord Brouncker had let the Dutch fleet escape in an attempt to propitiate a Protestant Deity.

In the capital, those who could flee packed their linen, plate and cash and went up the Thames or down to the Medway towns until it was all over. The poor, and officials who could not leave their posts, soon became resigned to the searchers passing from house to house to make sure the dead had been brought out to the carts; resigned to the carts themselves, full of stinking corpses drawn to mass graves; resigned to the carters and gravediggers kept drunk at the public expense so they could cope with their wretched task; resigned to the church bells tolling and the handbells clanging before the dead.

In the first week of the Plague there were over a hundred corpses; by September the figure had risen to over a thousand a day in a population of about half a million.

There were no medical services, no notions of public health. The wooden houses were rotten with damp (the spire of St Paul's had fallen down), and into the narrow streets housewives threw garbage and the contents of

chamberpots, praying for rain to wash it all away. The open sewers
worsened the pollution of the Thames and Fleet below and, above, the air
poisoned by brewers, soapboilers, dyers and others who ran their effluent
into the rivers and thus noxious gases into the sky. Not that the behaviour of
the better-off set much of an example: Pepys' wife fouled Lincoln's Inn
Walk several times when she was taken short away from home. There was
also the anti-social problem of the looter, and many middle-class
householders found themselves in Pepys' straits, paying for his own lodgings
(at the Admiralty evacuated to Greenwich), his wife's emergency lodgings
(Mrs Pepys and three maids were at Woolwich) and a caretaker for their
house in the City, 'a damnable expense'.

Nell Gwyn and her mother lodged for a time with her grandfather, the
canon, at Christ Church, Oxford, where he had rooms. They were not the
only refugees from the metropolis, and gossips forecast a season as heady as
that of 1642-3. Before the Court arrived, however, old Mrs Gwyn's
addiction to brandy and startling vocabulary made a move necessary, and
Charles Hart, who had joined them, found them a house just outside the
town. He brought with him strange tales. Most physicians had left London,
and innumerable quacks had taken their places; there was a Plague Specific
consisting of powdered roots and herbs simmered in Málaga wine. Rumour
also had it that syphilis somehow worked as a vaccination against the
Plague, and Madame Ross and her sisters were seeking out old whores they
had discharged as being notoriously poxed. This medical fiction was perhaps
not surprising when Aubrey records that William Butler 'causes a cow to be
killed and opened and the dead parson putt into the cowes warm belly,
which after some time brought him to life'.

The King set a good example. He confined his wife to Hampton Court,
though most of his and her courtiers had gone as far away as Salisbury, but
stayed in his capital for most of the summer. Pepys accompanied him on a
tour of inspection of the fleet refitting at Greenwich on 26 July (arrears of
wages had been paid) and noted that the bastard Duke of Monmouth, never
far from his father, was a 'skittish, leaping gallant ... always in action,
vaulting or leaping or clambering'. In August the King joined his Court at
Salisbury, reviving morale, then took the opportunity to tour the West
Country, thanking in person for the first time many who had helped him
escape, a decade and more ago, from Cromwell's Roundheads. In October
the King and Queen and both their entourages moved to Oxford, where
Barbara Castlemaine gave birth to her third royal bastard in the lodgings of a
Fellow of Merton (she also relieved herself habitually in his fireplace).

In late November a sudden severe frost did more to halt the spread of the
Plague than the Specific, and deaths fell to just over five hundred a week and
went on falling; this was just as well because, 'In Westminster there is never
a physician and but one apothecary left.' Pepys consoled himself by buying

two barrels of oysters and chatting with the shopkeeper, 'a fine woman', who had survived. Life in the capital was still grim, however, and as Defoe commented later, 'All the Plays and Interludes ... were forbod to act. ... The Gaming Tables, public Dancing Rooms and Music Houses ... were shut up and suppressed; and the Jack-Puddings, Merry Andrews, Puppet Shows, Rope Dancers and such-like doings ... shut up their shops.' Sir Edmund Berry Godfrey wrote to the Earl of Newport on 19 December: 'The poor people cry out upon the dearness of fuel and want of employment by reason of the King and Court having been so long out of town, and some of the courtiers, nobility and gentry forgetting of their debts as well as their charity.'

By Christmas, however, Plague deaths had fallen to double figures and the King became more cheerful. He lifted the ban he had imposed in Oxford on all divertissements, and the university town came to life immediately. La Belle Stewart sang in French in the evenings but still kept the King at arm's length at night. Balls were given and gallants strolled again in the gardens of Christ Church. Nell was joined by her sister, and they lived with other members of the King's and Duke's Houses on the fringe of the Court, flirting with the gallants and keeping up with the latest fashions. A great many public feasts were given that Christmas by the King and the burgesses, the King in genuine gratitude for the approaching end of a nightmare, the burgesses in the hope that the Court would move on as soon as possible.

At the end of January 1666 Charles took his wife back to Hampton Court and a fortnight later returned to Whitehall amid general rejoicing. Pepys started to go to church again but resolved not to walk through churchyards, past the sinister mounds still picked over by the crows. Nell Gwyn and her friends seem to have taken lodgings for a while in the City, which was soon 'almost as full again of people as ever it was'. Covent Garden was still deserted, though hammering and clattering were to be heard as places of public entertainment were refurbished. The King's House was 'all in dirt, they being altering of the stage to make it wider', when Pepys visited it on 19 March. He had disapproved of 'the narrowness of the passages in and out of the Pit, and the distance from the stage to the boxes, which I am confident cannot hear (and the music being below, and most of it sounding under the very stage, there is no hearing of the bases at all, nor very well of the trebles)'. Tom Killigrew assured him that all these faults would be remedied. Pepys reported: 'My business ... was to see the inside of the stage and all the tiring-rooms and machines; and indeed it was a sight worth seeing. But to see their clothes, and the various sorts, and what a mixture of things there was; a wooden leg here, there a ruff, here a hobby-horse, there a crown would make a man split himself to see, with laughing: and particularly Lacy's wardrobe and Shotrell's.' He was also curious about the survival of the company, and Killigrew reassured him. Lacy and the Shatterels (William and Robert) were well, as were the rest of the men: Mohun, Hart, Clun, 'Scum' Goodman, Kynaston, Burt, Bateman, Baxter, Cartwright, Duke Hancock, Wintershall and some new recruits. All the women were well too: his favourite Mrs Knipp, the Marshall sisters, Mrs Rutter, Mrs Boutel, Mrs Knight, Mrs Verjuice, Mrs James, Mrs Uphill (now Lady Howard and only an occasional performer) and, of course, little Mrs Gwyn.

There was a new note of scandal: Clun was said to be the bastard of Ben Jonson – that was why he had 'one eie lower than t'other and bigger'.

After the refurbishing of the House, the players needed new clothes, including a new set of the livery they were entitled to wear as King's Servants. On 30 June 1666 'Ellen Gwyn' and the other 'eleven women comedians in His Majesty's Theatre' were sent four yards of bastard scarlet cloth and one quarter yard of velvet each, with which to make their cloaks.

Major Mohun had an ingenious idea, to build lodgings for all the company in Playhouse Yard, Drury Lane. They could be better supervised there, their health protected if not their virtue. Davenant had tried something similar before the Plague but the rooms had been too bleak and the Duke's company had not been enthusiastic. Mohun's project met a similar fate: only Elizabeth Weaver and the Shatterels joined his little club. There was one very good reason for the failure – the actresses who were not being kept by some generous nobleman had to make shift to earn what they could in the brothels, because the allowance the King was supposed to pay them was insufficient to feed and clothe them.

There is some evidence to suggest that Nell Gwyn and her mother did not stay long in the City, and delayed their return to the old lodgings until the end of the year. They may well have gone to live in converted stables ('neat houses') in the old Manor of Eye, 'a detached portion of St Martin-in-the-Fields', divided into the three Manors of Neyte, Eybury and Hyde (Geo. Saunders FRS); the Grosvenor Estate archives suggest that the exact location was Warwick Street, Pimlico. It would no doubt have been healthier in semi-rural Chelsea, and there were certainly temporary camps there and on the south bank of the Thames; though the main parish area was declared free from plague on 30 January 1666, this was probably wishful thinking or a device to get commerce back on its feet again.

The Dutch War came to life in the early summer. The English fleet was divided into two, half under Prince Rupert and half under Albemarle (the King forbade his brother to risk his life again), and put to sea to show that the Plague had not lowered its morale. From 1-5 June a naval battle was fought in the Channel. The Dutch, under Admiral de Ruyter, showed that they had improved their gunnery. It was said that the sound of battle could be heard in London as 130 men-of-war shot at each other at point-blank range, destroying ships, men and, accidentally, a fishing fleet. When the ammunition was gone, the battle ceased and both sides claimed victory; the wounded were banned from the streets of London so that victory should not be in doubt.

This bloody exchange does not seem to have affected Killigrew, Davenant or their companies. The work of refurbishing the theatres went on, new costumes were made, new plays were rehearsed and all was ready by the beginning of August; a number of performances were given at Court. The Bear Garden at Bankside reopened with bear- and bull-baiting for the *aficionados*. There was a general feeling of optimism, encouraged by hot, sunny weather and news of fresh skirmishes, undoubtedly successful this time, with the Dutch at sea.

According to Pepys (29 August 1666), the King's House re-opened on 18 August; Orange Moll was his informant, though she was not forthcoming about which play was done, nor even for how many days the show ran. There is no other evidence of the reopening, and if Killigrew did presume the Lord Chamberlain's ban had lapsed then, Davenant would certainly have had it invoked. The best interpretation of the conflicting evidence is that there were dress rehearsals for either *The Maid's Tragedy* or *The English Monsieur*, and that an invited audience saw them – a sort of trailer, as it were. What is known is that sixteen-year-old Nell Gwyn had already been chosen to play the leading female role in *The English Monsieur*, opposite her lover Charles Hart. Once more, Fate was to be unkind to her.

As he was dressing on the morning of Sunday 2 September, Pepys looked out of his window. When he had gone to bed in the early hours, a red glow in the sky had presaged fine weather; now the glow was still there but framed in smoke, and there were great shouts in the streets. Hurriedly finishing his dressing, he ran from his house in Seething Lane towards the City.

The Great Fire, which was to destroy most of old London, had begun in a baker's shop in Pudding Lane earlier that morning. The old wooden houses and shops, the warehouses full of silk, tar, oil and spirits, burned for six days, devouring 13,000 houses and many churches, including St Paul's Cathedral, 'after an incredible manner' (Evelyn). On Tuesday morning the King and his brother rode to the City, where the Fire was still being fought hard, in vain. He stayed in the front line all day, passing leather buckets of water, even taking a pick in his hand to make a firebreak. He ordered the Lord Mayor, Sir Thomas Bludworth, to take powder to blow a *cordon sanitaire* round the worst of the blaze so that the fire should not get up Fleet Street. The unfortunate Sir Thomas told him that he had been pulling down houses as fast as he could, but his citizens would not obey him; they had only just moved back in with all their treasure, after the exile from the Plague, and hung on until they were driven out by the heat and the smoke.

In his poem *Annus Mirabilis*, Dryden paid tribute to Charles' heroism:

Now day appears and with the day the King,
Whose early care had robbed him of his rest;
Far off the cracks of falling houses ring
And shrieks of subjects pierce his tender breast.
Near as he draws, thick harbingers of smoke
With gloomy pillars cover all the place;
Whose little intervals of night are broke
By sparks that drive against his sacred face.

John Dryden and Nell Gwyn were very close companions at this time, but it is almost certain that they were nothing more. He might have spent some hours dallying with her sister Rose while her husband was on the road, but she was generally available; Nell was not promiscuous by Restoration standards and, anyway, knew that it was in her interests at this stage in her career not to offend Charles Hart. The same sort of reasoning probably stayed Dryden's hand. He was only thirty-five and had had one great success on stage, due to Hart and Nell. Though he enjoyed the King's patronage (his poem, written as a schoolboy, on the premature death of Lord Hastings in 1645, had first endeared him to his royal contemporary), he suspected that his contemporaries George Etherege, William Wycherley and Thomas Shadwell were better playwrights. For Dryden, the fact that he had insinuated himself into the inner circle of the King's House and could use the theatre to keep himself ahead of his rivals was more important than the perlaceous delights of the body of even a talented sixteen-year-old girl; he, too, did not want to offend Hart.

What did Nell and John Dryden have in common? Perhaps, as one critic has it, the fact that she was common. Professor Arthur Humphreys wrote wisely that the works of Sidney, Spenser, Bacon, Donne, Herbert and Milton 'appear to be written partly for their own sakes and partly for the reader as a single person, a private auditor, not one of a wide community. On the other hand ... the satires and prefaces of Dryden call up an inescapable notion of an extended public.' In Restoration times there was an audience 'out there', not just in the theatre. Charles II had given his patronage and warrant to the Royal Society because he did not believe knowledge to be the prerogative of an elite. His own adventures had taught him that there were quick minds far from Court circles; maybe he really believed in 'cultural democracy' – and as the *History of the Royal Society* puts it, 'preferring the language of Artizans, Countrymen and Merchants, before that of Wits or Scholars'. Dryden was convinced that it was 'easier to be Greate' under Charles if he did not lose the common touch; he probably found in his *gamine* companion a key to the language of the ordinary people who were coming to frequent the theatres in increasing numbers. She found in his use of language, in his skill with rhymed couplet and quatrain, and in his patience, a great help to learning parts which she could not read.

Whatever it was that made them find pleasure in each other's company, they were both anxious to get back to work. The risk of a new outbreak of the fire had almost disappeared with the coming of autumn (though ruins still smouldered in January), but the Lord Chamberlain gave no sign of lifting his ban. The actors and actresses were starved of applause and very short of money; the King's allowance to his Servants was still paid erratically. There was also the irritating knowledge that plays were being put on at Court. On 18 October 1666 Evelyn noted that: 'This night was acted my Lord Brahal's Tragedy called *Mustapha* before their Majesties at Court: at which I was present, though very seldom at any time going to the publique Theatres, for many reasons, now as they were abused to an atheisticall liberty, fowle and indecent; Women now (and never 'til now) permitted to appear and act, which inflaming severall young noble-men and gallants, became their whores, some to their Wives.'

At the end of October the Lord Chamberlain relented. Davenant was given permission to reopen the Duke's House, which he did on 29 October with Etherege's new play *Love in a Tub*. Killigrew, perhaps to punish him for an illegal performance in August, was made to wait until the end of November before his licence was renewed; perhaps the King intervened, in response to a petition by his Servants to reopen, promising to show their gratitude by donating the takings one day a week for the care of victims of Plague and Fire.

On 7 December the King's House opened its doors with a performance of *The Maid's Tragedy*, but this was really only a warm-up for the comedy produced next day, *The English Monsieur*, by Dryden's brother-in-law, the Honourable James Howard. Howard had done some unsuccessful re-writing of Shakespeare for Davenant, who put on *Romeo and Juliet* in the new and revised versions on alternate days to stave off criticism. *The English Monsieur* was less controversial, and Pepys, who was at the opening night, commented: 'To the King's playhouse, and there did see a good part of *The English Monsieur*, which is a mighty pretty play, very witty and pleasant. And the women do very well, but above all, little Nelly, that I am mightily pleased with the play, and much with the House, more than I ever expected, and very fine women.'

It is interesting to compare the comments by Evelyn and Pepys, if only to see how alive still was the debate on women's direct participation in the life of the theatre. Evelyn was not worried about what would now be thought of as the 'racist' undertones of *Mustapha*, nor Pepys about the cynicism of *The English Monsieur*; it was the women on stage, fine or corrupting gallants and noblemen, witty or silly, which got the tongues wagging. Six years after the Restoration, there was a current of Italian Cinquecento morality running through the thoughts of men like Evelyn. The honour of the family had to be protected at its sexual fount; it was right that Prince Lelio Massimo's sons should murder his second wife because her low social status was an insult to the honour of the family (one of the murderers, Luca, was acquitted on these grounds) – so it was right that sons of noble families in England should be protected from actresses.

Nell Gwyn's audiences liked women and did not see why they should not be as unscrupulous as men as long as they were witty with it. She was cast as Lady Wealthy, a rich widow, and the fact that she was so credible in this role though not yet seventeen says much for her talent. Many of the lines had been written for her by James Howard, who knew her well: 'This life of mine can last no longer than my beauty; and though 'tis pleasant now – I want nothing whilst I am Mr Wellbred's mistress – yet, if his mind should change, I might e'en sell oranges for my living; and he not buy one of me to relieve me.' Everybody in the audience knew that she had been an orange-girl, and Mary Meggs, 'Orange Moll', is reported to have cackled every night when her former protégée spoke these lines. The social morality of a fortune hunter, in exchange for a name, being able to make off with a rich relict's goods, was not questioned. Anyway, everybody knew that she was living with 'Mr Wellbred' (Charles Hart) and that, just as he had no nobility, she had no fortune. The pit appreciated the blows dealt in repartee:

> *Lady Wealthy*: Go, hang yourself.
> *Wellbred*: Thank you for your advice.
> *Lady Wealthy*: Well, then, shall I see you again?
> *Wellbred*: When I have a mind to it. Come, I'll lead you to your coach for once.
> *Lady Wealthy*: And I'll let you for once.

Though the play was a great success and was performed on and off for years (long runs of the same play were almost unknown), Tom Killigrew did not rest on his laurels. He was determined to make the repertory of his House larger and more popular than that of the Duke's. His management was European rather than English, very personal and dictatorial, determined to work his company hard, playing, rehearsing, refreshing their knowledge of past efforts. The archives of the present-day Theatre Royal Drury Lane show that Nell had to learn or re-learn at least seven roles, including that of Lady Wealthy, between Christmas and Easter 1667; on 20 December she was playing the lead in *The Humorous Lieutenant* and rehearsing another play by James Howard, *All Mistaken*.

Pepys, who had enjoyed *The English Monsieur*, found it difficult to get a seat for *The Humorous Lieutenant*, and it was not until 23 January 1667 that he could get in, with his wife and maid, in his favourite middle-tier box. He wrote in his Diary:

... a silly play, I think; only the spirit in it that grows very tall, and then sinks again to nothing, having two heads breeding upon one, and then Knipp's singing did please us. Here in a box above we spied Mrs Pierce; and going out, they called us all in and brought us to Nelly, a most pretty woman, who acted the great part of Ceolia today very fine, and did it pretty well: I kissed her and so did my wife; a mighty pretty soul she is. We also saw Mrs Hall, which is my little Roman-nose black girl, that is mighty pretty: she is usually called Bett. Knipp made us stay in a box and see the dancing preparatory for tomorrow for *The Goblins*, a play of Suckling's not acted these twenty-five years; and so away thence, pleased with this sight also, and specially of kissing of Nell.

Kissing Nell was now on the agenda of a number of gallants, and Charles Hart must have suspected that he could not hold her for long. An admirer who was to become a lifelong friend, and her political mentor, appeared on the scene at this time. George Villiers, second Duke of Buckingham, had been a childhood friend of the King; his father had been an intimate (perhaps he was bisexual) of Charles's grandfather. They had been companions of misfortune; the first Duke of Buckingham had been assassinated; King James VI and I had seen his life degenerate into wretchedness; King Charles I had been executed. Both Charles II and the second Duke, after sharing the personal tragedies and the privations of exile, were determined to avoid misfortune in later life, but the Duke was 'everything by starts and nothing long' and lacked the subtlety and suppleness of his boyhood playmate. He was enormously ambitious but intellectually shallow and did not know how to conceal it. He would have liked to have been President of the Royal Society, but put his trust in alchemists rather than chemists. He was a great patron of the arts (especially music) but offended nearly all those he patronized.

The Duke's long-time mistress was a Roman Catholic, Anna-Maria Brudenell, daughter of the Earl of Cardigan and wife of the Earl of Shrewsbury, former mistress of Harry Killigrew and Thomas Howard (who killed Giles Rawlins and wounded Henry Jermyn in a duel to protect her 'honour'). Anna-Maria's fervent Catholicism, and that of her father and husband, moved Buckingham to cast himself in the role of defender of the Protestant faith; he helped John Wilkins, Cromwell's brother-in-law, to the See of Chester, and his self-appointed task was to protect the King from Catholic plotters. During the New Year of 1667 he was known to be plotting the removal from power of the indefatigably Protestant Lord Chancellor Hyde; he was also trying to set up a Venetian glassblowing works in London and re-writing Fletcher's *The Chances*.

Buckingham spoke about his new play to Nell at the wedding of their mutual friend the Earl of Rochester, on 29 January. Rochester had abducted Elizabeth Malet, an heiress, and had been arrested and committed to the Tower. Aubrey says: 'His youthly spirit and opulent fortune did sometimes make him doe extravagant things, but in the country he was generally civill enough. He was wont to say that when he came to Brentford the devill entered into him. ... ' Rochester was eventually released and, as Elizabeth swore she would marry no one else, eventually acquired her £2,500 a year. At the wedding both Buckingham and Rochester declared that Nell should 'being constant play Constantia' in *The Chances*, which they would have Tom Killigrew put on as soon as she could learn her lines, say by the middle of February.

The allusion to constancy was one of their little jokes. There are two Constantias in *The Chances*, a virtuous heroine and a whore; Nell was cast as the latter, playing opposite Charles Hart as Don John, 'a getter of maidenheads'. Constantia meets Don John by chance when she is wearing a mask. Unmasking, she excites him so much that he says, aside: 'I'd best fall to presently, though it be in the street, for fear of losing time.' A few lines later he is so excited that he starts to undress on stage. The bawdy dialogue and the 'reaching for his breeches' made the play, overshadowing the performances of the hero and heroine, who were planning a wedding before the bedding.

Pepys was seldom far from the theatre that winter. His career was blossoming (he had had a special commendation from the King for not deserting his post during the Plague), and he used his new-found favour to promote the cause of Knipp and ingratiate himself generally backstage at the King's. Knipp had a mediocre talent but full breasts, which Pepys liked fumbling, and a good singing voice – he managed to get her a raise of £30 a year. At Lord Brouncker's, Killigrew told him that Knipp had a great talent, but he was much more excited at the prospect of being able to put on two shows a day, at three and seven, so much better were the new wax candles than the old tallow dips.

On 2 March 1667 Dryden presented his latest play, *Secret Love, or The Maiden Queen*, with Nell in the leading female role of Florimel, opposite Charles Hart as Celadon. It was the first play he had written specifically to exploit her comic genius, and contains an accurate word portrait of her: 'A turned-up nose that gives an air to your face – Oh, I find I am more and more in love with you! – A full nether lip, an out-mouth that makes mine water at it; the bottoms of your cheeks a little blub, and two dimples when you smile. For your stature, 'tis well; and for your wit, 'twas given you by one that knew it had been thrown away upon an ill face.'

Hart and Nell made the most of Dryden's wit. As Professor P.A.W. Collins has written:

The early plays of Dryden and Etherege are a hotchpotch of gay-couple adventure, low farcical intrigues and humours, and romantic-heroic love-and-honour plots in verse, but the vitality clearly belongs to the gay couples, Etherege's Sir Frederick Frolick and Widow Rich in *The Comical Revenge* (Duke's House 1664), Dryden's Loveby and Constance, Celadon and Florimel ... in his *Wild Gallant* (1663) and *Secret Love* (1667). The recent introduction of actresses on to the English stage contributed, of course, to the success and popularity of these sharp encounters between the sexes. One prominent element in Dryden's plays was the 'Proviso-Scene' in which hero and heroine bargained about the conditions under which each might contemplate matrimony; Dryden's success with these scenes established them as a sterotype, and they were much imitated and burlesqued ... [his] gay couples begin from such premises as these:
Florimel (A Maid of Honour): But this marriage is such a bugbear to me! Much might it be if we could invent any way to make it easy.
Celadon (A Courtier): Some foolish people have made it uneasy by drawing the knot faster than they need, but we that are wiser will loosen it a little. [Act V, Scene i]
The couple traverse some familiar grounds for marital discord: Florimel hopes that Celadin may find 'marriage as good as wenching', if they are married not under the damning titles of 'husband and wife' but 'the more agreeable names of mistress and gallant'.

Dryden said that he based the play on a story in *The Cyrus (Queen of Corinth)*, the tragi-comic story of Queen Christina of Sweden (daughter of Gustavus Adolphus), but there is good reason to believe that the idea came after a not-too-serious conversation with King Charles himself, 'who grac'd it with the title of *his* play'. If so, Dryden misunderstood the King's views on marriage, which were very strict for a monarch whose extra-marital behaviour was so free, though the play certainly reflected the views of the Court; Professor Bonamy Dobree noted that these views were healthy and sane and that Restoration comedy expressed 'not licentiousness but a deep curiosity, and a desire to try new ways of living', rather like a chemical experiment at a meeting of the Royal Society. The play was enormously popular with King and Court (perhaps the King's reported protests were echoes of the Queen's), and Charles, who saw it many times, used to remark in later years, to all who would listen, that Nell was superb. One sign of royal approval was a command performance at Court on 18 April 1667, with extra costumes for Nell paid for by the King ('Rhinegraves and other furniture for Mrs Gwyn – £10 7s') who liked her in her 'rhinegraves' (breeches cut wide to show a lot of thigh when she danced).

Nell's appearance in the clothes of a gallant, and her description of them,

stopped the show: '*Looking into a pocket glass*: Faith, methinks you are a very
jaunty fellow, *poudré et ajusté* as well as the best of them. I can manage the
little comb, set my hat, shake my garniture, toss about my empty noddle,
walk a courant slur, and at every step peck down my head. If I should be
mistaken for a courtier now, pray where's the difference?'

Pepys was at the opening night of *Secret Love*, 'mightily commended for
the regularity of it, and the strain and wit; the truth is there is a comical part
done by Nell, which is Florimel, that I can never hope to see the like done
again, by man or woman. The King and Duke of York were at the play. But
so great a performance of a comical part was never, I believe, in the world
before as Nell do this both as a mad girl, then most and best of all when she
comes in like a young gallant; and hath the notions and carriage of a spark
that most I saw any man have. It makes me, I confess, admire her.'

The cast of the play was about as strong as the King's House could
muster: apart from the leads, Major Mohun played Philocles, Mary Knipp
was Asteria, Anne Quinn Candiope and Rebecca Marshall the Queen of
Sicily.

Never slow to seize an opportunity, Killigrew revived Beaumont and
Fletcher's *The Knight of the Burning Pestle* as a burlesque of *Secret Love* – the
debt was acknowledged in the epilogue Nell spoke:

> The prologue durst not tell, before 'twas seen,
> The plot we had to swinge *The Maiden Queen*;
> For had we then discovered our intent,
> The fop who writ it had not given consent,
> Or the new peaching trick at least had shown,
> And brought in others' faults to hide his own.
> Thus our poor poet would have 'scaped today,
> But from the herd I single out his play.
> Then heigh along with me –
> Both great and small, you poets of the town,
> And Nell will love you – for to run him down.

Dryden was not offended; his original was much better.

Pepys's opinion was general: 'Sir W. Pen and I in the pit, and here saw
The Maiden Queen again; which indeed the more I see the more I like, and is
an excellent play, and so done by Nell, her merry part, as cannot be better
done in nature, I think.' The popularity of the play and the cast was so great
that men fought each other as supporters of this or that player 'and would
not have it said that another was as good'. The women especially were
sought after for supper parties and more intimate encounters. Rebecca
Marshall turned down an offer from Sir Hugh Middleton (who had made a
fortune piping water from Ware to the City) and when she refused he had
her beaten up on her way home one night.

In April Killigrew revived Sir Robert Howard's *The Surprisal*, not a very good play, though Nell starred as Samira in it. More to her liking was *All Mistaken, or The Mad Couple*, written for the King's House on condition that Nell played Mirida, opposite Charles Hart as Philidor and John Lacy as Pinguister. James Howard, the author, knew that this was a virtual guarantee that the King would be present. He was said to be already interested in Nell, and John Lacy was his favourite actor, the only one whose portrait he ever commissioned. (The painting, by Michael Wright, showed Lacy in three roles, as a gallant, as a Highlander and as a Presbyterian minister, and hung in Charles' dining-room at Windsor.) Lacy had grown rather fat, and his costume exaggerated this; his pursuit of the petite Nell brought howls of glee from the audience:

> *Mirida:* Dear Love, come sit thee in my lap,
> And let me try if I can enclose thy
> World of fat and love within these arms.
> See I cannot nigh compass my
> Desires by a mile.

> *Pinguister:* How is my fat a rival to my joys!
> Sure, I shall weep it all away.

> *Mirida:* Lie still, my babe, lie still and sleep,
> It grieves me sore to see thee weep
> Wer't thou but leane, I were glad;
> Thy fatness makes thy dear love sad.
> What a lump of love have I in my arms.

There was a lot of frolicking and repartee as Pinguister tried to press his suit, only to be disarmed and rolled across the stage like a barrel.

Nell Gwyn was lucky not to be beaten up by supporters of her rival Moll Davis, now starring at the Duke's House as Celania, in an adaptation of Fletcher's *The Noble Kingsmen*. There is a song in this play, sung by Moll sitting on a bare stage, which begins:

> My lodging it is on the cold ground
> And very hard is my fare,
> But that which troubles me most is
> The unkindeness of my dear.
> Yet still I cry 'O turn, love,'
> And I prithee, love, turn to me,
> For thou art the man I long for
> And alack what remedy?

James Howard wrote a parody of this song for Nell:

> My lodging upon the cold floor is
>   And wonderful hard is my fare
> But that which troubles me most is
>   The fatness of my dear.
> Yet still I cry 'O melt, love,'
>   And I prithee now melt apace,
> For thou art the man I should long for
>   If 't'were not for thy grease.

Nell sang this pouting, sitting on the bare stage and showing all her legs, to the shouts and whistling of the pit, and in a voice which was a perfect imitation of Moll Davis's rather coy and petulant tone. Everybody at the King's House thought it was inspired, but the Duke's House gallants heard of it, and several times Nell was waylaid and abused; she always escaped unhurt, thanks to her ready wit, but she took to having a permanent escort of gallants of her own, a sort of private police force.

Trouble was in store for Lacy, too, because of his role in the *Change of Crownes* by Edward Howard, which alternated with *All Mistaken*. On 15 April 1667 Pepys reported in his Diary: 'Lacy did act the country gentleman come up to Court with all the imaginable wit and plainness about selling of places, and doing everything for money.' The King was less lenient than he was with Tom Killigrew in person, and Lacy was immediately confined for three days in the Porter's Lodge at Whitehall, a sort of penalty box for the King's Servants. When he was released, Lacy angrily told Edward Howard that he was more of a fool than a poet and, when Howard tried to hit him (with a glove or stick), went for him with a wooden sword; within hours he was back in the Porter's Lodge for a week.

Warm weather came in May, and tempers cooled. On Mayday itself, Pepys walked to Westminster 'in the way meeting many milkmaids, with their garlands on their pails, dancing with a fiddler before them; and saw pretty Nell standing at her lodgings' door in Drury Lane in her smock sleeves and bodice, looking upon one; she seemed a mighty pretty creature'. There was still some murmuring over the cynicism of *The Maiden Queen* but Dryden defended her and himself in a new Epilogue, taking on a 'typical critic':

> But he condemns their malice, and defies
> The sharpest of his censurers to say,
> Where there is one gross fault in all his play.
> The language is so fitted for each part,
> The plot according to the rules of art,
> And twenty other things he bid me tell ye;
> But I cried, E'n go do't yourself for Nelly!

The King had more to worry him than the vagaries of actors, actresses and playwrights. As Pepys had reported to his master, the Duke of York, shortage of money had forced the Navy to lay up many of its capital ships and just keep a force of frigates with which to harass Dutch merchantmen; locally raised funds were used to strengthen coastal defences and re-arm the militia in preparation for any invasion attempt. Hearing of this (the Dutch had paid informers, including Andrew Marvell, in the House of Commons), Admiral de Ruyter sailed his fleet up the Medway, cut the chain which was supposed to protect the river and set fire to as many of the laid-up capital ships as he could. It was an extraordinary scene. The English on land and on the estuary seemed helpless. The ultimate humiliation came when de Ruyter towed away the disarmed *Royal Charles*, the very man-of-war on which the King had sailed from Holland to England and his Restoration. At that moment, Charles and Barbara Castlemaine, naked in the summer heat, were chasing butterflies around her salon. When the news reached the Admiralty, Pepys said the cry was: 'By God, I think the Devil shits Dutchmen!'

To add to his naval humiliation, Charles then heard that La Belle Stewart had decided to marry the ugly Duke of Richmond. The King wrote to his sister, Minette: 'You know my good nature enough to believe that I could not be so severe if I had not great provocation, and I assure you her carriage towards me has been as bad as breach of friendship and faith can make it, therefore I hope you will pardon me if I cannot so soon forget an injury which went so near my heart.' The *affaire Stewart* was soon known to all the Town, and 'Old Rowley' (as the King was called, after one of his stallions) became the subject of many more ballads and lampoons.

Yet Charles had the last laugh, at home and abroad. The Dutch were as anxious as he to put an end to the long war, and made peace at Breda on very reasonable terms. De Witt, their leader, observed that, 'If the Devil himself were sovereign of England, it would be necessary to live on friendly terms with him', so New York was not lost, nor were several useful African trading stations. On the home front, the new Duchess of Richmond soon realized that, though she had sold her virginity for a high price, there was little physical and no intellectual satisfaction to be got from the Duke, and she pleaded for Charles's forgiveness. The Richmonds were summoned back to the Court from which they had been banned and took up residence at Somerset House. The King was soon taking trips down the river or walking to taste the once forbidden sweets, and Pepys, who lived not far away, saw him climbing over the wall of Somerset House late at night, after taking his revenge.

Nell, too, had some domestic upsets in midsummer. Her brother-in-law, John Cassells, was arrested for causing an affray, and she had to bail him out to please her lachrymose sister Rose. Then her mother seems to have crept back to Town from Chelsea, and made drunken scenes in Drury Lane; this might have been tolerable a year before, but a rising young actress, anxious for social promotion as well, could not afford this sort of embarrassment, and she sent her mother back to the 'neat houses'.

As if there were not enough, the fiasco with the Dutch in mid-June caused the theatres to close, and Nell found herself with only her royal dole to live on. She turned for help to her new friends, Buckingham and Rochester. Buckingham had just decided to give himself up to the serjeant-at-arms (he had been on the run since February for causing the King's horoscope to be cast, an act of *le lèse majesté,* reported the French Ambassador), so apart from an invitation to dinner at the Sun Tavern on 28 June, on his way to the Tower, he could offer nothing. Rochester was still on his honeymoon, watched by his wife like a hawk, but he had an idea. Nell had met Charles Sackville, Lord Buckhurst, a patron of the King's House. He was rich, heir to the earldoms of Dorset and Middlesex. He was amusing, if a little extravagant. he was certainly grand, a Member of Parliament and a Deputy Lieutenant. He was also an admirer of hers. Why not come to some sort of arrangement with him until things improved? Rochester, no mean procurer for himself and his friends, had a word with Buckhurst, and the bargaining began.

Nell had no moral scruples about hiring herself out to Buckhurst. He had given her 'ardent glances', and he was certainly a step or two up the social ladder from Hart, who now needed her as much as she had needed him. Charles Hart had been invaluable, but he was very poor and had told her that before he was too old he ought to find a Lady Wealthy in real life who would keep him in the style to which he would have liked to have been accustomed; maybe even Barbara Castlemaine would be interested – she had already a muscular rope-dancer and knew she was losing the King's favour because of her greed and infidelity. If Hart was moving on and up, then so should Nell. Rebecca Marshall and Elizabeth Weaver had already climbed the royal backstairs into the royal bed – the sea seemed 'fluttered by a breeze which could have brought many vessels to port'.

Once Nell's mind was made up, the bargain was struck quickly. Hart was approached and, a ballad said, handed her over:

> Take her, my lord, quoth Hart, since you're so mean
> To take a player's leavings for your quean,
> For though I love her well, yet as she's poor
> I'm well contented to prefer the whore.

In a poem to Sir John Denham, Andrew Marvell noted the speed with which Hart consoled himself, and in the direction desired.

> Paint Castlemain in colours that will hold
> Her, not her picture, for she now grows old.
> She thro' the Player's Drawers as he ran,
> Discern'd Love's Cause, and a new Flame began.

It was a hot summer; Buckhurst decided to take Nell out of London to Epsom and rented a house next door to the King's Head there.

Epsom had become famous during the Commonwealth for the 'bitter purging salt, which was then erroneously named calcareous nitre, but which has since been a named sulphate of magnesia, in common parlance Epsom salt', and was a favourite place for gluttons. According to a local history of Epsom by Gordon Home, 'The dissolute Court of Charles II repaired to rural little Epsom' in large numbers. Pepys's cousin had a house nearby at Ashted, and there was a Court Yard and Bowling Green in the little town itself. Barbara Castlemaine demolished Non(e)such Palace, given to her by the King, and built a country house called Durdans there. The Well, on private land, was far enough out of town for the vomiting and other body reactions to the waters to be ignored, and Buckhurst's was not the only love-nest on the High Street. (It fell on hard times and has been a wine shop, grocer's, cakeshop and now jeweller's.)

On 13 July 1667 Pepys confided to his Diary: ' ... home to dinner, where Mr Pierce dined with us, who tells us what troubles me, that my Lord Buckhurst hath got Nell away from the King's house, lies with her, and gives her £100 a year, so as she hath sent her parts to the house and will act no more. And yesterday Sir Thomas crew [Carew?] told me that Lacy lies a-dying of the pox, and yet hath his whore by him, whom he will have to look on, he says, though he can do no more.' He could scarcely contain his curiosity. Next day: 'We go to Epsom by eight o'clock, to the well, where much company, and there we 'light, and I drank the water ... it growing hot in the sun, and so we took our coach again and to the town to the King's Head, where our coachman carried us, and there had an ill room for us to go into, but the best in the house that was not taken up. Here we called for a drink, and bespoke dinner, and hear that my Lord Buckhurst and Nelly are lodged at the next house, and Sir Charles Sidly with them: and keep a merry house. Poor girl! I pity her; but more the loss of her at the King's house.' The loss was, in fact, considerable. When the theatre reopened on 1 August, Pepys went 'to see *The Customs of the Country*. The house mighty empty – more than I ever saw it and an ill play. After the play we went into the house and spoke with Knepp ... who told us the story that Nell is gone from the King's house, and is kept by Lord Buckhurst.'

Nell's house at Epsom was a merry one. Both Sedley and Buckhurst were good company, though they were not often invited twice to great houses; the Countess of Warwick noted in her diary that Sedley dined with her on 5 August and 'It pleased God to restrain him.' Most of the time Nell and her two companions, and Sedley's young daughter, rode on the Downs, ate and drank and laughed the days away. When the drink flowed too fast, Sedley's wife Katherine would arrive and take young Catherine away, though whether the girl was safer with her mad mother (she thought she was the

Queen) than with her drunken father was a matter for dispute.

About the middle of August Buckhurst and Nell seem to have had a quarrel. He was not used to being railed at by pretty girls with such ripe vocabularies, and he was offended, so he said; the girl in question was also using his credit to buy clothes at local shops. They patched up the quarrel, but by the 20th Nell was back in London and on the 22nd was on stage in the role of Cydaria. Pepys noted: 'After dinner with my Lord Brouncker and his mistress to the King's playhouse, and there saw *The Indian Emperor*, where I find Nell come again, which I am glad of; but was most infinitely displeased with her being put to act the Emperor's daughter.' There was more news on 26 August: 'I walked to the King's house there to meet Sir W. Pen, and saw *The Surprisal*, a very mean play, or else it was because I was out of humour ... I had a great deal of discourse with Moll [Orange Moll]; who tells us that Nell is already left by my Lord Buckhurst, and that he makes sport of her, and swears she hath had all she could get of him; and Hart, her great admirer, now hates her; and that she is very poor, and hath lost Lady Castlemaine, who was her great friend also; but she is come to the House, but is neglected by them all.'

This news was about as reliable as the report that Lacy was dying of pox. Buckhurst, when he got over the shock, became a good friend. Her colleagues soon tired of mocking her, and Lady Castlemaine had other things in her mind. For some time she had been in the Buckingham plot to get rid of the Lord Chancellor, though she was not sure that the Duke (still in the Tower) was the right man to rule England. And get rid of the Lord Chancellor they did. Evelyn noted in his diary for 27 August 1667: 'Visited L Chancellor to whom his Majestie had sent for the Seales a few daies before: I found him in his bedchamber very sad: the Parliament had accused him, & he had enemies at Court, especially the boufoones and Ladys of Pleasure, because he had thwarted some of them and stood in their ways.' Clarendon, his house stoned by a mob which blamed him for the fiascos with the Dutch, had to flee the country. A man of immense dignity, he would only take his dismissal in person from the King, whose companion and adviser he had been since the years of exile. The Court and Parliament forced Charles to make him a scapegoat for the mismanagement of the Government, and as Clarendon left London for the last time he looked back at Whitehall where the buffoons and ladies of pleasure 'looked out of her [Castlemaine's] open window with great gaiety and triumph'. It was a shoddy episode.

Nell Gwyn was indifferent to Clarendon's fate. It was enough for her that Buckingham wanted him out of office, and anyway she had problems of her own. Pepys reported some backstage quarrelling. Rebecca Marshall had called her 'Buckhurst's whore', to which she had replied: 'I was but one man's whore, though I was brought up in a bawdy house ... and you are a whore to three or four though a Presbyter's praying daughter.' She was soon back at the top of the bill, though she had missed a chance to star in *Sir Martin Mar All*, perhaps his funniest play, based on a translation by Newcastle from Molière, Dryden had put it on at the Duke's House to spite her. Worse, the leading role of Mrs Millicent was given to Moll Davis. She quickly made her peace with Dryden, and told him she thought of him as *her* playwright.

During the autumn, Nell took leading roles in *The Indian Emperor* and *Surprisal*, as Panthea in Beaumont and Fletcher's *A King and No King* and in Richard Rhodes' comedy *Flora's Vagaries* (as Flora). Pepys, who had heard her cursing prettily 'for having so few people in the pit' on 5 October, went to see *Flora's Vagaries* on 3 November and was pleased to see a full house; after the play he 'went down to the women's shift, where Nell was dressing herself, and was all unready, and is very pretty, prettier than I thought'. He also enjoyed her as Bellario in Fletcher's *Philaster*, perhaps because she wore breeches and he liked to see the shape of her legs; this play about a love-sick girl, which saw her friendship with Hart restored at a platonic level, attracted a great deal of critical praise, and a quarter of a century later her successors could say, in the Prologue:

> That good old play Philaster ne'er can fail,
> But we young actors, how shall we prevail?
> Philaster and Bellario, let me tell ye,
> For these bold parts we have no Hart, no Nelly,
> Those darlings of the stage that charmed you here.

About the end of November, when she was parodying Barbara Castlemaine as the greedy mistress of Edward III, in Lord Orrery's *The Black Prince*, Nell seems to have struck up a friendship with Moll Davis. Though rivals, they were at different houses, and neither was so much better than the other that she could feel superior. Nell was the better comic actress, Moll the better dancer; Pepys noted that season that, 'Little Miss Davis did dance a jig ... and the truth is that there is no comparison between Nell's dancing [as Florimel] and this, thus being infinitely beyond the other.' Both girls were beautiful but coarse. Nell was the more natural and less pretentious; Moll, though she was a blacksmith's daughter from a village in Wiltshire, always hinted that she was a bastard of the first Earl of Berkshire and so a half-sister of the Howard playwrights.

Whatever the basis of this friendship, both Nell and Moll seem to have made up their minds to find rich, aristocratic protectors on as permanent a basis as possible; they would never make a fortune in the theatre. They were both anxious to have a comfortable house not too far away from the Court. At hilarious suppers, they are said to have discussed, too, potential candidates as protectors, almost as if they were reciting their roles in *The*

Comical Revenge or *Secret Love*. What they did not, perhaps, realize was that they themselves were being manipulated. Buckingham, now convinced that Barbara Castlemaine was not going to help him to power, was conspiring with the Howards, and possibly with Tom Killigrew and Davenant, to replace her in the King's affections with an appetizing actress.

In late December the news broke that the King was making one last effort to get the Queen pregnant. The whole Court would move to Tunbridge Wells for Christmas, and the Queen would take the waters again, 'a certain cure for sterility'. If it did not work, the King was used to looking elsewhere and had already seven bastards by most reckonings. It was hinted to Nell Gwyn and Moll Davis that, if they were looking for a protector, perhaps they should look for the best of them all, who never cast a girl off with £100. Quick to take the hint, they hurried to their seamstresses and started to pack for Tunbridge Wells.

Centre Stage, 1667-9

In pious times, ere priestcraft did begin,
Before polygamy was made a sin:
When man on many multiplied his kind,
Ere one to one was cursedly confined ...
Then Israel's monarch after Heaven's own heart,
His vigorous warmth did variously impart
To wives and slaves; and wide as his command,
Scatter'd his Maker's image thro' the land.

Annus Mirabilis, John Dryden

The contest between Nell and Moll does not figure prominently in present-day guidebooks to Tunbridge Wells. This is a pity, for, as Dryden was to write later: 'This critical age indeed was like Polonius, he's for a jig, or a tale of bawdry, or he sleeps.' All the ingredients for a timeless farce were there, and the bards and chroniclers were in the wings, even the promoter of rival fields of battle (Thomas Shadwell in *Epsom Wells*).

Lord North's early advertisements had attracted great attention. Medical men noted that, 'The Tunbridge waters are impregnated with a chalcanthous or vitriolate juice; which, with its sulphureous particles, irritates and moves the belly to a blackish excretion ... with their saponary and detersive quality clean the whole microcosm or body of man from all feculency and impurities.' The fashionable soon heard of 'the long walk, shaded by spreading trees, under which they walk while drinking the waters; on one side of this walk is a long row of shops, plentifully stocked with all manner of toys, lace, gloves, stockings, and where there is raffling, as at Paris, in the Foire de Saint Germain: on the other side of the walk is the market. Here young, fair, fresh-coloured country girls with clean linen, small straw hats, and neat shoes and stockings, sell game, vegetables, flowers and fruit: here one may live as one pleases: here is, likewise, deep play and no want of amorous intrigues: (Comte de Gramont).

Whether it was the waters or the opportunities for amorous intrigue Tunbridge soon acquired the reputation of a place in which a woman got pregant with little or no difficulty. By 1664 there were already prints of *The Springs at Tunbridge Wells* on sale in London booksellers. The following summer the Queen, still not pregnant, decided to take the cure and 'a procession of gilded coaches, each drawn by six lumbering great horses and escorted by scarlet-cloaked courtiers on horseback, was seen cutting its way through the rough Kentish lanes. In its train rumbled coach and waggon loads of the Queen's Portuguese attendants – swarthy, coarse-featured waiting-women, disfigured in English eyes by their top-knots and comically out-of-date in their ruffs and farthingales, a score of dirty black-robed monks ... physicians, barbers, grooms, cooks and scullions.' The French Ambassador was soon writing to Paris: 'The Queen is now physicking herself as a preparation for the waters, in the hope that it will facilitate the result she intends, and for which she goes there.'

The sheer effort involved in getting her entourage to Tunbridge Wells persuaded the Queen to leave a sort of garrison there and make trips every year. There was also the question of expense. In spite of her enormous dowry and theoretical entitlement to £50,000 a year, she seldom succeeded in getting more than £3,000 every month or two out of her husband's treasury.

By the time the move of 1667 had been planned, the town had increased in size and improved the quality of its entertainments. Large houses had been built or rebuilt – Summerhill or Somerhill, and Mount Ephraim were the largest – and clusters of cottages near the Wells and as far as Rusthall and Southborough could accommodate hundreds of visitors. Lord and Lady Muskerry were resident hosts, Lady Muskerry alone after her husband's death fighting the Dutch. There were balls and banquets every day, not to speak of assignations by the fish pond, 'an ornamental waterpiece with swans and waterfowl', adjoining the bowling green at Mount Ephraim, where the royal family lodged.

With the arrival of the King, the pace of life accelerated. The day started very early with 'the Waters'. Rochester, who always took wine before hand to settle his squeamish stomach, describes the scene:

> At five this Morn, when Phoebus rais'd his head
> From Thetis' Lap, I rais'd my self from Bed,
> And mounting Steed, I trotted to the Waters,
> The Rendezvous of Fools, buffoons and Praters,
> Cuckolds, Whores, Citizens, their Wives and Daughters.

The King would ride back from the Wells to breakfast, then hear petitioners and start to transact the business of State. When breakfast was done, the Queen would be accompanied to the Drinkers' (as opposed to the Dippers') end of the portico (the end of the present-day Pantiles) and drink several glasses of the water. About noon there was a little indoor tennis, a brisk rub-down and the main meal of the day. This meal went on interminably, as it always did in Whitehall, and there was plenty of time for the ladies of the Court to exchange gossip; those who were attached had to make sure they had not become semi-detached, and those who were unattached tried to remedy this state of affairs as quickly and profitably as possible. The crude hedonism of life led what Rochester called 'a Tribe of Curates, Priests, Canonical Elves' to protest that the waters had become a fount of scandal not of good health and natural fertility.

The French Ambassador, de Gramont (or de Grammont) commented in his despatch: 'Well may they be called the *eaux de scandale* for they have nearly ruined the good name of the maids and the ladies (those who are there without their husbands). It has taken them a whole month and for some more than that to clear themselves and save their honour; and it is reported that a few of them are not quite out of trouble yet.' Husbands, having been flagrantly unfaithful to their wives in Town, played scenes of outraged virtue when they heard of what went on in the Lower Walk. Fortunately, better actors and actresses were to hand.

The French Ambassador's Memoirs, which were a great *succès de scandale*, record that it was the Queen herself who sent for the players, from both the King's House and the Duke's. They seem to have commuted from London, arriving for lunch and a three o'clock performance. Nell Gwyn was seen by Pepys at the Duke's House, watching Moll Davis perform, and on 28th December Moll returned the gesture. Pepys noted that, 'Nell's and Hart's mad parts are most excellently done, but especially hers: which makes it a miracle to me to think how ill she do any serious part, as the other day, just like a fool. ... ' (he was referring to *The Surprisal* on the 26th). But both actresses were at Tunbridge Wells on at least seven occasions over Christmas and the New Year; Nell spoke several prologues and sang her favourite songs; Thomas Betterton and Moll spoke duologues, and Moll danced, in excerpts from Shirley's *Love Tricks*, enchanting one local bard:

> Who would not think to see the dance so light,
> Thou wert all *air*, or else all *soul* and *spirits*?
> Or who'd not say to see thee onely tried,
> Thy *feet* were *Feathers*, other *feet* but *lead*? ...
> ... none like thee ere charmed with *feet* before.
> Thou Miracle! whom all men must admire.

It was Moll's dancing which helped her to the first victory in the tournament of whores. Late one afternoon, early in the New Year, 1668, she did a particularly provocative 'jig'. The Queen, offended, left the room. The King carried Moll Davis away to his apartments. Barbara Castlemaine ('When she saw Moll Davis, she looked like fire') went off with Charles Hart. There was a game of sexual musical chairs, and Nell Gwyn, having refused to settle for a second best, was left out.

Moll must have given instant satisfaction, for Pepys recorded on 11 January: 'Knepp came and sat by us, and her talk pleased me a little, she telling me how Mis Davis is for certain going away from the Duke's house, the King being in love with her; and a house is taken for her, and furnishing; and she hath a ring given her already worth £600: and that the King did send several times for Nelly and she was with him, but what she did she knows not. ... She told me also of a play shortly coming upon the stage, of Sir Charles Sidly's, a comedy that, she thinks, will be most pleasing and also another play, called *The Duke of Lerma* (for Nell); besides *Catelin* which she thinks, for want of the clothes the King promised them, will not be acted for a good while.'

Moll's colleague Peg Hughes seems to have 'brought down and greatly subdued the natural fierceness' of Prince Rupert during the same season at Tunbridge Wells. De Gramont wrote to Paris that there had been 'a complete farewell to all mathematical instruments and chemical speculations: sweet powder and essences were now the only ingredients that occupied any share of his attention'.

John Wilson in his *Life* worries about Moll's triumph at the Wells: 'What was wrong with Nell? ... Buckingham, Nell's manager, made a serious blunder. As he told Bishop Burnet some years later, when Nell was "first brought to the King, she asked only £500 a year". The King refused. ... Moll Davis, more wisely managed by Colonel Howard, accepted the King's gifts and throve.' It is probably nearer the truth to say that Nell was enjoying her life as an actress too much at that stage to want to risk pregnancy and early retirement. Perhaps a ring worth £600 was just not enough, bearing in mind Evelyn's comment on 4 February, at a performance of *The Trajedie of Horace* ('written by the virtuous Mrs Philips'): 'The excessive galantry of the Ladies was infinite. Those especially on that ... Castlemaine esteemed at £40,000 or more.'

Whatever the truth of the matter, Nell had her revenge, in the long and short term. According to legend, she invited Moll to a 'collation of sweetmeats which she had mixed with jalap', which had the effect of loosening Moll's bowels that night and sending her scurrying from the royal bed to the 'little chamber' next to it. This little feline gesture, accompanied as it was by a note of congratulation, Wycherley called 'that heinous and worst of women's crimes, hypocrisy' but raised Nell's stock in the 'Women's Shift'. She was also touched to receive a letter from the Duchess of Monmouth to say that Her Grace had acted her part in *The Indian Emperor* at Court (14 January) with the Duke and Mrs Cornwallis, and all were 'mightily pleased'.

On 20 February 1668 Pepys went ' ... to the King's House: a new play

The Duke of Lerma, of Sir Robert Howard's: where the King and Court was; and Knepp and Nell spoke the prologue most excellently ... . The play was designed to reproach our King with his mistresses, that I was troubled for it, and expected it should be interrupted; but all ended well, which salved all.' The play itself is not a significant one, about the Duke of Lerma, trying to prostitute his daughter, but the King's presence without Moll Davis suggests that she was proving either too exhausting or too greedy; she was already pregnant and installed in a house in Suffolk Street.

Nell had a very busy season. In addition to *The Duke of Lerma*, she was playing Samira in *The Surprisal* again, and Lady Wealthy in *The English Monsieur*. At eighteen she was the toast of the Town, and Buckingham was cheered to think that he might after all achieve his aims of installing her as an official royal mistress and himself as chief minister.

Both the French and English Courts were buzzing with the news that the Duke of York was about to announce officially that he had been received into the Roman Catholic Church. The Duke's conversion was not news. It was well known that his mother had pestered him about 'getting in the right way' until he had been received, and he had made no objection (though he had protested at the attempt to convert, forcibly, his younger brother Henry). There is some support for the contention that he was pushed to declare himself in 1668 by his wife, Anne, also a convert. He said: 'What I have done was not done hastily, but upon mature consideration', but the Duchess was certainly an active agent. She was a woman of great intellectual gifts, and not at all of the lax morals of which she was accused at the time of her marriage. She was genuinely fond of James and anxious to improve him. She seldom took part in Court life but read to him for hours from the works of the Fathers of the Church, and probably wore her husband down. What became immediately obvious after the 'declaration' was that he lost interest in his House and went there less and less.

One of the last occasions on which the Duke of York did grace the theatre of which he was patron was in April 1668. It was the first night of Etherege's *She Would If She Could* (Nell had seen his first play four years before and probably hoped that this obviously talented man would write for her). The King and the Duke of York were in their box, and next to it was Nell with a relative of Buckingham. As soon as Charles saw her, he struck up a conversation and at the end of the play invited them to dinner at a nearby tavern. The King was on his best form, though Nell said the Duke was 'a dismal Jimmie', and two hours passed in eating, drinking and badinage. When Nell said she had to leave because she had an early rehearsal next morning, the King called for the bill. The landlord pretended not to recognize him and was very angry when he was told that they had drunk too deep for the royal pocket. Would James settle matters? But the Duke of York had only a very thin purse, and Villiers one even thinner, so in the end

Nell had to pay for the evening's entertainment: "Odsfish,' she said, echoing the King's favourite expletive, 'this is the poorest company I ever was in.'

At the end of the month, Sir William Davenant died, dealing another blow to the Duke's House and reinforcing the prestige of the King's. Davenant, a great trimmer in an age of trimmers (he had managed to be Poet Laureate under Charles I, the two Cromwells and Charles II), was given a good send-off. Aubrey says: 'I was at his funerall. He had a coffin of walnutt-tree; Sir John Denham sayd 'twas the finest coffin he ever saw. His body was carried in a herse from the playhouse to Westminster-Abbey, where, at the great west doore, he was received by the singing men and choristers, who sang the service of the church to his grave, which is in the south cross aisle, on which a paving stone of marble is writt, in imitation of Ben Jonson, "O rare Sir Will. Davenant". '

Before Davenant was cold in his grave, Tom Killigrew had appropriated his translation from the French of *The Man's the Master*, with Nell in Moll Davis' old role of Lucilla. Pepys had seen it at the Duke's on 26 March and had not liked it: 'Most of the mirth was sorry & poor stuffe, of eating of sack posset and slabbering themselves and mirth fit for clownes.' Killigrew made an excuse to put the new star of the play into breeches and quickly captivated Pepys: 'I called Knepp from the King's house, where going in for her I did see Beck Marshall come dressed off stage, and looks mighty fine and pretty noble; and also Nell in her boy's clothes, mighty pretty.' He was in the habit, that spring, of taking Knipp ('Knepp') to Chelsea and during May went several times to the Nete House and its 'Neat houses', where there were now fruit and vegetable stalls and a wine stall probably kept by Nell's mother (Nete House was on Willow Walk).

Sir Charles Sedley's new play, announced in advance by Knipp, was *The Mulberry Garden*; the leading role, Victoria, was written for Nell and had a royal première on 18 May. Pepys wrote that this was a memorable first night indeed. He had at first lunched at the Rose to see if the reports of Nell's supper with the King and his brother were true, then got himself a box from which he could watch the royal family (the Queen was making one of her rare appearances, perhaps to reassure her husband's subjects that she did not mind not being pregnant). Everybody who was anybody was there, from plotting Buckingham to Etherege looking for a new patron or patrons. Aubrey remarked on the periwigs universally worn, 'though not commonly until 1660 ... one Gregorie in the Strand was the first famous periwig maker and they were than called Gregorians'; the King, who had naturally long, thick, wavy hair encouraged his balding courtiers to patronize Gregory, perhaps an early instance of a Royal Warrant.

The Mulberry Garden was a great success, though Pepys did not like it, perhaps because Knipp did not have a major role in it. Etherege liked it and said it would last as long as the garden itself, a grove of mulberry trees laid out by James VI and I where Buckingham Palace is today. Pepys noted that the King seemed touched and unusually serious throughout the afternoon. The title, with its reference to one of his grandfather's artefacts, moved him, devoted as he was. The two monarchs had much in common, even physically, for James was a 'black boy', too.

James VI of Scotland and I of England has not been treated kindly by historians, though John Prebble describes him as, 'the most scholarly prince in the history of Britain and one of the finest in Europe'. Before he was fourteen he was a considerable Latinist; he had a little Gaelic to please his Highlanders and a lot of philosophy, natural and moral. He was a famous patron of mathematicians, and was especially kind to Napier, the Scots inventor of logarithms. He was interested in politics at an early age, managed his Scottish Parliament well and wrote (in 1598) *The Trew Law of Free Monarchies*, a textbook for discreet despots which was widely read on the Continent. He thought war futile and on his accession brought to an end the interminable English squabble with Spain. He was a great friend to literature and the arts, though to be a Jacobean poet was quite a different thing from being an Elizabethan; he thought Shakespeare greedy and overrated (he was upset by the genealogical errors in *Macbeth*) and replaced him in favour with Jonson. He appointed Inigo Jones Head of Works but encouraged him to design Court masques as well. He tackled the Church of England as well as he could, and commissioned the translation of the Bible which many people think is unsurpassed. He was the first great patron of science in Britain and did not deserve his nickname, 'the wisest fool in Christendom'.

His grandson was as quick to learn and never disappointed his tutors. His Latin was monkish, but he spoke French, Italian and Spanish well. He read widely when young, as many, it was said, as the six hundred books which had formed the hard core of his grandfather's education. He spoke English with grace and charm, with that special precision and timbre of voice which comes from living many years abroad. When he was restored to his kingdoms, he tried to contain his Parliaments. He, too, was a great friend to literature and the arts, not to speak of the theatre. He, too, was fascinated by the challenge of science, and formally founded not only the Royal Society but also Greenwich Observatory (and so the meridian from which longitude is reckoned and Greenwich Mean Time is calculated). As statesman and politician he was as devious and able as his grandfather, whose sexual morality he seems to have inherited (though they deviated in different directions). Like his grandfather he was anything but insular, and although he disliked the native Scots, he never made it so obvious as to arouse resentment. One asset Charles II possessed which his grandfather did not was an easy manner. James VI and I had wisdom and learning beyond that of nearly all his subjects, but he took no care to hide it. Charles wore his understanding of men more lightly, and deceived and conquered fools, as Guicciardini the Italian statesman recommended.

One of Charles' most devious servants was William Chiffinch. Appointed in 1668 to look after the King's private apartments, Chiffinch, (who succeeded his rather dull brother) was officially Page of the Royal Bedchamber and Keeper of the King's Private Closet, and Mrs Chiffinch was a well-known procuress, so it now became essential for an ambitious girl to get into their good books. Charles would occasionally order a girl suddenly, as he sometimes did saddle of mutton (to which he was also partial) and did not always care what social rank she was so long as she could be procured quickly; the Chiffinches soon organized a register and a chain of pages to bring to the King the best whores in Town, as well as ladies afflicted with 'frailty and dishonesty' (Wycherley) who just wanted an hour or two with their sovereign to add to their sexual souvenirs. William Chiffinch specialized in getting husbands drunk if his master fancied their wives and was useful when it came to causing ambassadors to commit indiscretions. He also marketed 'The King's Drops' or 'Godard's Restorer' said to help drunkards keep a clear head. Nell Gwyn became a great friend of both the Chiffinches and was often their guest for lunch and gossip, even when she was not in the royal apartments on her own business.

Dryden had promised Nell a new play as soon as he could finish it, and by the end of May had it ready, *An Evenings Love or The Mock Astrologer*. Dryden had found his inspiration in Calderón's *El Astrologio Fingido*, of which he speaks highly and recommends the orginal in his Preface to the play. The new work opened on 12 June 1668 with 'Mrs Ellen Gwyn' in the leading female role of Donna Jacintha. Charles Hart played opposite her as Wildblood and Major Mohun as Bellamy, 'a young English gentleman in Madrid'. Pepys' Mary Knipp was Beatrix. Mrs Pepys did not like the play, but then she was 'in a fusty humour' and perhaps spoilt the play for her husband, too – he said it was 'very smutty and nothing so good as *The Maiden Queen* or *The Indian Emperor*'. Langbaine did not like the play either, but then he did not like Dryden and was furious at the rumour that Dryden had been made Poet Laureate *in pectore* instead of his protégé Shadwell; though Dryden had made generous acknowledgement of his debt to Calderón, Langbaine sneered that the play had 'little hints borrow'd from Shakespeare, Petronius, Arbiter and other authors'.

The new play seems to have alternated with *The English Monsieur*, *The Man's the Master*, Sir Robert Howard's *The Committee* (first produced at Court on 8 February) and *Philaster*, but the King seems to have liked *An Evening's Love* best of all; to Dryden's critics he observed that those who accused him of plagiarism should set to and steal plays as good as his. The criticisms continued, however.

The play is set in Madrid at Carnival time but the scenes played there would, in real life, have had every episcopal policeman on the streets. The characters of Wildblood and Jacintha are neither as comic nor as crisp as those of Celadon and Florimel. Nell Gwyn was wasted as Jacintha, and it was a crime to put an actor of such long standing as Charles Hart in such an inferior role as Wildblood. Only Major Mohun escaped the barbs. In the end, Dryden wrote a special epilogue for Nell:

> I have had time today
> To mark your various censures of our play.
> First, looking for a judgement or a wit,
> Like Jews I saw them scattered through the pit;
> And where a knot of smilers lent an ear
> To one that talked, I knew the foe was there.
> The club of jests went round; he, who had none
> Borrowed o' the next and told it for his own.
> Among the rest, they kept a fearful stir,
> In whispering that he stole th'Astrologer;
> And said, betwixt a French and English plot,
> He eased his half-tired muse, on pace and trot.

There was a clear reference to Langbaine, who held court at one side of the pit called Fops' Corner.

The King, who knew Langbaine's prejudices well, was amused by an exchange in which Nell makes it quite clear just what a gentleman may hope for from her:

Jacintha: To be admitted to pass my time with, while a better comes; to be the lowest step in my staircase, for a knight to mount upon him, and a Lord upon him, and a duke upon him till I get as high as I can climb.

And the promises in return for royal favour:

Jacintha: None but fools confine their pleasure: what insurer ever thought his coffers held too much? No, I'll give myself the swinge, and love without reserve. If I'll keep a passion, I'll never starve it in my service.

Evelyn was horrified by the cynicism, perhaps even more by the amoral generosity (he kept his wife cheaply in the country). He seldom went to the theatre in eager anticipation of an evening's enjoyment and was always scathing about 'the women of the playhouse, still piquing at each other, who shall go the best drest and in the richest habits'. However, as on other occasions, some out-of-town visitors 'persuaded' him to take them to the

King's House, and he could complain: 'To a new play with several of my relations, *The Evening Lover* [*sic*], a foolish plot and very prophane; it afflicted me to see how the stage was degenerated and polluted by ye licentious times.'

It was during the run of this play that Nell quite often got as high as she could climb. Chiffinch himself came several times to take her up the royal backstairs. It is hard to say at this stage just how interested the King was in her, other than as a delightful sexual object. He had spent hours in her company, often in public, and knew she was not a bore. He had seen her often on the stage and admired her acting ability. She was, after all, one of his Servants, and many of them had served in his bed. Whatever his motivation, she quickly became his first choice of company. He was getting very tired of Barbara Castlemaine, ever greedier for money and notoriously promiscuous; she seldom excited him now, which astonished Pepys, her great admirer. And Moll Davis, whose delightful jig had enlivened his days in Tunbridge Wells, seemed set to become as greedy. Mrs Pierce, who was Pepys' principal informer at the Duke's House, said she could not see what the King had ever found in Moll to make him lose his head: she was 'the most homely jade' and 'a bastard of the Earl of Berkshire and he hath got her for the King', and even 'the most impertinent slut in the world'. Mrs Pierce seems to have been right about Moll's impertinence. Not satisfied with Suffolk Street, she insisted that the King give her the freehold of 22 St James's Square (since demolished to make way for the Army and Navy Club); in the end she was pensioned off with £1,000 a year, and her bastard daughter was given the name of Lady Mary Tudor (she married Francis Ratcliffe, second Earl of Derwentwater, and their son became a prominent Jacobite, executed after the '15).

By the end of the summer, everybody at the King's House knew that their favourite actress had become the King's favourite whore. The event rated several verses in 'The Song of Old Rowley', a sort of endless chronicle of the royal progress through Restoration England. (The subject of the chronicle once heard a maid of honour singing it in her room at Whitehall, knocked on her door and said: 'Old Rowley, at your service.') Pepys, during a visit to his cousin near Epsom, reported that Charles had given Nell some stables at Epsom, (in present-day Church Street, opposite St Martin's), for the only thing he vowed she could not do was ride a horse.

Buckingham was always at Nell's elbow, making sure that no one usurped the new royal prerogative. He even sat through a revival of Lacy's *The Old Troup* and, worse, on 15 September, Flecknoe's *Damoiselles à la Mode* in which the author had written the part of Lysette for her. Pepys said the play was so bad, 'so mean a thing that when it was announced that it would be acted again on the next day, the Pit fell a 'laughing'. Flecknoe put the failure down to enemies among the critics and sent Nell a poem:

She is pretty, and she knows it;
She is witty, and she shows it;
And besides that she's so witty,
And so little and so pretty,
Sh'has a hundred other parts
For to take and conquer hearts.

There were better plays in store. In addition to the revivals of Nell's earlier successes, there was a new production of Ben Jonson's *Cataline's Conspiracy* paid for by the King, who gave the company sixteen scarlet robes for the occasion; Nell spoke the prologue 'in an Amazonian habit' which seems to have comprised a crested helmet, a belted tunic hanging down to just above her knees, and not much else — she carried a bow and arrows. There was a furore halfway through the play when the actress who was playing Sempronia slowly developed a role parodying the well-known meddling of Lady Elizabeth Harvey (whose husband had just been sent to Turkey as Ambassador); Barbara Castlemaine, who hated the Harveys, interrupted the actor playing Cicero, who had just asked: 'But what will you do with Sempronia?' with a shout: 'Send her to Constantinople.' The epilogue acknowledged only the heroine of the prologue: 'The House hath cause to thank Nell more than Ben.'

It was at about this time that Buckingham recruited the Duke of Monmouth (Baron Tyndale, Earl of Doncaster, Duke of Buccleuch, Earl of Dalkeith, Baron Scott of Winchester and Eskdale). The cause was always the same, the advancement of Buckingham's own interests, which he identified with 'the Protestant interest'. Rochester had taken up residence in the City of London, where he was wooing the merchants and even, the French Ambassador reported, seducing their wives. Monmouth's role, as the recently appointed Captain of the King's Guard (he was soon to be promoted Captain-General of all the armed forces), was to assure the loyalty of the troops. Rochester was triumphing with the 'delicate and magnificent ladies' of the City; Monmouth was described by de Gramont as 'the universal terror of lovers and husbands'; and in the front line, of course, was Nell. A conspiracy based largely on the assumption that sex guaranteed loyalty did not seem ridiculous to Buckingham, Rochester and Monmouth, all three blinded by ambition to the shallowness of that assumption; Buckingham saw himself as Chief Minister in the way his father had been at the Court of King James VI and I; Rochester saw himself as a Solomon of vice; Monmouth believed that England would not tolerate a Roman Catholic succession and that, as the King's eldest male child, he should inherit the throne. The conspiracy does not seem to have been taken seriously at first in England, but in France the advantages of having a Catholic King of England, and the disadvantages of having a Protestant of

Monmouth's ilk, were immediately obvious. What should be done? What sexual piece could France place on the chequerboard?

At eighteen, Nell's eyes were still on the stage, her ears tuned to applause. Not even the King could persuade her to leave the theatre and join the other royal mares more or less active in the stable (it always amused her that he was so reluctant ever to let any of them go, even when they were out of favour). Dryden no doubt encouraged her in this. The Poet Laureate designate had a new play half written, in which she was to star. She was one of his most precious assets, and Dryden, who loved money, did not want to see it wasted. He had managed to raise his salary as Laureate to £200 a year (a twentieth-century Laureate gets much less in real terms), and he had an assortment of paid appointments at Court (among others, Historiographer Royal) but he was never satisfied. From a play, especially one with Nell Gwyn in it, he could expect at least another £200 a year; all this money would give him time to concentrate on very profitable translations (he was to get £1,400 for his Virgil and 250 guineas for 12,000 lines of verse in his *Fables*) and more plays.

With everybody extolling Nell's virtues, it was not surprising that some change became noticeable in her attitudes. It would have been too much to expect of any eighteen-year-old girl, of any nation, at any period of history, that she would not exult at the speed of which she had risen from fishcart to royal flesh-taster.

An African President Leopold Senghor once said that, as long as she was no worse off than her peers, a woman could live happily in the jungle, naked. Difficulties arose when the girl in the next hut acquired a copper bangle and a second cooking pot; at this point the possession of a copper bangle and two cooking pots became the absolute minimum necessary for happy domestic life. So, in another century, Nell Gwyn, having improved her social status in the dense, competitive jungle of whores, demanded material recognition from her peers. She moved out of the Women's Shift and got a tiring-room of her own, with a chimney. She moved out of her lodgings into a house in Lincoln's Inn Fields, so that she had, as it were, the Duke's House on her doorstep, too. Her costumes had to be re-made. She became 'Mrs Ellen Gwyn', 'Nelly' only to a few intimates and her 'public'. She had Orange Moll arrested by the Lord Chamberlain's steward for insulting her old enemy, Rebecca Marshall, an act of revenge in magnanimity of which only a woman who has overtaken them all feels capable. In Dryden's words, she worked up her rivals 'by your high flying, as heron and falcon do' – or, as she herself sang in *An Evening's Love* (to Charles Hart as Demon):

> Passion's but an empty name
> Where respect is wanting.

Pepys, too, noticed the change in status, to the detriment of his Mary Knipp. At a performance of Massinger and Decker's *The Virgin Martyr*, he noticed the other actresses waiting for Nell to pass (she was playing Angelo, in boy's clothes again), and how even the 'confident gallants' gave her respect. Pepys was always afraid of being 'horned' by the pit, and rightly so: Knipp was arrested several times in 1668 for misbehaviour and was notorious for quick, cash, sexual transactions.

The King came regularly to the play, to see Nell act and carry her off to supper and to bed. He trusted Buckingham to provide her with a suitable escort when he was busy with unavoidable affairs of State, though he was not jealous by nature: Welwood writes that he was 'a great votary to love, and yet the easiest and most unconcern'd Rival. He was for the most part not very nice in the choice of his mistresses, and seldom possess'd of their first favours, yet would sacrifice all to please them.' Pepys saw Nell on 7 January 1669 escorted by Villiers, watching Beaumont and Fletcher's *The Island Princess* – 'a bold, merry slut who lay laughing there upon people'. It was generally appreciated that her own clothes were better, and she had some expensive jewellery. She became very particular, too, in the dress of those who came near her, and reproved William Fanshaw, husband of another of Lucy Walter's bastards and Master of Requests, for having a stinking periwig: he was to go 'straightways to Mr Gregorie and get a new one, so that she might not smelle him stinke two stories high'.

On 14 January Nell upset Evelyn by doing a series of dances as *entr'actes* to the *Trajedie of Horace* by his 'virtuous' Mrs Philips. Tom Killigrew, if he was not concerned about the virtue of his actors, was worried about absenteeism, and told Pepys on 24 January 'that he is fain to keep a woman on purpose at 20s a week to satisfy 8 or 10 of the young men of the house, whom till now he could never keep to his business, and now he do'.

Though she continued to work hard, Nell was now often with the King for days at a time. She had inherited from her mother a weakness for gambling, and she liked horses, though was an indifferent performer in the saddle. She did not like Epsom, perhaps because her mother refused to be exiled there, perhaps because it reminded her of the Buckhurst episode, but she shared Charles' love of Newmarket. When Wren was asked to build her a house there, there was irony of a sort in the choice of site, opposite the Maiden's Inn. Charles also decided that spring to enlarge his stables at Newmarket and take racing more seriously, and from then on certainly spent many weeks there every year, always with Nell and sometimes with the Queen and a small Court. This rural idyll, the simple clothes he wore in the country, his general affability and love of horseflesh endeared him to the common people of England, and these breaks enabled him to recover from the hectic pace of life in Town. Nell was credited with this bucolic turn to the reign, but Charles had always loved country life (a passion for hunting was the only interest but one he shared with his brother), and the weeks spent out of Town enabled her to get a firmer grip on the slippery heart of the monarch.

In May 1669 rehearsals began for Dryden's new play, *Tyrannic Love, or The Royal Martyr*. The King complained to Tom Killigrew that so much work for the actress made *him* a royal martyr but was promised a good play and a fine cast as consolation. Though Tom was worried about the health of his son, 'Lying Harry', who had been beaten up by the footman of his former mistress, the Countess of Shrewsbury (who had now transferred her affections permanently to the Duke of Buckingham), he was as good as his word. Charles Hart was chosen to play Porphyrius, and Major Mohun the Emperor Maximin, father of the heroine Valeria (Nell Gwyn); Peg Hughes inappropriately (she was pregnant by Prince Rupert) played St Catherine. Killigrew even patched up Edward Kynaston, an ageing matinée idol but still the darling of the ladies – they vied with each other in driving him round and round Hyde Park dressed in the costumes he wore on stage. While he had played recently in a satire called *The Heiress*, he had decided to dress like Sir Charles Sedley (whom he resembled) and promenade with his admirers; this was a mistake and he had been set upon next day and beaten up, so that he should keep his 'piercing eyes and imperious vivacity' for the theatre, and his own station in life when abroad.

All the best actresses were recruited, too. Mary Knipp (Pepys' wife was complaining about the liaison) had two parts, Felicia and the spirit Nakar. Rebecca Marshall was Berenice, the Empress, and Susanna Uphill was Erotian. Dryden had sidetracked the usual criticism that he should not put Nell into tragic parts, by limiting the amount she had to say and giving her lots of 'business', flouncing about, striking poses and, in the end, dying. She managed to add her own comic touches. When she stabbed herself at the end of the play (not a dry eye in the house), she was supposed to fall up front, then be picked up and put onto a bier to be carried off. As they approached the wings, she leapt off the bier and cried:

> Hold! Are you mad, you damned confounded dog?
> I am to rise to speak the epilogue.

Walking back up front again, she spoke an epilogue which eventually went:

> I come, kind gentlemen, strange news to tell ye,
> I am the ghost of poor departed Nelly.
> Sweet ladies, be not frightened, I'll be civil,
> I'm what I was, a harmless little devil.
> For after death, we sprights have just such natures,
> We had for all the world, when human creatures;
> And therefore I that was an actress here,

Play all my tricks in Hell, a goblin there.
Gallants look to't, you say there are no sprights,
But I'll come dance about your beds at nights.
And 'faith you'll be in a sweet kind of taking,
When I surprise you between sleep and waking?
To tell you true, I walk because I dye
Out of my calling in a Tragedy.
O poet! damn'd dull poet, who could prove
So senseless, to make Nelly dye for love,
Nay, what's worse, to kill me in the prime
Of Easter-Term, in Tart and Cheesecake time! ...
Here Nelly lies, who, though she liv'd a slattern
Yet died a Princess acting in St Cathar'n.

The allusion to dancing about beds was intelligible to all in the pit. The
Queen had paid a visit to her husband, unnannounced, in the middle of the
night, when, solicitious as ever, she had heard he had a bad cold. Nell was
woken hurriedly by Mrs Chiffinch and hid under the bed. Unfortunately,
one of her slippers was visible when the Queen came into the royal
bedroom: 'Ha,' said the Queen, 'I will be off then. I see it is not you who has
the cold.'

Dryden had assured himself both of Buckingham's favour and of regular
royal visits to the theatre by dedicating the play to the Duke of Monmouth.
He had also tried to forestall criticism by writing a long Preface explaining
that he did not want to be attacked for filling his writings with faeries and
spirits: 'Whether there are such Beings or not, it concerns not me: 'Tis
sufficient for my purpose that many have believed the affirmative: and that
these Heroick Representations, which are of the same Nature with the
Epick, are not limited, but with the extremist bounds of what is credible.' It
was, after all a superstitious age, with astrology booming as well as
astronomy, and with 'faeries' everywhere. (Aubrey says that about this time,
'Not far from Cirencester, was an apparition: being demanded, whether a
good spirit or bad, returned no answer, but disappeared with a curious
perfume and most melodious twang.')

Superstitious or not, the play was an immediate success and ran for two
consecutive weeks, something which very seldom happened in Restoration
times. The King was delighted and gave presents to all the cast.

During the run, the heir to the Grand Duke of Tuscany, Prince Cosimo,
was on a visit to London; he was taken to see the play, and several others in
which Nell starred, in April, May and June. He was much impressed by the
theatre, 'superior to anything in Florence', and a member of his entourage,
Count Magalotti (Magliotti) has left a Memoir, in which he writes: 'The
theatre is nearly of a circular form, surrounded in the inside by boxes
separated from each other, and divided into several rows of seats, for the

greater accommodation of the ladies and gentlemen, who in conformity with the freedom of the country sit together indiscriminately.' He admired the actors and actresses, and the scenery, which he thought beautifully painted. He complimented Tom Killigrew on the ensemble and on his Italian. He anticipated Canaletto's fascination with the Thames and its innumerable craft (he estimated that there were at least 10,000 boats of one sort or another on the river) and used to have himself rowed up and down until Charles lent the party a royal barge. He was very sharp about the excessively favourable comparison with the Arno, which, he agreed with the Venetian Ambassador Mocenigo, was 'ill cared for, full of filth'.

The future Grand Duke was lavishly entertained, as part of the foreign policy of the day, which was to strengthen relations with the Italian States (especially Venice and Tuscany) and find an alternative to the eternal shuffling of the principal alliance between France and the Netherlands. On 19 May Evelyn notes that there was a special meeting of the Royal Society to see how the Prince should be received. On 9 July he was taken to see the inaugural concert of 'the New Theater so magnificently built by the munificence of Dr Gilbert Sheldon, Archbishop of Canterbury ... it was now resolved to celebrate its dedication with the greatest splendour and formalitie that might be and therefore drew a world of strangers and other Companie to the University [Oxford] ... after loud Musique from the Corridor above (where was placed an Organ) there follow'd divers Paneygyric Speeches both in Prose and Verse ... mingl'd with excellent Musique both vocal and instrumental to entertain the Ladys & '.

Count Magalotti was amazed also by the quantity of alcohol consumed by men and women alike. Even the Court put away 'wines from Florence and Naples and those of Provence and Languedoc', not to speak of 'delicious and exquisite bottled beers'. The Duchess of York: 'Colonel Popham's great tankard [she] dranke it off at a draught.' The Count ought not to have been surprised. Aubrey writes of Sir John Dunstable: ' ... the cellar he calls his library. Parliament men prepare themselves for the business of the nation with ale in the morning. Some justices doe sleepe on the bench every assizes. At Chippenham, the Deputye Lieutenants meet to see the order of the militia, but *quales* D: Lieutenants, *tales officiarii*. After the taedious setting (at dinner and drinking after dinner) the drummes beate and the soldiers to marche before the windows to be seen by the Deputye Lieutenants. Justice Wagstaffe (colonell) had not march't before 'em many yardes but down a-falls all along in the dirt. His myrmidons, *multa vi*, heav'd him up, and then a-cry'd put "Some drinke, ho!" and so there was an end of the business.' Sir Charles Sedley's motto was:

> Drinke about till the day finds us,
> These are pleasures that endure.

The Grand Duke and the Count were astonished to see Nell Gwyn, at a banquet 'quaff a great goblet of canary'.

It was at this feast that the word went round that 'sweet Nell' was pregnant and the stage would soon lose its brightest star. It was true. By the end of August the fact could not be hidden. Pepys was sad. Evelyn rejoiced. Everybody wondered if they had seen the last of her. Would she ever be seen again in Drury Lane? Buckingham knew there would be many other roles for her to play in the future, this time on the wider stage of the State.

Resting, 1669-72

A Church Papist loves Popery well but is loth to lose by it. Once a
month he presents himself at the church [of England] to keep off the
churchwardens, kneels with the congregation, but prays by himself and
asks God's forgiveness for coming thither. He would make a bad
martyr and a good traveller, for his conscience is so large he could
never wander from it, and in Constantinople would be circumcised
with a mental reservation.

Contemporary chronicle

The King's behaviour towards Nell Gwyn that autumn was very touching.
Mrs Chiffinch, who was paid £1,200 a year to supply him with whores,
must have been worried by this fidelity and paternal interest; his health
improved noticeably. He would walk from Whitehall down the Strand, and
up Maypole Alley or Wych Street (her old lodgings were where Wych
Street led into Drury Lane) and across to the house in Newman's Row (the
whole area demolished to make way for Aldwych and Kingsway). He would
eat at least one meal a day with Nell, play cards and gossip with her.
Diplomats and petitioners (more familiar with the brothels of nearby
Whetstone Park) had to find their way to the little house to do their
business, and remarked on the atmosphere of domestic bliss – the King had
'putt off Majestie'. Moll Davis sulked in St James's Square; Barbara
Castlemaine, put out of the Palace, brooded in Berkshire House, to which
Charles had exiled her.

The conversation at Nell's was not entirely frivolous. In 1669, with the
Thirty Years War on the Continent, and the Commonwealth of Cromwell at
home, still fresh in people's mind, the manner of worship was a topic for
lively, even ferocious debate. When it was raised with a leaven of personal
ambition, as in Buckingham's case, the mixture of ideas became explosive.

The conversion of the Duke of York was the starting-point for most
debate. Would a Roman Catholic succeed Charles? What would this mean
at home and abroad in terms of alliances? And of what religion was Charles,

anyway? He did all the things an Anglican was supposed to do, attending Divine Service regularly. As Head of the Anglican Church he received and appointed bishops, even listened to lengthy theological discussions, but he had many Catholic friends on the one hand and encouraged that old atheist Thomas Hobbes on the other. His wife was a Catholic, but his Poet Laureate (the appointment was confirmed in 1670) was an admirer of Hobbes and, as Aubrey says, 'oftimes makes use of his doctrines in his plays'. The King was both sceptical and tolerant, an unpopular stance. He approved of an exchange between Aubrey and Sir William Petty: 'I remember one St Andrewe's day, which is the day of the meeting of the Royall Society for annuall elections, I say'd methought 'twas not so well that we should pitch upon the Patron of Scotland's day, we should rather have taken St George or St Isidore. "No", say Sir William, "I would rather have had it on St Thomas' day for he would not believe until he had seen and putt his fingers into the holes". '

The French diplomats accredited to the Court had at one stage hoped to use Barbara Castlemaine to further the interests of both Louis XIV and the Pope; it is not quite clear whose idea this was, that of de Bordeaux (who had remained after the Restoration as an extra emissary), of de Barthes (who spent most of his time in business in the city), of de Gramont (who had become a Restoration rake and had recently married the notorious Lady Elizabeth Hamilton) or of the titular Ambassador, Colbert de Croissy; they all styled themselves 'Ambassador' at one time or another and carried on an official correspondence with Louis XIV's Secretary of State, de Lionne. In 1667 de Lionne had written to Colbert de Croissy: 'The King thinks well of your efforts to obtain the help of the Countess of Castlemaine, and read with interest of her point-blank way of telling you that Lord Arlington would not hear of an alliance with France.' By 1669 Lord Arlington had become a Catholic and a potential ally of His Most Catholic Majesty of France, and the Countess of Castlemaine was out of favour. A new initiative seems to have been taken in France itself by Charles' sister, 'Minette'. She had recently turned her attention to religion and was looking for an outlet for her zeal. In an audience with Louis XIV she convinced him that it was possible to 'turn' his royal cousin, bring the Kingdoms of Scotland and England back into the Church of Rome and make of her brother's realm a faithful ally of France. Louis was not particularly devout at that stage in his life but he could see the advantages of an alliance with his neighbour across the Channel. Charles' armies needed reinforcements and the Royal Navy was in some disrepair, but the English, Irish and Scots were good soldiers and sailors – indeed, he had thousands of them in his own service.

What Minette proposed was a Secret Treaty (it became known as the *Traité de Madame*) under whose terms Charles would receive 2 million livres a year; in return he would become 'a perpetual ally', remove the discriminatory laws against Catholics from the Statute Book, be received into the Church of Rome and in due time 'turn' England and Scotland again. Charles, who was by nature a tolerant man, liked the idea of a general indulgence. Catholics and Dissenters were victims of a whole penal code: proselytizing and harbouring priests were capital crimes; not taking the sacrament at Divine Service in the Established Church brought a fine of £20 for a first year of refusal, and fines on a rising scale thereafter; even not attending Divine Service was punishable with a fine of one shilling, a day's wage for a workman. Many Catholics dissimulated, many others stuck to their 'known principles by the strict practising of which we shall live and die with comfort, though poor and passing to our last home by the gibbet' (William Blundell). The Duke of York had toyed with the idea of attending Anglican services, to avoid embarrassing his brother, but had been told that year that such hypocrisy was inadmissible; he could not be a 'Church Papist'.

Colbert de Croissy revealed the terms of the treaty over lunch at Nell's house. He reported to Paris that the King was much entranced by her and 'how he loved her buffooneries'. He did not see how she could be used in their cause. She was known to be a close friend of the Duke of Buckingham, who was at the moment anti-French and anti-Catholic. Charles' other ministers were, perhaps, more tractable: Clifford (Thomas, Lord Clifford of Chudleigh) was a practising Roman Catholic from birth; Arlington (Henry Bennet, Earl of Arlington) was, as de Lionne knew, a recent convert; Anthony Ashley Cooper (soon to be Earl of Shaftesbury) was a trimmer, having served both Charles I and Cromwell, but was a firm Protestant and pro-Dutch; Lauderdale (John Maitland, first Duke, and Master of Scotland) hated most things, including the bagpipes, the Scots and the Pope. These five ministers (known as the Cabal from their initials – Clifford, Arlington, Buckingham, Ashley and Lauderdale) seldom met together. Clifford and Arlington would accept the Treaty. Lauderdale was usually in Scotland, but something might be hinted to him during one of his trips to his retreat at Ham House, Surrey. Ashley Cooper had to be kept ignorant of what was going on for as long as possible; he was distracted by a project to 'bring back the spectacle of judges riding with their foot cloathes to Whitehall'. Buckingham would be the great obstacle.

De Croissy under-estimated the difficulty of dealing with this 'most inconstant and forgetful of men' (Burnet). During the winter of 1669-70 Buckingham was seen as the companion of Lord John Roos, heir to the Earl of Rutland, not a man with whom he had much in common. Roos, to restore the honour of his family, had petitioned to have his wife declared an adultress and her children bastards. Having succeeded in this, he was preparing a Bill of Divorcement, so that he could marry again and produce legitimate heirs with an honest woman. In March 1670 the Bill was presented, and Buckingham spoke to it himself; on 12 April 1670 the Bill was accepted by the House of Lords, and Roos was free. It was during the discreet celebrations that Buckingham's interest was revealed.

He said he was about to introduce a Bill to put an end to the King's marriage to Catherine of Braganza, as Henry VIII had done with her namesake of Aragon, because she could not produce an heir. When the King said Buckingham was mad and that he would have him arrested for *lèse majesté*, Buckingham is said to have suggested the Queen be kidnapped and taken to America – well looked after, of course – and then the marriage could be dissolved for desertion by a spouse. The King said again that he was mad, and even Nell Gwyn, coming near to her time, agreed that the idea was not workable. Charles' next reaction was to hurry on the final negotiations for the *Traité de Madame*.

Louis XIV did not haggle about the financial terms of the Secret Treaty, and entrusted Minette with the last details. As an earnest of his goodwill, he sent Charles a number of presents by de Gramont, and an astrologer whom he thought would interest the Royal Society; the King kept the astrologer, Pregnani, until the Easter meeting at Newmarket, then, when he forecast wrongly the result of three successive races, he was sent back to Paris.

At the beginning of May 1670 everything was ready for Minette. Charles virtually moved the Court to Dover, then Canterbury, for what was supposed to be just a family reunion. In addition to the Treaty, Minette brought with her over two hundred courtiers, priests, spies, secretaries and advisers, not to speak of 'boxes of perfumed gloves, little mirrors, apricot paste and the other small wares of love' for the young actress who she had heard was about to give birth to her brother's latest child (the gifts also included a silver fruit knife and fork now kept at the Army and Navy Club).

The King was touched by his sister's interest in Nell, but was not so paternal that he did not notice Louise Renée de Quérouaille, daughter of the impoverished Sieur de Penancoët. There were to be many spellings of her name. Saint-Simon wrote of her: 'Her parents intended her to be Louis XIV's mistress, and she obtained the place of Maid of Honour to Henrietta of England. Unfortunately for her, Mlle de la Vallière was also Maid of Honour to the Princess, and the King preferred her to that lady.' Louise may have missed her chance at home because she would not subdue her natural inclination and had already lost her virginity to the Comte de Sault and entertained other courtiers. To Charles she pretended to be virtuous and, helped by a baby face, she seems to have convinced him that she was. When she came to his suite with a casket of jewels from her mistress, to ask the King to choose one, he said she was the only jewel he wanted. Reluctantly, Minette said she had promised to return the girl to her parents.

In addition to his signature, the King gave his sister some fine silver and gold plate, paintings, two spaniels, several rings and necklaces of pearls. He also summoned the actors of the Duke's House to Canterbury to play *Sullen Lovers* (Shadwell) and *Sir Solomon of The Cautious Coxcomb* (Caryl). Star of the performances was James Nokes, a rising comic actor who so captivated the Duke of Monmouth that he handed Nokes his sword. Colley Cibber wrote of him: 'He was an actor of a quite different genius from any I have ever read, heard of, or seen, since or before his time; and yet his general excellence may be comprehended in one article, namely a plain and palpable simplicity of nature, which was so utterly his own, that he was often as unaccountably diverting in his common speech as on stage.' Minette's female attendants all wore the latest very wide-brimmed hats, and the men short coats and wide belts; Nokes, in a very short coat, enormously wide belt and the Duke's sword, used *Sir Solomon* as a vehicle for his own comment on the latest French fashions.

The 'family reunion' over, gifts exchanged and the Secret Treaty of Dover signed, brother and sister parted tearfully. Charles hurried back to London to fondle his latest child: Anthony à Wood recorded that on 12 May, 'One that belongs to the King's Playhouse was brought to bed of a boy in her house in Lyncolns Inn Fields, next to Whetstone Park – the King's bastard.' The King found Nell well and approved when she said she would have the baby baptized Charles. (One of Barbara Castlemaine's bastards had been given the name, too, but had been first baptized by a Jesuit priest in the service of her husband; there had been a great furore and a re-baptism at St Margaret's, Westminster.) Nell's house was full of her friends and colleagues from the theatre – 'like a Bear Garden', the pleased and proud father said. John Dryden was there every day with the play he had written for Nell and which had had to be postponed because of her pregnancy. As he wrote in one of the epilogues:

> Think him not duller for this year's delay;
> He was prepar'd the women were away;
> And men, without their parts, can hardly play.
> If they, through sickness, seldom did appear,
> Pity the virgins of each theatre!
> For at both houses, 'twas a sickly year!
> And pity us, your servants, to whose cost
> In one such sickness, nine whole months are lost.

Nell was as keen as Dryden to get back to the theatre. She did not want to lose her public, and the extra hold she had on the King, 'yea, as one as popular as he'. The little house was warm, if noisy, but she knew that domesticity would soon pall. She was lucky that a tragic event prolonged the King's emotional dependence on her. On 29 June 1670 Buckingham, back in favour, brought the news that Minette had died (in all probability poisoned by her husband's latest lover, the Chevalier de Lorraine).

On 2 July 1670 Colbert de Croissy wrote to de Lionne: 'The King of England is inconsolable, and what still further increases his affliction and sorrow, is that there are many people who do not refrain from asserting that Madame was poisoned, and this malicious rumour is spreading so rapidly in the town that some of the rabble have declared that violent hands ought to be laid on the French ... The Duke of Buckingham is in the transports of a madman, and if the King were not more wise and prudent, and my Lord Arlington very reasonable and well-intentioned, affairs would be carried to the last extremities.'

Nell also added her doubts that anybody would be a party to such an absurd crime and took the King off to Newmarket, where the air would do them, and the child, good; it was with some difficulty that she persuaded her mother to stay behind with Rose. On 21 July Evelyn saw them at Newmarket and 'alighted to see his Majestie's house there now building new, the arches of the Cellars beneath are exceedingly well turned by the Architect Mr Samuel, the rest meane enough and hardly capable for a hunting house; many of the Roomes over had Chimnies placed in angles and Corners, a Mode now introduced by his Majestie which I do at no hand approve of besides this house is placed in a dirty Street without any Court or avenue like a common Burgers. ... ' Evelyn disapproved of the fact that the new 'palace' had not been built near the racecourse, though he knew well that its siting was partly determined by the presence of Nell's house, completed by a more important architect, on the other side of the street.

It seems to have been an idyllic summer. Nell even received a layette from Cosimo, who had just succeeded his father Fedinand II as Grand Duke of Tuscany. The Venetian Ambassador, who was a great admirer, bought a collection of ingenious toys for the young child. Unbeknown to Nell (and even the King, possibly), over the Channel the Duke of Buckingham was plotting. Charles' interest in Louise de Quérouaille had not gone unnoticed or unreported, and as the Marquis de Saint-Maurice, the Duke of Savoy's Ambassador in Paris, wrote to his master on 19 September: 'She is a beautiful girl, and it is thought the plan is to make her mistress to the King of England. The Duke of Buckingham would like to dethrone Lady Castlemaine, who is his enemy, and His Most Christian Majesty will not be sorry to see the position filled by one of his subjects, for it is said that the ladies have great influence over the mind of the King of England.'

Buckingham did not know that Barbara Castlemaine had already been dethroned in his absence. The King had gone up to Town on business and had stopped at Berkshire House to see his children. As he approached her bedroom, he heard a commotion and was just in time to see John Churchill (ancestor of Sir Winston) leg it out of the window and off through the garden. 'Nay, hasten not,' said the King, 'I know you only do it for money'. Barbara was raised to the dignity of Duchess of Cleveland and told that after the birth of her latest child (by Churchill) no more would be recognized as royal and given titles.

This *coup* did not establish Nell Gwyn as 'official mistress', and Burnet was perhaps right to be severe with Charles for never giving her this position; she was, however, a commoner and could not even claim, like Moll Davis, to be a noble bastard. There is no doubt, however, about his ever-deepening feelings for her as something more: a whore, a friend, a discreet political hostess whose opinion he valued. On their return to Town he moved her to a house at the end of what is now Pall Mall (possibly the site of the Reform Club today); it was not much of a house (the rates were only 16 shillings a year) but it would do until something better came along, and at least 'it is near to the best friend I have', as Nell said herself.

The Duke of Buckingham was not pleased. Louis XIV had charged him with the delivery of Louise de Quérouaille, and he was on his way with her to Dieppe when he heard the news. He had under-estimated Nell's influence and had been deprived of the satisfaction of tumbling Barbara Castlemaine from her perch. He hurried to Calais with a few of his gentlemen and forgot all about Louise; in the end the British Ambassador in Paris had to make arrangements for her further journey to London – she never forgave the Duke for the slight.

At the beginning of October Colbert de Croissy reported: 'It is certain that the King of England shows a warm affection for Mlle de Keroualle, and perhaps you may have heard from other sources that a richly furnished lodging has been given her at Whitehall. His Majesty repairs to her apartment at nine every morning, and never stays there less than an hour, and sometimes two.'

Nell Gwyn certainly under-estimated the attractions of the woman who was to become her greatest rival. She heard that the Bretonne was not yet fully 'in service' and perhaps thought there would be a lengthy and amusing courtship, like that of La Belle Stewart, followed by a sweet revenge and then obscurity. In any event, Nell had the immediate consolation of knowing that the whole theatre-going public was counting the days until her re-appearance at the King's House in the new play – *Almanzor and Almahide, or The Conquest of Granada.*

The play was another resounding success. Again the cast was strong: Kynaston was Mahomet Boabdelin, the last Moorish ruler of Granada; Charles Hart played Almanzor, and Michael Mohun Abdelmelech; the Marshalls, Boutel and Jeames had the supporting female roles. Nell was cast as a 'chaste, highminded heroine' who married Boabdelin out of a sense of duty and had to wait for a year after the death of her husband before she could marry her 'true love', Almanazor. This bit of casting produced some ribald comment, none more so than Etherege's celebration of her relationship with the King:

> Permit me, Sir, to help you to a whore:
> Kiss her but once, you'll ne'er want Cleveland more.
> She'll fit you to a Hair, all wit, all fire –
> And Impudent to your own Heart's desire.
> And more than this, Sir, you'll save money by her.
> She's Buckhurst's whore at present, but you must know –
> When sovereign wants a whore, the subject must forgo.

Buckhurst had not been Nell's lover for years, but gossip had it that he was always being sent abroad on pointless diplomatic missions to keep him out of the way of his royal rival.

The play started with a Prologue spoken by Nell in a wide belt and a hat like a sun umbrella. Waldon in his *Roscius Anglicanus* explains: 'At the Duke's theatre, Nokes appeared in a hat larger than Pistol's, which took the town wonderful, and supported a bad play by its fine effect. Dryden, piqued at this, caused a hat to be made the circumference of a timber coach wheel; and as Nelly was low of stature, and what the French call *mignonne* or *piquante*, he made her speak ... under that hat, the brims thereof being spread out horizontally to their full extension. The whole theatre was in a convulsion of applause, nay, the very actors giggled, a circumstance none had observed before. Judge, therefore, what a condition the merriest Prince alive [King Charles] was in at such a conjecture! 'Twas beyond *odso* and *ods fish*, for he wanted little of being suffocated with laughter.'

Dryden acknowledged the parentage of this fresh parodying of French fashions:

> This jest was first of the other house's making,
> And, five times tried, has never fail'd of taking;
> For 'twere a shame a poet should be kill'd
> Under the shelter of so broad a shield.
> This is the hat, whose very sight did win ye
> To laugh and clap as though the devil were in ye.
> As then, for Nokes, so now I hope you'll be
> So dull, to laugh once more for love of me.
> I'll write a play, says one, for I have got
> A broad-brimm'd hat, and waist-belt, towards a plot.
> Says the other, I'have one more large than that
> Thus they out-write each other with a hat.

Gerard Langbaine was there at the opening night, on 10 December 1670, and inevitably accused Dryden of plagiarism, of 'borrowing' from Mlle de Scudéry's *L'Esclave Reine* and 'purloining' the historical characters of Ferdinand and Isabella (who were undeniably responsible for the conquest of Granada). Dryden, who had taken the wind out of the sails of all criticism with his Prologue, repeated that 'I have no difficulty, nor ever shall to take the foundation (of a Romance, Novel or foreign play), to build it up and make it proper for the English stage.' Very shrewdly, he divided the play in two parts and showed the second, in which Nell's love and virtue triumph, on 9 January 1671. Even the Queen approved of the sentiments, and the play was performed at Court by royal command on 10 and 11 February; by then even the disapproving Evelyn had seen it (6 February) – he describes it as *The Siege of Granada* – and when he saw it again on the 10th at Court he noted: 'There were indeed very glorious scenes and perspectives, the work of Mr Streeter [Robert Streeter, His Majesty's Serjeant Painter] who very well understands it.'

A fire at the King's House on 25 January had caused more damage than had been originally estimated, and from the end of February the company led a peripatetic life for the next three years. Nell seems to have worked with them for the first few months of 1671, but she had other things on her mind. She was not satisfied with her little house near what is now Trafalgar Square and managed to get herself moved, on the strength of her latest success on the stage, to a much grander establishment at 79 Pall Mall, where she was to live for the rest of her life (it is now the offices of the P & O Shipping Line). She was in good company. The Duchess of Cleveland and Moll Davis were both near neighbours, and she was even nearer to her protector, now over forty and easily tempted on a cold night to stay in the Palace itself.

On 1 March, Evelyn saw Nell shortly after she had moved in. He was walking with the King from St James's Park to the Private Gardens (now Marlborough House) discussing matters of State and the visit of the Tsar, not to speak of the preferment of his friend May, when he heard a loud cry: 'Charles!' The garden of 79 Pall Mall was contiguous with the Private Gardens, and Evelyn had to put aside 'some sheetes of my Historie [and] both saw and heard a very familiar discourse between [the King] and Mrs Nellie as they cal'd an impudent comedian, she looking out of her garden on a Terrace at the top of the Wall, and standing on the greene Walke under it; I was heartily sorry at this Scene.'

Having got her house, with its two floors of public rooms and three for servants and services, Nell proceeded to decorate it in style. It was easy to get the necessary money from Charles (in addition to the £4,000 a year he now allowed her) because she was pregnant again, and she even managed to get a pardon for her brother-in-law, who had been arrested while burgling Sir Henry Littleton's house. Andrew Marvell celebrates this event and its sequel:

> Our good King Charles the Second,
> Too flippant of treasure and moisture,
> Stoop'd from the Queen infecund
> To a Wench of Orange and Oyster.
> Consulting his Catzo, he found it expedient
> To waste time in revels with Nell the Comediant.

> The lecherous vainglory
> Of being lim'd with Majesty,
> Mounts up to such a story
> This Bitchington Travesty,
> That to equal her lover, the Baggage must dare
> To be Helen the Second, the Cause of a War.

> If the sister of Rose
> Be a whore so annointed
> That the Parliament's Nose
> Must for her be disjointed,
> Then should you but name the Preoragative 'whore',
> How the Bullets would whistle, the Cannons would roar.

The Parliamentary nose in question was that of Sir John Coventry, MP for Weymouth, who had been astonished by the money lavished on the two 'Comediants', Nell and Moll Davis, the more so because 79 Pall Mall had formerly been leased by the Coventrys, though it had fallen into the hands of the Earl of Scarsdale (who conveyed the lease in trust for its new menagère). Sir John proposed in the House that a tax be levied on all theatres and as an aside wondered 'whether the King's pleasure did lie among the men or among the women who acted?'. This was a very foolish remark, and a few days later he was beaten up by Nell's friend Sir Thomas Sandys (whose wife Lucy was a lifelong intimate and later a witness to her Will) and had his nose slit to the bone. More questions were asked in the House, but more discreetly.

Having silenced the Coventrys (and got rid of their bric-à-brac from her home), Nell made friends among the tradesmen. She bought herself a carriage and spent £146. 5s. decorating it to her taste. One bill for upholstery was for £74. 4s. 3d., and 'for gilding the hinges and Nayles for a cabinett £3. 10s.' There are many accounts, usually settled promptly, in Cunningham's collection and she prided herself on being a better paymistress than any other of the King's favourites.

This domestic activity, however, pleasant though it was, caused a hiatus in Nell's slow but steady advancement, and smoothed the path for Louise de Quèrouaille. Nell knew that the King would 'take his Greate Engine elsewhere', perhaps nearby to Mary Knight, Catherine Pegge (Lady Green) or an actress. Actors were in the ascendant. In March William Wycherley had had a great success with his first play at the Duke's, *Love in a Wood*. Barbara Cleveland went to see every performance and one day stopped him in the Park with the remark: 'You, Wycherley, are the son of a whore', alluding to one of his songs, in the play, which ended:

Great wits and great braves
Have always a punk to their mother.

They made an assignation on the strength of this exchange of pleasantries;
the next evening they slept together, and Barbara found the young
playwright even more vigorous than her rope-dancer, Jacob Hall or the
young Churchill (she had given him £5,000 to buy some new clothes but he
had invested it in an annuity). By Easter 1671 Wycherley was a regular
performer, at her house and at Mary Knight's, where he sometimes obliged
both ladies. The King could not believe this at first but one night crept into
Mary Knight's with Rochester and met Wycherley coming downstairs
muffled in his cloak. Upstairs, Barbara hurried to compose herself and said
she was staying with a friend to prepare herself better for her Easter duties.
'Ha!' said the King, 'and I suppose that was your confessor I met going
downstairs.'

Louise, though her inclinations had not changed, was more circumspect.
Her sister, who was not at all *sage*, advised her to be so in England so that
the 'rumours' of her sexual athletics in France could be discounted. She was
also advised by Philibert de Gramont, who had become an ambassador in
England because La Motte Houdancourt had preferred Louis XIV's
patronage to his reputed potency; Elizabeth Hamiliton had amused her with
the story that at the end of his 'exile' he was about to return to France,
unwed, when the Hamilton brothers stopped him at Dover with the
reminder that he had forgotten to wed their sister.

Louise had no virginity to lose, but she had to pretend that she had. She
taunted the King, even hinted to others that she had given in. On one
occasion during the summer of 1671 she was so convincing that the French
Ambassador could report ' ... that the affection of the King of England for
Mademoiselle increases every day, and the little attack of nausea which she
had yesterday when dining with me makes me hope that her good fortune
will continue, at least all the remainder of my embassy' – de Lionne and the
Minister of War, Louvois, were toying with the idea of replacing him with
a Huguenot.

But Louise held out, notwithstanding repeated reminders that she had
been sent over to England to console the King on the death of his sister and
protect French interests in the battle of the bedchamber. The Queen had
accepted her as a maid of honour, and indeed she was very slow to surrender
her 'honour', once reminding the King solemnly of his marriage vows. More
advice was forthcoming. The Chevalier de Saint-Evremond wrote to her:
'Happy is the woman who knows how to behave herself discreetly without
checking her inclination! For 'tis scandalous to love beyond moderation, as
'tis a great mortification for a woman to pass her life without one amour. Do
not too severely reject temptations, which in this country offer themselves

more modestly than is required, even in a virgin, to hearken to them. Yield, then, to the sweets of temptation instead of consulting your pride.'

It was not pride, and not of course virginity, which held Louise back, but greed and a preoccupation with security. She had to be assured that she would be provided for handsomely, given a house and servants and titles for any children who might be forthcoming, and that her parents would be received at the English Court. Lord Arlington was approached to reassure her, and Colbert de Croissy wrote to Paris: 'My Lord Arlington said to me quite recently that he was very pleased to see that the King was becoming attached to her; and that, though His Majesty was not the man to communicate affairs of state to ladies, nevertheless it was in their power on occasion to render ill services to those whom they disliked and defeat their plans, it was much better for the King's good servants that His Majesty should have an inclination for this lady, who is not of a mischievous disposition, and is a gentlewoman, rather than for actresses and such-like unworthy creatures, of whom no man of quality could take the measure.'

Lord Arlington added that it was necessary to 'counsel this young lady to cultivate the King's good graces, so that he might find with her nothing but pleasure, peace and quiet.'

During the month of September, even Lady Arlington was brought into play and told to 'urge this young lady to yield unreservedly to the King's wishes, and tell her that there was no alternative for her but a convent in France ... '. It was explained to her that time was running short, that within a few days the King would be off to Newmarket with Nell Gwyn, for most of the month of October, and by the time they got back Nell's latest child would be born. By good fortune, the Arlingtons had a house, Euston Hall, near Thetford, and there would be a large house party in October; the King *always* came over, with the Duke of York, and there would be an opportunity for her to show she realized the 'obligation she was under to My Lord'.

The yielding was done, and there is an impeccable witness, John Evelyn, to the fact that the terms of her 'surrender' had been settled and her 'honour' offered up during the race meeting nearby. On 9 October 1671 Evelyn (also a house guest) recorded: ' ... the fair lady was bedded one of these nights, and the stocking flung after the manner of a married bride. I acknowledge that she was for the most part in her undress all day, and that there was fondness and toying with the young wanton. Nay, it was said that I was at the former ceremony, but it is utterly false. I neither saw nor heard of any such thing whilst I was there, though I had been in her chamber and all over that apartment late enough, and was observing all passages with much curiosity. However, it was with confidence believed that she was first made a Miss, as they call these unhappy creatures, with solemnity at the time.' Evelyn's tone is always less censorious when writing of Louise, a distressed gentlewoman trying to repair her family fortunes, than when he recorded

Nell's adventures; perhaps this is because he was an incorrigible snob and, for example, enjoyed letting one of his houses to Peter the Great, although the Tsar, drunk, used to push his servants in a wheelbarrow through the privet hedges 'for fun'.

Having got his way with Louise at last, the King divided his time more or less equally between her (at Lord Arlington's) and Nell (at her own house in Newmarket). On 22 October 1671 Colbert de Croissy wrote to Louvois: 'The King comes frequently [to Euston Hall] to take his repasts with us, and afterwards spends some hours with Mlle de Keroualle. He has already paid her three visits. He invited us yesterday to Newmarket, where we were entertained very splendidly, and he showed towards her all the kindness, all the little attentions and all the assiduities love can inspire. And since she has not been wanting, on her side, in all the gratitude that the love of a great King can deserve from a beautiful girl, it is believed that the attachment will be of long duration and that it will exclude all others.' The French Ambassador did not comment on a meeting at Newmarket between the new 'attachment' and the old but, as Buckingham was there, still convinced he could use the one to his own advantage, it was certainly well staged. Evelyn accompanied his hosts on one occasion to Newmarket and 'found the jolly blades, Dauncing, feasting and revelling more resembling a luxurious and abandoned rout than a Christian Court; the Duke of Buckingham was now in mighty favour, and had with him that impudent woman the Countesse of Shrewsbury'. He says nothing about an episode in a brothel in Newmarket recommended by Nell (who could not oblige herself), in which the King was attacked by thieves, was stripped and escaped murder only when his royal ring was recognized.

As the time came for Nell to give birth to her second child, she moved back to London and excited the ballad-makers. According to one, Parliament was to be recalled to vote money for the layette, and Sir John Coventry, his nose repaired, was to present it. Another suggested that a warship was to be converted into an enormous cradle. Unperturbed, Nell was delivered of a healthy boy on Christmas Day. She had a rather touching visit from her former lover, Lord Buckhurst, who had married the widowed Lady Falmouth (a former royal whore), and visits from the King and his brother James, Duke of York, after whom the child was named.

There was another fire at the King's House in January 1672, and Killigrew, another frequent visitor to Nell, told her they had decided to give up any idea of repairing the scene of her many triumphs and build a 'great new playhouse'. She also heard of the death of a young actor, Richard Bell, in the fire, an event which prompted a ballad-maker to write:

> He cries just judgement, and wishes when poor Bell
> Rung out his last, 'had been the stage's kNell.

Nell disdained the ballad-mongers, or enjoyed them. She was more worried by the news that Louise was pregnant, knowing how the King enjoyed these proofs of his virility.

The French King was worried, too – about the lack of action on the front of both the reconversion of England and Scotland and, even more important, the containment of the Dutch. The Dutch, for their part, were extremely worried about their future. The complex, democratic government of the Netherlands (in reality ruled by the de Witt brothers), was beset by internal and external problems. It was quite obvious to them that Louis XIV, who had become more and more autocratic since the death a decade earlier of Cardinal Mazarin, intended to dominate all Continental Europe as the Holy Roman Emperor Charles V had done. Who was to stop him? The Emperor's descendants in Spain and Austria were still recovering from the Thirty Years War and in any event were looking not west but east, to a holy war against the Turks. There was in existence a Protestant Triple Alliance with England and Sweden, but Sweden was still recovering from the War, too. England was not to be trusted. Louis had got this new girl into the King's bed, and the Catholic Duke of York had been named Lord High Admiral again (he was desperate for employment after the sudden death of the Duchess Anne). The English Parliament (to Pepys' great relief) had granted a substantial sum for the refurbishing of the Royal Navy, though this had produced a lampoon:

> And ten to one before the spring be over,
> Our cavalry must march again to Dover,
> To guard the shore against the Dutch and French,
> When all this means but new supplies for wench.

The Dutch were not reassured. The refurbished fleet would certainly be used against them.

French historians have often accused Charles II of being half-hearted about keeping his side of the bargain struck in the *Traité de Madame*, but already an army of 20,000 men had been raised in Scotland under Lauderdale, and 18,000, mostly militiamen, were being drilled outside London – all this in spite of the fact that Louis had not paid the first year's subsidy in full (he was never to pay in full or on time). The French Ambassador complained that all political life seemed to have stopped to celebrate the birth of Nell's second son, but this was unfair. Charles and James were delighted with the child and its auspicious birthday, but the fact that they spent so much time at 79 Pall Mall was in part due to the need for security while plans were being made for the next stage in the implementation of the Treaty; Whitehall was full of spies, and many MPs were in the pay of the Dutch.

On 13 March 1672 Charles took the courageous step of publishing a

The Sculpters part is done the 'features' hitt
of Madam Gwin, No Arte can shew her Witt
An engraving of Nell Gwyn by G. Valck

Hortense Mancini, one of the King's mistresses and the Duchess Mazarin, telling her sister's fortune. A portrait by Pierre Maynard

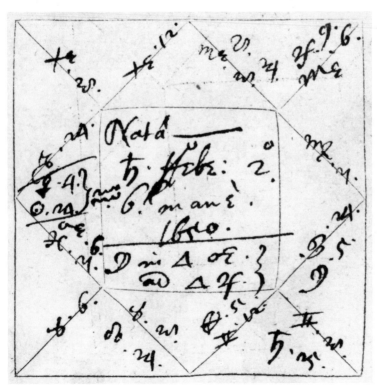

Nell Gwyn's horoscope, cast by Elias Ashmole

Barbara Villiers, who became Lady Castlemaine and Duchess of Cleveland, mistress of Charles II in the 1660s and mother of five of his children

Louise de Keroualle, the French maid-of-honour who became Charles II's mistress in 1671 and whom he created Duchess of Portsmouth

A miniature of Nell Gwyn which was worn by Charles II. Note the set of costumes on mica overlays which could be inserted into the picture's frame

James II, when Duke of York, with his first wife Anne Hyde whom he married secretly abroad

Nell Gwyn and her eldest son the Duke of St Albans portrayed as Venus and Cupid by Sir Peter Lely

Portrait of Nell Gwyn in a brown satin dress by Sir Peter Lely. Charles II
liked to watch his mistress being painted by Lely

A romantic idyll: how the Victorians saw Charles II and Nell Gwyn. The disapproving bystander is John Evelyn. A portrait in the garden by C. M. Ward

Declaration of Indulgence, giving official tolerance to all sects and religions. He did not consult Parliament, which was officially Anglican (though it contained known Catholics and Dissenters), and risked the beginning of a struggle with the House of Commons like this one which had cost his father his head. Some put down the gesture to Louise de Quérouaille's influence. Madame de Sévigné wrote to her daughter on 30 March 1672: 'You will be pleased to hear that Little Keroualle, whose star was divined before she left, has followed it faithfully. The King of England, on seeing her, straightway fell in love, and she did not frown on him when he declared his passion. The upshot is that she is in an interesting state [pregnant]. Isn't it all astonishing? Castlemaine is in disgrace. England is really a very strange country.'

While Madame de Sévigné was weighing up Louise's chances, James, Duke of York, had ordered the interception of the Dutch Smyrna fleet, and two days later war was officially declared against the Netherlands. Simultaneously, French armies under Turenne and Condé crossed the Rhine and invaded the common enemy. The Duke of York went to sea in the *Prince* (100 guns) and after a certain amount of skirmishing engaged the Dutch at Sole Bay on 28 May. It was as bloody a battle as the last one he had fought. Dutch vessels soon picked him out and battered *Prince* until it could fight no more; James had himself rowed to the *St Michael* until she was holed, then to the *London* for the rest of the day. There were some French men-of-war at Sole Bay but they kept out of harm's reach – they had been ordered to study closely the tactics of the more expert English and Dutch. Losses of men and ships on both sides were great and included the Earl of Sandwich (Pepys' patron) in *Royal James*, and the result was inconclusive. Prince William of Orange was appointed virtual dictator of the Netherlands in place of the de Witts, and declared that he would fight France and England for as long as it took to defeat them both.

The House of Commons seethed with anger. Members could not refrain from joining the general celebration of the undoubted heroism of the Duke of York and the 'victory at sea', but what angered them was that the King had gone ahead with his Declaration of Indulgence and the declaration of war without consulting them. What was more, he had put a Stop on the Exchequer, which was a way of freezing interest on public loans. How many more 'absurd adventures' could there be? Not being able to criticize the war, Members turned their wrath on the royal whores. No man, monarch, lord or commoner needed all those whores. A lampoon confirmed that one of them, Nell Gwyn, shared their disapproval. The King had asked her if she would invite the Countess of Shrewsbury to his birthday party at 79 Pall Mall in May, and she had refused, saying: 'One whore at a time is enough for you, Sire.' The Duchess of Cleveland (did he have to create them all duchesses and ennoble their bastards?), though pensioned off like Moll Davis and the others, flaunted her jewels and gambled vast sums of the country's money.

Then there was this new one, with the unpronounceable name, Kerouaille or Quérouaille or Keroualle – because she wore French, wide-brimmed hats, the common people called her Cartwheel or Carwheel. While the Battle of Sole Bay was raging, he had Nell and Louise both at Windsor, the one pregnant inside the walls and the other in a little house (now a gift shop) connected by a tunnel to his apartments in the castle.

On 29 July 1672 Louise gave birth to a child whom she named Charles, in case there should be any doubt about its paternity. In the House, it was said that this woman would be as expensive as Castlemaine-Cleveland had been and, worse, was a Catholic, a foreigner and certainly a spy.

And the 'impudent comedian' with her large establishment in Pall Mall, openly frequented by the Saviles, the Killigrews and all the 'Merry Gang'? She was only an actress, and so anathema to the Puritan Members, but she was said to be the only whore of whom the King was jealous. She seemed to have eclipsed her former 'manager', Buckingham, and had slapped his face recently when he had been too familiar. The Venetian Ambassador in one of his *relazioni* reported to the Doge and Senate: 'Buckingham is now in disgrace with the King for an audacious attempt on His Majesty's private pleasures.' The French Ambassador wrote to Paris that the Duke had tried to fumble 'Mrs Neslie' in the King's own apartments. However, said some Members, she was undoubtedly a Protestant, and the problem with the other one was that the King of France was said to be paying for her. Anyway, Charles had been granted substantial revenues for life, so how could they limit his 'private pleasures'? The Earl of Shaftesbury, who had deserted the Cabal as soon as the Grand Design (for the reconversion of the kingdoms and the alliance with France) had become obvious, did organize some stone-throwing and public insults for the 'ladies' when they went abroad, but it was ineffective. There were hundreds of bawdy songs and ballads printed, but they often had the opposite effect from the one intended, and turned their targets into folk heroines; the reaction of most women was of envy not moral disapproval, and they made this clear to their menfolk. The King was still extremely popular, and they knew that his good humour depended largely on Nell:

> When he was dumpish, she would still be jocund,
> And chuck the royal chin of Charles the Second.

As the House of Commons, foreign embassies and chancelleries (perhaps for the only time in English history) debated the fortunes of whores, the King, their master, felt very much alone. He had no effective ministers except the procurer Arlington; Lauderdale was a long way off in Scotland; Clifford's Catholicism had become common knowledge (he had been discovered on his knees in his carriage with a Jesuit confessor); for different reasons,

Buckingham and Shaftesbury were estranged from him. His armies could not be moved without Parliament's say-so and subsidies, which were not forthcoming. His Navy was refitting. Again he seemed to be doing nothing in the Franco-Dutch War and was nagged incessantly by the French Ambassador. He tried to stay away from Whitehall as much as possible and seems to have fled from time to time to Rose Gwyn's house in Princes Street (she rented it from her sister) or to Bagnigge House, which Thornbury (*Old and New London*) says was 'a summer residence of Nell Gwyn, near the Fleet and amid fields, where she entertained Charles and his saturnine brother with concerts and merry breakfasts in the careless bohemian way in which the noble specimen of divine right delighted.' The house (demolished in 1862) had 'the royal arms, the garter, and other heraldic bearings, and between them the bust of a woman in Roman dress let deep into a circular cavity of the wall, which is said to represent Nell Gwyn'. Cunningham says she came to take the plunge in Cold Bath Fields nearby and 'half a century later a nude statue was shown by the proprietor of the baths as her portrait.' The King also had his racing to console him, at Newmarket, and was often seen at Windsor in the summer and early autumn. The Queen liked Windsor, and so did Nell; Louise de Quérouaille said the air of the country affected her and stayed in Town.

It was during this period of retreat, if not flight, from politics that Nell decided it would be relaxing for the King to learn to fish. The Venetian Ambassador, Girolamo Alberti, a keen fisherman himself (he translated *The Compleat Angler* into Italian), was often with them; he always likened the 'villas of the English on the Thames to those of our families along the Brenta'. He reported that he had seen her teach her monarch how to bait a hook but chided him for his lack of patience. The streams they fished were well stocked, but Charles found it difficult to get the hang of the new sport. One day he looked so miserable after five fruitless hours that Nell bought a bag of fried smelt and strung them on his hook when he was not looking. 'Pull in,' she cried. 'You have the hook full!' When he saw his catch, the King was restored to his usual good humour and told the story against himself for years. As a reward, he had her portrait painted by Sir Peter Lely, as a shepherdess in a lace-edged smock, open at the left breast; she was shown caressing a lamb, a bunch of flowers in her other hand.

As Louise nursed her child and Nell basked in royal favour, Barbara Cleveland cashed in with grim determination like a defeated gambler about to leave the tables for ever. She got the Garter for her eldest son, the Earl of Southampton; her second son was made Earl of Euston (at the age of nine) and betrothed to Arlington's five-year-old daughter; her third son by Charles was given the title Lord George Fitzroy; her two daughters by the King, Anne and Charlotte, were granted 'the royal arms in a lozenge with a baton sinister ermine'. In the absence of Churchill, she got the Earl of Mulgrave for herself.

Outraged by this, the House of Commons prepared to give the King what

Colbert de Croissy called 'an unhappy year'. As the bells rang in 1673, the only buzz of non-political gossip was that Nell Gwyn was to make a last appearance on stage in a new comedy by Dryden, *The Assignation, or Love in a Nunnery*. The news and the title of the play kept the balladeers busy for weeks.

Entr'acte, 1673-5

The author dreads the strut and mien
Of new praised poets, having often seen
Some of his fellows, who have writ before,
When Nell had danc'd her jig, steal to the door,
Hear the pit clap and with conceit of that
Swell, and believe themselves the Lord knows what.

The Chances, George Villiers, Duke of Buckingham

In the spring of 1673 the House of Commons set up a Commission to see
how the 'illegal' war could be brought to a satisfactory conclusion; after all,
the Dutch were now ruled by a man who had a good Protestant claim to the
English throne. The full House debated at length the legality of the
Declaration of Indulgence, concluding that 'Penal Statutes in matters
ecclesiastical cannot be suspended except by Parliament'. A Bill was drafted
to nullify the Declaration. Its opening words give some idea of the
atmosphere in the House: 'What a Tempest should we have had, if this
Black Italian Cloud had broken over our Heads? Never was Hurricane so
double charged with Death and Destruction: It would certainly have Rain'd
Fire and Faggots, and all Instruments of Cruelty, upon the Innocent Heads
of Poor Protestants. But GOD have the praise That we are in hopes to see it
not only Blow over, but that the Storm is likely to fall on the Heads that
raisd it. Some of these treacherous Dealers, who have dealt so very
treacherously with us, are already fallen into the Pit which they have digged
for Others.' Even the Queen was suspected of dark dealings on the Pope's
behalf:

Imperial Lust does o're your Scepter sway
And though a Soveraign, makes you to obey.
She that from Lisbon came with such Renown,
And to enrich you with the Africk Town.
In nature mild, and gentle as a Dove;
Yet for Religion can a Serpent prove.

(Marvell)

109

The King was summoned to the House and asked to withdraw his Declaration of Indulgence. At first he refused and said he was resolved to stick by it, but he soon realized that there was nothing to be done and gave in with as good a grace as he could muster. Fortunately for the Crown, he did not have his father's stiff, hectoring manner. A mixture of the famous charm, and a hangdog look as if he had been fishing unsuccessfully all day, softened the hearts of most of the Members and he was forgiven. New revenues were allocated to him, though not before he had made a formal withdrawal of the Declaration and signed the Established Test, the Act which made it compulsory for any servant of the Crown to swear exclusive allegiance to the Church of England. There was a certain amount of finger-wagging:

> Shake off the brandy slumbers ...
> Players and Scaramouches are your joy;
> Priests and French Apes do all your Land annoy.
>
> (Marvell)

> Restless, he rolls about from Whore to Whore,
> A merry Monarch, scandalous and poor.
> To Carewell the most Dear of all thy Dears,
> The sure relief of thy declining Years;
> Oft he bewails his fortune and her fate,
> To love so well, and to be lov'd so late;
> For when in her he fettles well his T ... ,
> Yet his dull graceless Buttocks hang an Arse.
> This you'd believe, had I but time to tell ye,
> The pain it costs to poor laborious Nelly,
> While she employs Hands, Fingers, Lips and thighs,
> E're she can raise the member she enjoys.
>
> (Marvell, attr. Rochester)

'Carewell' (Quérouaille) was certainly restless. She wanted to be a duchess, now that Castlemaine was one, and if possible a duchess at home in France as well as in England. Colbert de Croissy, preparing to hand over to the Marquis de Ruvigny (Henri de Massue) at the end of the year, wrote in June that Louise had asked for the duchy of Aubigny, vacant on the death of La Belle Stewart's husband without an heir. The King, who had not had much chance to show his sense of humour that year, was willing, but the King of France had to approve his rewarding the new with the *tabouret* of the old. Colbert de Croissy did not feel she had done enough for her country to deserve the honour and wrote on 17 July to the new French Minister in charge of Foreign Affairs: 'I own I find her on all occasions so ill-disposed for the service [of Louis XIV], whether she feels herself despised or whether from the effect of caprice, that I really think she deserves no favour of His

Majesty. But as the King of England shows her much love and so visibly likes to please her, His Majesty can judge whether it is best not to treat her according to her merits ... I have, however, told him upon what conditions alone the fief could be granted [she could have the land but not the title], and what he asks is just the contrary.' Louise was furious and said she would become a naturalized English subject, 'as a necessary means to profit by the gifts which the King of England might have the kindness to bestow upon her'. On 19 August she was created Baroness Petersfield, Countess of Fareham and Duchess of Portsmouth, and sworn as a Lady of the Queen's Bedchamber.

There is some doubt whether or not Nell reacted by performing at Windsor that summer in *Love in a Nunnery* or in Lord Orrery's *The Black Prince. Love in a Nunnery* was certainly published earlier that year with a dedication to her, and the songs and dialogue were written for her exchanges with the pit: 'Are you fit, at fifteen, to be entrusted with a maidenhead? It is as much as your betters can manage at full twenty.' This was taken as a direct insult to the newly created Duchess of Portsmouth, as was Marvell's:

> The Misses take place, and advanc'd to be Dutchess
> With Pomp great as Queens in their Coach and six horses:
> Their bastards made Dukes, Earls, Viscounts and Lords,
> And all the high Titles that Honour affords.

The coach and six horses were Barbara Cleveland's latest acquisition. When Nell heard about them, she hired a rustic cart and six oxen and drove slowly past Berkshire House cracking an enormous whip and shouting 'Whores to market, Ho!' She met Louise Portsmouth on her way to Chiffinches and was taken aback to hear her say: 'Why, Nelly, you 'ave such beautiful clothes. You could be a queen.' To which she replied: 'And you, Cartwheel, look whore enough to be a duchess.'

This and other exchanges of pleasantries so angered the two duchesses that they (it was rumoured) invited Nell to a supper party at Berkshire House and tried to get her drunk. They accused her of having got £20,000 from the King for her new baby, 'and they did set about poor Nell and choke her with a kerchief, of which she is since dead'. The rumour was laid to rest when she was seen next day in the park.

The person who suffered most that year was the naval hero, James, Duke of York. The House of Commons petitioned the King to have him resign as Lord High Admiral, and the Royal Navy was put into the charge of Commissioners, with Pepys as Secretary. Unfortunately, James was not a man to show tact, least of all humility, and he lacked his brother's suppleness. Instead of vanishing from the scene of public affairs for a year of two, by which time things might have changed for the better, he did the things most likely to enrage the House and reopen the question of the

Succession: he sent his friend Lord Peterborough to find a successor to his late wife, Anne. There were several suitable Protestant candidates in Sweden and German states, but they were rejected as unattractive. In Italy Peterborough found several princesses and sent their miniatures for James to see; they were all, of course, Catholics. After some hesitation, James said he liked both Leonora of Modena and her niece Maria. He could not make up his mind between them, so he sent a marriage contract out to the duchy and told Peterborough to fill in the name himself, taking into consideration 'nature, devotion and the dowry'. His emissary settled on the seventeen-year-old Maria, who had tantrums for several days when she was told she was to go to England and marry a middle-aged man; she had declared her intention of becoming a nun. Obedient, however, to reasons of State, she agreed to do her duty, and the betrothal was witnessed in October. She arrived at Dover on 21 November 1673 and a wedding ceremony took place immediately, in the Roman Catholic rite; she was deflowered before midnight.

In London, the King heard the news gloomily. The House of Commons was furious. The Lord Mayor told him that there would be no official welcome, no bellringing and no bonfires to greet the woman who would probably become the next Queen. A broadsheet depicted the new Duchess of York as the Pope's eldest daughter, and her confessor, Father Petre, as a lamb driven by a wolf along the path of the conversion of England.

As if this were not enough, the Queen Consort was taken ill in early December, probably as a result of immersions in cold spa baths and drinking excessive amounts of Epsom and Tunbridge waters. The Duchess of Portsmouth, instead of showing (even false) sympathy, hung about the sick Catherine as if she were about to take her place in the royal bed at any moment, and had to be told she was 'at the wrong monarch's pillow'. Colbert de Croissy, making his farewells at Euston, reported to Paris: 'The King is going to sup and dance at Lord Arlington's, and I am to be of the party. So also is the Duchess of Richmond. Her great talent is dancing. Mademoiselle de Keroualle [he did not give her her new English title] may be taken in by all these parties, and all the more so because she does not keep her head sober since she has got into it that it is possible she may be Queen of England. She talks from morning till night of the Queen's ailments as if they were mortal.'

Nell confided in her new secretary, James Booth, that she was not worried by such a prospect as 'the nation will never have her'. The new tone of remarks recorded by Booth suggests that she was very close to the centre of power, the more so since the suicide of Clifford and the appointment of Buckingham's protégé, Sir Thomas Osborne (soon to be Earl of Danby), a Protestant, as chief minister. Buckingham and Nell were close friends again, and she had his mistress, Anna Maria Brudenell, Countess of Shrewsbury, as a house guest over Christmas; the Duke had killed Shrewsbury in a duel and the Countess was homeless until Buckingham had time to send his duchess home to her mother. The Lord Treasurer and the Speaker of the House of Commons were also her guests at about this time, and when Nell is said to have complained that she had not yet got the freehold of 79 Pall Mall, an anomaly since she 'always conveyed free under the Crown', the Speaker (Seymour) promised to see what he could do in the matter, in view of the fact that she was the only Protestant lady in the King's orbit, after which 'they all supped at 3 a.m. and drank smartly.'

The new chief minister was not averse to having at least one Protestant in the King's bed, but he did see it as one of his most urgent tasks to put the royal finances into some sort of order; this did not make him much loved by any of the Misses, irrespective of their religion. Charles was in the habit of handing out jewels and royal warrants (to pay over customs and excise duties) to whichever of his mistresses and whores pleased him at the moment. Sometimes, in his euphoria, he made what must have been mistakes. One day he granted the Duchess of Portsmouth some wine licences (worth £10,000 a year) in perpetuity; on another, he made over some import duties which brought her the astronomical sum of £136,668 in a twelvemonth. Nell was not so greedy and settled for an average of £10,000 a year for herself and her children, but she was not above complaining (to Sir Joseph Williamson in January 1674) that she was not as well treated as her rivals, young and old.

The King's House reopened on 26 March 1674, and Nell was given a box of her own. There were many opportunities for public mockery of her rivals, and she lost none of them. She felt secure now in her general popularity and was abroad day and night, notwithstanding the fact that bands of robbers roamed the streets. (As the Earl of Essex wrote to the King: 'They are becoming a reproach to ye Government, and look almost like petit rebellions, they are going by 20 or 30 in a company, and breaking open Houses even in ye day time.') Nell's constant companion at the theatre was the King, though the 1752 memorialist goes so far as to say that during the daytime she kept her monarch's nose to the royal grindstone:

Nell was undoubtedly the least offensive of the contending parties; she raised no enemies by her ambition and lost no friends by her insolence; so far was she from drawing aside the King from an attention to his affairs that she often excited him to diligence; and in the hours of dalliance would drop a hint that if he ever fell into distress, he might thank his ladies for it. One day when he had been struggling in the Council, and torn to pieces by the multiplicity of petitions presented to him for redress, the outrageous behaviour of the ministers, and the fierce contentions of the Parliament, he retired to Nell's very pensive,

and seemed entirely under the influence of grief. She took the liberty
of asking His Majesty the cause of his disorder: 'O Nell!' says he.
'What shall I do to please the People of England? I am torn to pieces
by their clamours.' 'If it please your Majesty,' says she, 'there is but one
way left, which expedient I am afraid it will be difficult to persuade
you to embrace. ... Dismiss your ladies and mind your business; the
People of England will soon be pleased.'

Another chronicler puts it more directly and alleges that Nell 'told his
Majestie to lock up his codpiece'.

Danby's most important task, however, was not to lock up the King's
codpiece but to stop an even greater drain on the royal purse, the war with
the Dutch. This he did successfully in that same March of 1674, and also
persuaded the King to prorogue Parliament. With the Members in recess, he
was able to approach them individually and buy as many of them as he
could afford – they become known as the Court Party, or 'Tories' (after the
nickname of Irish outlaws). The Earl of Shaftesbury (as Ashley Cooper had
become) counter-attacked by forming the Green Ribbon Club or 'Whigs'
(after 'Whigamores' – Scottish brigands). The Dutch bribed the Whigs
heavily, and it was estimated that they owned a third of the House of
Commons. The French bribed the Tories to support the King, not Danby
(Louis XIV thought he was anti-French). Some shrewd and greedy MPs
took bribes from the Dutch, the French and Danby; the Dutch never
discovered that the woman playwright Aphra Benn was spying for the King
in Holland and paid her handsomely to spy for them. Danby was at the
birthday party Nell gave for the King on 29 May 1674 and tried to explain
to her the situation. Her comment was that, 'Not even Etherege could write
such lines.'

The new French Ambassador was at the party and reported that,
whatever the result of the contest to amass wealth (the Marquis de Ruvigny
tipped Louise Portsmouth to win this), Nell Gwyn seemed to have by far the
greatest number of influential friends. The Ambassador was known as a
protector of the Huguenots (and much admired by Evelyn for this) and was
probably a Protestant himself (which was why he had been sent to England
at this time), but his judgement does not seem to have been influenced by
his religious loyalties. He reported that Louise made a fool of herself
regularly by behaving as if she were Queen, going into mourning for
potentates to whom she was not related; the real Queen found this offensive.
Nell Gwyn profited by this vanity by periodically dressing herself all in black
to mourn for non-existent dignitaries – the Boog of Oronooko was one.
When the Prince de Rohan died and Louise put herself into a mantle of
sable, Nell came to Court dressed identically and, when asked for whom she
was wearing black, said: 'The Cham of Tartary. I am the same relation to

him as Cartwheel is to Rohan.' When the King of Sweden died, Louise went into mourning again. So did Nell, and said to her rival, 'Let us settle this matter. We shall divide the world. You shall have the Kings of the North and I shall have those of the South.'

Charles was amused when Nell showed him her new bedstead. She had Jacob Hall the rope-dancer climbing up the Duchess of Cleveland, and an Eastern potentate lying with Louise in a tomb; this famous silver bedstead by John Coques was a wonder of the age and cost £1135. 4s. 1d. Louise burst into tears when she heard about it, and Nell christened her 'The Weeping Willow.' She was also known as 'Squintabella' since she may have had a squint in one eye.

Andrew Marvell was not amused:

> ... Charles without acre did swear by his Maker,
> If I ever see England again,
> I'll have a religion all of my own,
> Whether Popish or Protestant shall not be known;
> And if it prove troublesome, I will have none.
>
> I'll have a Long Parliament always to friend,
> And furnish my Treasure as fast as I spend,
> And if they will not, they shall have an end.
>
> I'll have a Council shall sit always still,
> And give me a licence to do what I will;
> And two secretaries shall piss through a quill. ...
>
> My insolent brother shall bear all the sway;
> If Parliaments murmur, I'll send him away. ...
>
> And whatever it cost me, I'll have a French whore,
> As bold as Alice Pierce, and as fair as Jane Shore;
> And when I'm weary of her, I'll have more. ...
>
> I'll wholly abandon all publick affairs,
> And pass all my time with buffoons and players,
> And saunter to Nelly when I should be at prayers.

With the reopening of the King's House came a new antagonism between the two companies. Dryden was accused of being a secret Catholic and urged to resign the Poet Laureate's post, which he had enriched, and hand it over to Thomas Shadwell. Etherege, who had been at the Embassy in Constantinople for three years on Montagu's staff, was accused of being a secret Muslim in the pay of the Sultan of Turkey; Otway had an injunction laid on him to stop him pestering Elizabeth Barry, an actress Rochester was pursuing.

The greatest theatrical scandal of the day was over the religious allegiance of William Shakespeare, whose work was enjoying a new popularity – Nell went to see *The Tempest* four times during the autumn of 1674. Shakespeare had been 'taken up' by the Protestant Whigs as a counter-attraction to the Tory Dryden and to Etherege (who was to die a Jacobite exile), and as an example of all that was best in the Tudor Reformation. Even a hint that the 'Sweet Swan of Avon' might not have been a conforming Anglican was heresy, though Ben Jonson's devotees had always held him in contempt as a non-intellectual, businesslike but not very artistic theatre manager, with 'little Latin and lesse Greek'. Aubrey says: 'His father was a butcher, and I have been told heretofore by some of the neighbours that when he was a boy he exercised his father's trade, but when he kill'd a calfe he would doe it in high style, and make a speech ... He was wont to say that he never blotted out a line in his life; sayd Ben Jonson, "I wish he had blotted out a thousand." ' When James VI and I expelled Shakespeare from Court (because he refused to correct the gross historical errors in *Macbeth*), Ben Jonson generously suggested that what the butcher's son would like most as a parting gift was a coat of arms. A boar's head was suggested, with the motto *Not Without Merit*; Jonson approved of the device but said the motto should be *Not Without Mustard*.

As David Norbrook has written: 'This Shakespeare has the characteristic Roland Barthes ascribes to myth: it turns history into nature, and thus impedes critical political analysis. Not only the Englishman's constitution, but also the English constitution are traditionally felt to be "natural": Shakespeare's plays are seen as embodying a characteristically English balance of opposites, neither too radical nor too conservative, neither too popular nor too elitist. Shakespeare, like his Queen, is held to be above politics' (review of Honigmann, London Review of Books). In 1674 there were other arguments: a Puritan resentment of the elaborate scenery as opposed to Shakespeare's almost empty stages; the presence of women, real women, on the boards and the theatrical *demi-monde* it created; the feeling in Shakespeare that 'All mobs and foreigners are always the same.'

There had always been gossip about the so-called 'lost years' of Shakespeare's life, from his documented marriage in 1582 until his first success in London in 1592. What was he doing in that anti-Catholic decade, so similar in tone to that from 1672 to 1682? Had he really been an apprentice (to an apothecary, a solicitor?), a sailor or a soldier, even a gardener? Where would a young adventurous Protestant or Catholic have gone if not into the fray? And here was the controversial rub. Was he in fact a Protestant? There is substantial evidence that William Shakespeare's father was a recusant, an unrepentant Roman Catholic.

Where would a young Catholic, son of a recusant, go in 1582, as Anglican England under Elizabeth prepared to resist the onslaught of Catholic Spain?

An enterprising Tory suggested that he would have gone to Catholic Lancashire, and hey, as in the rebuilding of London, the old registries are dusted down, here is one Alexander Hoghton, a Lancashire landowner, mentioned in his will William Shakeshafte and John Cottom (a master at the grammar school at Stratford-on-Avon attended by the boy Shakespeare). The suggestion was that Shakespeare, after leaving school, had gone with Cottom to work as a tutor in the family of Alexander Hoghton, like Cottom a Catholic. In the twentieth century, E.A.J. Honigmann (*Shakespeare: The Lost Years*, Manchester UP, 1985) has further documented the thesis that the young tutor helped to stage family versions of mystery plays, and was seen so doing by Sir Thomas Strange (later Lord Strange, Earl of Derby) who supported a company of strolling players. Honigmann says there is a wealth of evidence to show Shakespeare's connections with the Lancashire gentry and 'that the history plays and *The Phoenix and the Turtle* reflect Shakespeare's links with the Derby dynasty'.

Shakespeare's private life, or rather the fact that so little is known of it, suggests a secretive man with something to hide – in Elizabethan as in late Restoration times almost certainly his religion.

When the Shakespeare scandal broke in 1674, it brought even Pepys and Aubrey into the lists. Pepys had been seen less in Town (he was incessantly nagged by his wife) but, as the public servant closest to the Catholic Duke of York, for years he knew the strength of recusancy. Charles Hart, who had Shakespearian blood, was for a Catholic playwright. Aubrey came down on the side of a Catholic birth and then a business-like, quiet passage into the Established Church.

Broadsheets and ballads about recusants rivalled those about the Misses. There were comments about the surnames given to their children (Cleveland's were Fitzroy, Nell's Beauclerk, Portsmouth's Lennox) but spicier titbits about their extravagant purchases. There was a religious flavour to Nell's warming-pan, inscribed: 'Fear God. Serve the King.' Coques, who made her bed, also supplied 'a sugar box, a pepper pot, a mustard pot, two Kruyzes, a gold hourglass and two silver bottles'. In January 1675 she bought herself a sedan chair, carved and gilt (£34. 11s.), though when she kept a public chair waiting for a whole day, she received a bill only for 11s. 6d. Her brother-in-law died, and she paid for the funeral (not a very luxurious one) and bought a whole new wardrobe for her sister, Rose. When she was made a Lady of the Queen's Privy Chamber that spring (a sure sign of her rising political star among the Protestant factions), she bought several bolts of silk for her new Court dresses.

Louise Portsmouth did not have Barbara Cleveland's property-hunger, nor does she seem to have spent much on clothing; she collected a lot of easily movable plate and jewellery, just in case things went wrong. She managed to get the King to pay for her apartments in Whitehall Palace itself and a house at Barn Elms, and never seemed to enjoy making a splash; she seldom entertained and when she did she tried to charge the French Embassy with the cost on the grounds that she was working in the interests of the French Crown. When she had her parents over in the summer, Evelyn used the occasion to ingratiate himself with her. On 15 June 1675 he noted: 'This afternoon came Monsieur Quierwell and his Lady, parents to that famous beauty and favourite at Court to see Sir Richard Bro: my Father in Law with whom they were intimately acquainted at Brest. He seemed a soldierly Person, & a good fellow as the Bretons generally are, his Lady had been very handsome & seemed a shrewd understanding woman.' Evelyn seems to have been influential in marrying Louise's sister to the Earl of Pembroke and was invited to see the Duchess's apartments in September – 'luxuriously furnished, and with ten times the richnesse and glory beyond the Queene's'. He was never allowed into 79 Pall Mall, nor for that matter into Berkshire House, and sneered that Barbara Cleveland nearly always dined out, preferring disreputable taverns or ordinaries along the waterfront.

It was well known that the best place to eat among the 'ladies' was at Nell's. At one dinner she served six ducklings (£1. 10s.), four geese (£2), six 'rabets' (7s.), two chickens (4s.), two young hares (4s.) and a dozen boiled partridge (£3). The King liked her 'pidgeon peys', which he sometimes ate in bed. Wine always flowed freely, and there was a fine cellar full of whiskies donated by Sir Robert Moray. Charles liked Canary (2s. 6d. a bottle) with his 'pey' (also 2s. 6d.). Nell also gave tea parties (tea was 28s. a pound and a teapot 16s.) and liked to have *corbeilles* of fruit everywhere. Buckingham always joked about the oranges in the baskets. Louise never joked about anything to do with her.

Defoe records: 'I remember that the late Duchess of Portsmouth in the time of Charles the Second, gave a severe retort to one who was praising Nell Gwynn, whom she hated. They were talking of her wit and beauty, and how she always diverted the King with her extraordinary repartees, how she had a fine mien, and appeared as much the lady of quality as anybody. "Yes, madam," said the Duchess (who had just heard that the King had given Nell £17,000), "but anybody may know she has been an orange wench by her swearing." '

Madame de Sévigné, writing to her daughter in September 1675, summed up the rivalry at that point:

With regards to England, Mademoiselle de Keroualle has been disappointed in nothing; she wished to be the mistress of the King, and she is so ... She amasses treasure, and makes herself feared and respected as much as she can. But she did not forsee that she should find a young actress in her way, whom the King dotes on; and she has not it in her power to withdraw him from her. He divides his care, his time and his health between these two. The actress is as haughty as the Duchess of Portsmouth; she insults her, makes faces at her, attacks her, frequently steals the King from her, and boasts of his preference for her. She is young, indiscreet, confident, meretricious and pleasant; she sings, dances and acts her part well. She has a son by the King, and wishes to have him acknowledged: she reasons thus: 'This Duchess,' says she, 'pretends to be a person of quality; she says she is related to the best families in France; whenever any person of consequence dies, she puts herself in mourning. If she be a lady of such quality why does she demean herself to be a courtesan? She ought to be ashamed of herself. As for me, it is my profession; I do not pretend to be anything better. The King maintains me, and I am constant to him at present. He has a son by me: I say he ought to acknowledge him, and I am sure he will for he loves me as well as he does Portsmouth.' This creature gets the upper hand, and discountenances and embarrasses the Duchess extremely.

Ambassadors and visiting dignitaries knew they would do well to cultivate the friendship of 'Mrs Neslie' and coveted places at her table. The King found it easier to entertain at 79 Pall Mall, and the Queen was always relieved when she could live in complete retirement. During the hot summer of 1675 Philip William, heir to the Count Palatine of Neuberg, was so impressed by Nell's hospitality that he sent her some fine lace when he went home.

Before he left, the German prince was given a State banquet and insisted (unnecessarily) that she be present; on this occasion the unfortunate Queen had to offer the use of her apartments, her husband's being large enough only for love. For hours the guests sweated under their periwigs, heavy clothes and jewels; women were fainting and the air was foul – the Queen had a Latin horror of fresh air. By midnight on that, the hottest night of the year, everybody had had enough until Nell suggested that the party should move into St James's Park – ladies, gentlemen, musicians, food and drink. The suggestion was greeted with applause and for a couple of hours a curious crowd watched while the Court amused itself *al fresco*. Then Nell had another idea – to take the royal barges up the Thames to Hampton Court and breakfast there. The guest of honour (travelling incognito with a retinue of fifty) was delighted, and Nell joined him and the King in the rear of the first barge. A light breeze refreshed them, and when they arrived as dawn was breaking, everybody was in a good humour. While most of the ladies went off to the *cabinets d'aisance* in the palace, Nell took the King and Neuberg and set them to fishing. The two men were equally unlucky with rod and line, so she provided a catch of her own – the King got a net full of marble minnows and Neuberg a purse of gold containing a miniature of his mistress.

During this period, Louise Portsmouth was out of commission, having caught a dose of the pox. Louis XIV sent her a large diamond and a pearl necklace to console her, but for nearly a year she was trundled about between Epsom and Tunbridge Wells, being sweated and medicated by French and English physicians. There was a lot of talk about who could have given her the pox – the King was said to be poxed and clapped regularly by the cheap whores Chiffinch brought up the Backstairs, but Nell does not seem to have been affected at this time. Louise was said to have been sampled by Danby and several French visitors, but nobody could lay the blame with any certainty. She came out of her enforced retirement in October 1675, when she heard that Nell had refurnished her bedroom at a cost of £1,700 (new Normandy glass, new hangings and two wainscot seats with compass ends engraved CR and NG). With two other great ladies (says the 1752 memorialist) Louise gave 'a costly banquet ... with divers sorts of music and variety of liquors ... the company had screwed their mirth to the highest pitch and the night [was] entirely dedicated to Bacchus and Venus'. In the small hours, she invited the King to a closet where she and her two friends undressed: 'Not unlike the three goddesses, Juno, Pallas and Venus before Paris, did those three naked ladies stand before the King, who was ravished with the sight, and examined every part about them with his own hands and eyes, with all imaginable curiosity.'

Nell retaliated by offering an entertainment at a different level. Though the object of the exercise was to show off her new furnishing, she described it as 'an evening concert of music'. She had, still, access to the best talent available at the King's House. There were recitals, and she gave some of her best-remembered songs and excerpts from Dryden's prologues. The star of the evening was Henry Bowman from the House, who sang love songs to music by performers from the theatre and the Chapel Royal. There was sincere, polite applause, after which Nell said to the King: 'Well, Sire, you will not speak and do like a courtier, I hope, but give these gentlemen a handsome purse.' The King said: ' 'Odsfish, I have no money. I will ask my brother.' The Duke of York had only 2 guineas. 'Again,' said Nell, 'I have fallen into poor company.'

The common people followed this contest with great interest. A goldsmith recalled that, 'When he was a prentice, his master made a most expensive service of plate [the King's present] for the Duchess of Portsmouth. He remembered well that an infinite number of people crowded to the shop out of mere curiosity; that they threw a thousand ill-wishes against the Duchess, and wished the silver was melted and poured down her throat; but 'twas ten thousand pities his Majesty had not bestowed this bounty on Madame Ellen.'

'Madame Ellen' had some domestic preoccupations. In addition to her eight servants, she had to keep her steward (Thomas Groundes) and secretary (James Booth), as well as her mother and widowed sister (who had moved in). The household devoured (according to surviving bills) vast quantities of oysters, beef, mutton, chickens, salmon, gudgeon, smelts, shrimps and sweetbreads, veal, cream, cloves and pastries, not to speak of 280 gallons of small beer a year and large quantities of wine and spirits. It is perhaps not surprising that her apothecaries' bills were substantial – purgatives and plasters (and some exciting medicine, 'cordial julep with pearls' for her elder son). Her mother was well on the way to dipsomania and was regularly dosed with Plague Water and glysters. Nell was healthy enough and seems to have used few cosmetics, for a former actress; she made do with oil of lilies and white roses for her eyes, 'Queen of Hungary's water' and rosewater for her complexion.

As John Wilson has written: 'Nell was in politics up to her elbows. ... Nell's home was a kind of neutral ground, and not infrequently the King, who wanted to know what his enemies were thinking, met and talked with them there.'

Danby had advised the recall of Parliament on two occasions in 1675. They were not agreeable meetings between a sovereign and his elected Commons, and Shaftesbury and Buckingham stirred up trouble in the Lords (they were now both living in the City under the protection of the Lord Mayor). In the main the carping and criticism were kept within discreet limits, but once tempers rose to such a temperature that committees were formed to see if and how Danby could be impeached and possibly despatched like Strafford. There was some grumbling about what Danby called his 'economical settlement' of the 'ladies': Cleveland had been settled with £6,000 for herself and £3,000 a year for each of her three sons; Louise had been given £8,600 a year for life; and Nell had had to take £4,000 a year only.

Nell was not too worried by this apparently shabby treatment, as she was being used as an intermediary to try to tone down criticism of the King in the Green Ribbon Clubs – the Secret Service Funds paid her about £10,000 a year for this purpose. Danby hinted that bribery and corruption in Parliament was now on such a grand scale that the 'ladies' had been overtaken. The Marquis de Ruvigny wrote to Paris that managing the House of Commons was becoming a fulltime occupation and was not to his taste – he would prefer to be replaced. Andrew Marvell, who as 'Mr Thomas' was the Dutch paymaster in the House, observed wryly that he sometimes forgot who was spying for whom, but he was convinced that it was only a matter of time before the King himself was brought to the Bar of the House and arraigned.

At Newmarket that autumn, Charles complained to Nell that 'they will not leave me in peace' and 'what could he do to content them?' She is said to have told him to give them a Scotch collop, a French ragout and a calf's head, and in return they would give him his revenues: the Scotch collop was Lauderdale, who held Parliament in contempt (it wanted to impeach him); the French ragout was Louise Portsmouth, 'a stewe which sucks up good like good beef wine', the calf's head may have been Danby with whom she had quarrelled, though he seems to have found a husband for Rose, Guy Foster, in his service.

The atmosphere of plot and counterplot is well illustrated by 'the coffee-house affair'. Nell Gwyn had taken to going out in the late mornings, so her son Charles could watch his father play tennis in the Private Gardens; afterwards she would take the boy in her new sedan chair on a tour of her old haunts in Covent Garden, and often into the City. Wherever she went, she noticed that she was cheered by the customers of the taverns she had frequented, but jeered by the habitués of the coffee-houses. When she complained to Dryden, mainstay of Will's, he told her that Shaftesbury was using the coffee-houses as meeting-places for his Green Ribbon Clubs, and as distribution centres for scurrilous ballads and cartoons, ridiculing life at Court. She was also told that the 'Misses' were often the butt of coffee-house wit, though not at Will's; the farther into the City, the more likely it was to find treasonable talk, and there was no doubt about it, the majority east of Temple Bar were 'payshoppes for the cripple's [Shaftesbury's] briske boyes'.

Nell was very angry whenever she heard of any erosion of what she believed was her universal popularity with the mob. Her complaints to the King were reinforced by others from a very respectable source. Thomas Hobbes had been frequently with the King that year; he planned to leave London for good and spend the rest of his days at Chatsworth, as guest of the Earl of Devonshire. Hobbes had fought a running battle with the Dean of Christ Church for over a year, because of some unauthorized alterations the Dean had made in Anthony à Wood's *History and Antiquities of the University of Oxford*, and in particular in the *Life* of the old philosopher. Hobbes had printed an *Epistle*, which he had distributed in the coffee-houses of London and Oxford with the King's permission: 'The king, seeming to be troubled at the dealing of the deane, gave Mr Hobbes leave, conditionally that he touch no-body but him who had abused him, neither that he should reflect upon the Universitie' (Aubrey). The customers of the coffee-houses treated the old gentleman with less than respect, and Hobbes gave it as his opinion that the places should be suppressed as 'meetinges for fooles and knaves'. Nell knew how much the King held Hobbes in esteem, so it is not perhaps surprising that at Christmas 1675 a Proclamation for the Suppression of Coffee Houses was drafted (Charles always spent part of Christmas Day with Nell, at their son's brithday party) and sent to the royal printers John Bill and Christopher Barker. The Proclamation noted that,

Whereas it is most apparent, that the Multitude of Coffee-houses of late years set up and kept within this Kingdom, the Dominion of Wales, and the Town of Berwick upon Tweed, and the great resort of Idle and disaffected persons to them, have produced very evil and dangerous effects; as well as for that many Tradesmen and others, do therein misspend much of their time, which might and probably would otherwise be employed in and about their Lawful Callings and Affairs, but also that in such houses, and by occasion of the meetings of such persons therein, divers False, Malitious and Scandalous Reports are devised and spread abroad, to the Defamation of His Majestie's Government, and to the Disturbance of the Peace and Quiet of the Realm; His Majesty hath thought it fit and necessary, That the said Coffee-Houses be (for the future) Put down and Suppressed, and both (with the Advice of his Privy Council) by this His Royal Proclamation, Strictly Charge and Command all manner of persons, That they or any of them do not presume from and after the Tenth day of January next (1676) ensuing, to keep any Publick Coffee-House, or to attempt to sell by retail, in his her or their house or houses (to be spent or consumed in the same) any Coffee, Sherbett or Tea, as they will answer the contrary at their utmost perils. ... Given at Our Court at Whitehall, this Nine and Twentieth Day of December, 1675.

It was an unwise Proclamation and doomed to be ineffective. Even the Vicar of St James and St Martin-in-the-Fields (at which Nell had had her sons baptized and which she still attended regularly) came nervously to 79 Pall Mall to urge her to beg the King to have the Proclamation rescinded, 'the better to curbe drunkennesse'. Lampoons and ballads multiplied. Louise Portsmouth was accused of inspiring the Proclamation, and models of her apartments were sold with the inscription:

> Within this place a bed's appointed
> For a French bitch and God's anointed.

> (Rochester)

The defence of the natural table and beverages was celebrated:

> The Duchess of Portsmouth one time supped with the King's Majesty;
> Two chickens were at table, when the Duchess would make 'em three.
> Nell Gwyn, being by, denied the same; the Duchess speedily
> Reply'd here's one, another two, and two and one makes three.

'Tis well said, lady, answered Nell: O King here's one for
thee,
Another for myself, Sweet Charles, 'cause you and I agree;
The third she may take to herself, because she found the
same:
The King himself laughed heartily, whilst Portsmouth
blushed for shame.

And more references to her misfortunes:

Coffee-houses shall stay free.
You get no pox from D'Arcy's tea.

In the end, having caused great amusement with which to end a year, it was
decided that the Proclamation should lapse before it was put into effect. Not
the least effective of all the pressures was that exercised by the tea, coffee,
and sherbet merchants.

The last joke of the year was at the expense of Barbara Cleveland. Henry
Savile, one of Nell's great friends came to see Nell with his new mistress,
Lady Mary Scroope (Scrope), the mother of another friend, the poet Sir
Carr Scrope. This was in itself an item of news because it was well known
that Savile had been kept by Cleveland for over a year, ever since his return
from France (he had been banished by the King for trying to seduce the
widowed Countess of Northumberland and force her into marriage – she
was worth £10,000 a year). According to Lady Mary, the notorious Barbara
was leaving England for France, where she would enter a nunnery.

This rumour was, of course, unfounded in part. But it was true that the
Duchess of Cleveland was about to leave England. She was frightened by
Danby's threat to reduce slowly, year by year, the allowances paid to the
King's whores and mistresses, and reasoned that, if she were absent, she
would be forgotten. The size of her income made this unlikely – in 1815, the
then Duke of Grafton converted one of the incomes she left him (Prisage
and Butlerage) via an annuity charged on the Consolidated Fund, into
£229,000 of Government Stock.

Barbara was also middle-aged and passed unnoticed often when she went
for drives in her splendid coach. Nell's rapid rise to fame and fortune, not to
speak of royal favour, had discouraged her, and she was having to pay more
and more to secure the services of impoverished 'mounts'; Rochester said
that after Churchill she had hired in swift succession the Duke of
Monmouth, the Earl of Cavendish, Sir Carr Scrope, her cousin Villiers, Lord
Newport, Will Henningham and Henry Savile at an average cost of £5,000.
But more important, she had fallen in love with Ralph Harvey, British
Ambassador in Paris (who had married the Countess of Northumberland
Savile had not won), and it seemed that Harvey (though as false as her old
enemy, his sister) was 'truly in love with her'.

When the news was confirmed, that Cleveland would be leaving for France as soon as she could get together her traps, Nell gave a splendid party to which she invited Barbara and Louise Portsmouth (again struck down with pox). She could afford to be generous. There was apparently not a real rival in sight, and she could at last, like any mother, catch up with the honours, showered on other women's children and procure some for her own.

She was wrong about a real rival. Though she had not seen her, one had just arrived, booted and spurred.

Disorderly House, 1675-8

When through the world fair Mazarin had run
Bright as her fellow traveller, the sun,
Hither at length the Roman eagle flies,
As the last triumph of her conquering eyes
As heir to Julius, she may pretend
A second time to make this nation bend;
But Portsmouth, springing from the ancient race
Of Britons, which the Saxon here did chase,
As they great Caesar did oppose, makes head,
And does against this new invader lead.

Anon.

Hortense Mancini, niece of the late Cardinal Mazarin, arrived booted and spurred in London (she had landed at Torbay and ridden to the capital), 'dressed as a cavalier, accompanied by two women and five men, without counting a little Moor, who takes his meals with her' (Ruvigny). A well-known international whore, she added another dimension to the domestic quarrels between Nell and Louise – and 'brought a new pox to the King's bed', as one commentator had it.

When she was sixteen Hortense had been married off to the Marquis de la Meilleraye, who was created 'Duc Mazarin' and given 28 million francs as a dowry because his bride was pregnant; the happy event had taken place on 28 February 1661. Mazarin's troubles had only just begun. He was something of a religious maniac (Saint-Simon wrote that, 'Piety poisoned all the talents that Nature had bestowed on him'), and when he discovered his wife's inclinations he broke up all the nude statues in his house, painted over the nude women in his pictures and tried to surround her with only ugly maids. It was not surprising that after five years she had fled to a convent and petitioned for a separation. At the Convent des Filles de Sainte-Marie Hortense had made friends with the Marquise de Courcelles and made the lives of the nuns so difficult that they asked her to leave. Leave she did, dressed as a man, with an officer she had picked up during an illegal absence

127

from the convent, and went to Savoy, where she stayed until the death of Carlo Emmanuele II, who apparently enjoyed her favours.

It was while Hortense was at Chambéry in Savoy that she met Ralph Montagu, British Ambassador to France, who had fallen into disgrace at the English Court and blamed Louise Portsmouth for it. Montagu hit on the idea of getting her to go to England to supplant Louise (and Nell), fill her own pockets and his and put his star back into the firmament. She would find it somewhat difficult to compete with the healthy vulgarity of Nell Gwyn, but the Duchess of Portsmouth was getting fat as well as poxed (she had been nicknamed 'Fubbs' and her boat 'Fubb's Yacht').

Hortense was intrigued by the idea, the more so because Carlo Emmanuel's widow had ordered her to leave Savoy, but she had no intention of arriving unannounced on the offchance of an introduction. She went first to her cousins the Martinozzi, who were related to the new Duchess of York, and they wrote to London hinting that the Duchess Mazarin had met the King when he was still in exile, and wanted to meet again this wise monarch. The Duchess of York replied immediately, offering her an apartment at St James's Palace; she was still 'Maria d'Este di Modena at heart and would welcome a guest with whom she could speak Italian'.

Hortense's arrival caused a flutter in the diplomatic dovecote. The French Ambassador wrote to Pomponne in Paris: 'Everyone here is in expectation of some important changes, and it is believed that a lady so extolled cannot fail to be the cause of adventures. M. de Grammont, who has undertaken the care of this lady's conduct, considers her as beautiful as ever. For myself, not having seen her since her marriage and remembering what she was like then, I have observed some alteration. ... I never saw anyone who so well defies the power of time and vice to disfigure.'

Saint-Evremond was more flattering: 'She is one of those Roman beauties who in no way resemble your dolls of France. The colour of her eyes has no name; it is neither blue, nor grey, nor altogether black, but a combination of all the three; they have the sweetness of blue, the gaiety of grey, and, above all, the fire of black. ... All the movements of her mouth are full of charm ... Her smiles would soften the hardest heart. ... The tone of her voice is so harmonious and agreeable that none can hear her speak without being sensibly moved. Her complexion is so delicately clear that I cannot believe that anyone who examined it closely can deny it to be whiter than the driven snow. ... '

The Town and the House of Commons were curious. Marvell reasoned that, as her uncle had left Italy to serve the French Crown, Hortense must be French not Roman and not so different from Louise. He wondered

> That the King should send for another French Whore,
> When one already had made him so Poor.

Nell Gwyn did not seem to resent the new arrival. Hortense had been on the scene for fourteen years, after all, and at thirty was five years her senior. The King, too, at first did not seem to notice her. He was always at 79 Pall Mall and promised that before the year was out he would ennoble Nell's children (Charles became Baron Heddington and Earl of Burford, with a pension of £1,000 a year). He also promised her the office of Registrar in Chancery for her elder son, and gave her the hereditary duty on all logs exported from England (her friend Laurence Hyde farmed it out for £500 a year). He also promised her the freehold of 79 Pall Mall, offering the Earl of St Albans 3½ acres in Soho in exchange.

However, by the early springtime, the new French Ambassador, Honoré de Courtin, could report that Montagu's sister, Lady Harvey, Lord Arlington and de Gramont were 'bringing Mazarin into play'. The 'Roman beauty' moved from St James's Palace to a house of her own in St James's Park, and began to receive the *beau monde* and London's intellectuals; her conversation was witty, she was extremely well read and kept a good table, if not as good as Nell's. She was a patron of writers and booksellers, and 'All marvelled at the three languages spoken at any soirée, and she is mistress of them all.' The Duchess of York paid calls, and even the Duke appeared from time to time, stayed for an hour or so, gave Hortense some religious tracts and departed 'quite cheerful'. The Conde de Castelmehor saw the King one day in St James's Park 'dying for the love of Madame Mazarin'; he would stroll there late at night and stand gazing up at her windows.

Louise Portsmouth wept and did not know what to do. She beat her head against her bedpost and gave herself a black eye. Her health was still indifferent and on 25 May 1676 she fled to Bath to take the waters, leaving a tearful message that she had been destroyed by love and hoped only that her sovereign would do something to restore her. The unfortunate King had little time for her but did ride to Bath once or twice a week to try to console her. When he got back, he would dine at 79 Pall Mall, then 'go through the elaborate ceremony of going to bed at Whitehall, but as soon as his gentlemen had left the room would steal away to St James's and arrive when Hortense's gambling parties had broken up, and not return to Whitehall until after five in the morning'. There was work aplenty for balladeers, painters and limners. The three contestants all had their portraits painted again in what they believed to be their most attractive attitudes, Nell virtually naked, Louise looking wistful and Hortense as an adventuress. Rochester was touched and wrote to Savile: 'I am sorry for the declining duchess and would have you generous to her at this time, for that is true pride and I delight in it.'

The declining Duchess fought back. Having recovered some of her strength, Louise returned to London after six weeks and gave the most lavish reception of her life. She persuaded Louis XIV to send over his own chamber orchestra (Lambert, Gilet, La Forest and Gandomeche), and as Charles arrived they struck up '*Mateme con'no mirar, mas no me mate con zelas*' ('Kill me with a look but not with jealousy'). Mean though she was, she had spent over £3,000 on food and drink and taken out her plate (normally locked away in great chests). As a show it was a great success, and was celebrated by the ageing Edmund Waller in *The Triple Combat* between Little Britain (Louise), the Amazon (Hortense) and Chloris (Nell):

> Legions of Cupids to the battle come,
> For Little Britain these, and those for Rome.
> Dressed to advantage, this illustrious pair,
> Arrived, for combat in the lists appear ...
>
> The lovely Chloris well attended came,
> A thousand Graces waited on the dame;
> Her matchless form made all the English glad,
> And foreign beauties less assurance had.

Louise had wasted her money. Next day the French Ambassador went to call on her and reported to Paris:

> I witnessed yesterday evening an incident which aroused in me the greatest pity imaginable and which would perhaps have touched you, wise and virtuous though you are. I went to Madame de Portsmouth's apartments. She opened her heart to me, in the presence of two of her waiting maids. The two maids remained glued to the wall, with downcast eyes. Their mistress shed a torrent of tears, and her sighs and sobs interrupted her words. In short, never has a spectacle appeared to me more sad or touching. I remained with her until midnight, and I neglected nothing to restore her courage and to make her understand how much it was in her interest to conceal her chagrin and seem not to mind the King's altered humour.

The Ambassador, however, was worried. Louis XIV had paid Charles £100,000 to get the Grand Design going again and re-establish the Anglo-French alliance, but the money would not last forever. Parliament would have to be recalled, and Shaftesbury had promised to do battle against the French interest. Hortense, who thought herself illtreated by Louis (he had refused to sponsor divorce proceedings), had the King's ear. De Courtin wrote: 'We have the whole Kingdom and the chief minister against us here, and if we are to have the mistress, too, I leave you to judge of the future.' His friend the Marquis de Louvois urged him to be patient, to trust in the King's inconstancy, but de Courtin was not to be so easily consoled. He was observed on 1 September throwing stones at the ducks on the River Fleet and muttering '*Hélas*' like an old tragedian.

Even Evelyn was intrigued. On 6 September 1676 he wrote in his diary:
'Supp'd at L Chamberlain's, here also supp'd the famous beauty and errant
Lady, the Duchesse of Mazarine (all the world knows her story), the Duke of
Monmouth, Countesse of Sussex, both natural Children of the King's.' He
did not know it, but he had stumbled on a secret. The Duchess of York, who
had given Hortense her first *logement*, seems to have changed her mind
about her protégée and urged her husband to have her out of the house in St
James's Park. This did not create any insoluble problems, as it happened.
One of the many young ladies at Court who were fascinated by Hortense
was Charles' own daughter Anne Fitzroy (by Cleveland), who had been
given as a wife to the Earl of Sussex. The Earl spent most of his time in the
country, at Hurstmonceux, and his wife occupied her mother's old
apartments just above the King's in Whitehall. William Chiffinch had an
extra key made for the Countess of Sussex's suite and she used to vacate it at
strategic moments so that the King could bed Hortense.

Charles gave numerous parties on the banks of the Fleet and the Thames
during that Indian summer. De Courtin reported that there was no mixed
bathing: 'The ladies do not go with the men ... it is the only decency which
they observe in this country. There is a great deal of laxness in the rest of
their conduct.' After the evening bathe, the couples formed, and the streets
were full in the early hours of the morning as husbands returned to their
wives after dalliance with somebody else's. De Courtin reported that
Charles seldom even visited Louise: 'I have ascertained beyond doubt that
he passes nights much less with her than with Mistris Nesle; and if I can
believe those who are most about him, his relations with the Duchess of
Portsmouth have subsided into a virtuous friendship. As to the Duchess
Mazarin, I know he thinks her the finest woman that he ever saw in his life.'
In return for her services, Hortense was allowed £4,000 a year and given a
house in Chelsea.

The balladeers put it rather more negatively:

> Since Cleveland is fled till she's brought to bed,
>   And Nelly is quite forgotten,
> And Mazarine is as old as the Queen,
>   And Portsmouth, the young whore, is rotten.

De Courtin, in spite of his doubts about Hortense's feelings towards the
country which had made her uncle's fortune, eventually fell under her spell
and used his own official residence at 8 York Street as a refuge for her; she
would play battledore and shuttlecock with the infatuated Countess of
Sussex while he tried to find out where her loyalties lay. Hortense was
always asking him for money, for 'her money', for a return of her dowry. In
one of his reports to Paris, he wrote: 'She had had a livery made more
magnificent than any with which you are acquainted. The lace costs three

livres and fiteen sols the French ell, and the coats disappear in it. There are
nine of them for the two porters, six lackeys and a page, and they cost, with
the cravates, 2,600 livres. She keeps an excellent table. ... With the appetite
which God has given her, she would certainly devour double the income
that she has ... .' He also used all his diplomatic skills (as Seigneur de
Chanteroine he had been Councillor of the Parliament at Rouen when only
fourteen years of age) to reconcile Hortense to Louise, and on one occasion
'accidentally' locked them in a room together so they would have to face up
to each other's existence; he was successful in this, and the Signora
Addolorata (as he called Louise) dried her tears and accepted the inevitable.

Once she realized that Hortense represented no long-term threat to her
position, Nell Gwyn accepted the situation, too. She even enjoyed
entertaining Louise and Hortense at home, and the three Misses ate, drank
and played cards together during the long autumn afternoons. All three were
compulsive gamblers. Hortense was the better card-player, and it was said
that she had been taught by Morin himself, the croupier who had introduced
the game of ombre into England. Whoever it was who taught her, she learnt
well. One afternoon she won £8,000 from Louise and £5,000 from Nell.
But they all lost from time to time, and all three turned to their royal
paymaster for extra money with which to pay their debts. The King was
always very angry about this and tried to stop them playing cards; at one
stage he tried to ban basset, or limit the playing of it to men, granting
patents to sons of courtiers who thereafter had the monopoly of the role of
tallière. But he was not the only one to lose when not at the tables; the
Duchess of Cleveland had struck a bargain with Wycherley and an actor,
Goodman, she had kept for years in Covent Garden, and her steward made
up their losses.

Where Nell scored in Town was at her table and in her frank appraisal of
herself. She had a long exchange with de Courtin one day at 8 York Street
about Frenchwomen, how they performed in bed and what sort of
underclothes they wore. De Courtin said he supposed all women wore the
same sort of underclothes, anywhere in the world, at which Nell said this
was nonsense – Hortense, nearly always in trousers, wore none, and Louise
always had dirty petticoats because she did not change them every day. To
prove her point, Nell raised hers and showed the French Ambassador what
she wore. He wrote next day to Pomponne in Paris: 'Never in my life did I
see such cleanliness, neatness and sumptuousness. I should speak of other
things which were also shown if M. de Lionne were still Foreign Secretary,
but with you I must be more grave and decorous.' Pomponne replied: 'I am
sure you forgot all your troubles when you were making Mistris Nesle raise
those neat and magnificent petticoats of hers.' De Courtin also reported on
Nell's passion for silver, which he shared, on the silver andirons at her
fireplace and other 'extraordinary appointments'.

When the King left Town, it was noticeable that he always took Nell with him; Hortense seems to have lived in Chelsea, commuting to the Countess of Sussex's apartment, and Louise left London only for treatment or when the whole Court moved to Windsor. One of the reasons for Hortense's fall, as rapid as her rise, was that she did not like tennis, pall mall or horseracing; when she realized this, Nell persuaded Charles to extend his stay that autumn at Newmarket and refurbish his stables. He was nothing loth; he loved the town, his horses and racing and was determined to repeat that year his 1675 triumph in the Twelve Stone Plate (himself up).

The Royal Palace at Newmarket was now complete and very comfortable, notwithstanding Evelyn's criticism of the site. The palace occupied the whole of Ram Hill (now Palace Street) covering the present-day site of Palace House or Palace House Mansion and several adjoining properties on the High Street side. By a stroke of irony, the United Reformed Church now occupies the site of one wing. Nell's house, begun the year after she gave up the stage, was opposite one of the suites used by the King, and there was a secret passage (now bricked up but with the entrance visible) which connected her cellar with a room below the suite: the King could give her a signal which she could see from her dining-room, and she could be with him in two minutes. The King's patronage of the town had made it fashionable, and the Hearth Tax collected, from 1674 on, assessed the Duke of Ormonde for fifteen hearths, Lord Suffolk for six, Lord Oxford for eight and Thomas Ellyot for twelve. (Mr Bruce Hobbs now keeps his horses where the old Confectionery used to be.)

Nell seems to have turned her attention to regularizing her roll of real estate. In addition to the house in Newmarket, in which she apparently had only a life interest (it is now subdivided into two private dwellings), she had at least one house in Windsor already, the stables in Epsom, Bagnigge House, a house at Mill Hill called Littleberries, Sandford House and some land in Chelsea and 38 Princes Street (now 53 Wardour Street), in addition to 79 Pall Mall.

While Nell and the King were at the races, Hortense did a very foolish thing. She accepted the attentions of the Prince of Monaco and put up little resistance to him. By the middle of October she was sleeping with him at his house, and at hers in Chelsea, and had admitted that she had almost become his mistress in Chambéry when she was entertaining Montagu and an abbé simultaneously. Chiffinch hurried off to Newmarket and told the King that this public scandal was making his master the laughingstock of the Court. Hortense's allowance was stopped. After a few weeks, she dropped her pose as a polyglot original and wrote asking to be forgiven. Charles, mollifed, gave her back her £4,000 a year, and the Prince of Monaco left England discomfited.

The Christmas season of 1676 was very merry, and Nell gave a lavish

birthday party for her younger son. The fashionable *monde* was there. The
Duchess of Cleveland sent a gift and begged Nell to dissuade her daughter
from acting as a sort of brothel-keeper for Hortense; in the end the Earl of
Sussex summoned his wife to Hurstmonceux and, like Baron Ricasoli's wife
two centuries later at Brolio, paid for her indiscretions with immolation at
the family seat (*see* Luigi Barzini *The Italians*). The King came with the
patent ennobling both Nell's sons, and she was now officially a lady, mother
of an earl; coats of arms for the boys and for her were quickly devised and
painted everywhere.

The New Year was a time for paying calls, and the three Misses tried to
outdo each other in courtesy. On 18 January 1677 Louise went in great state
to call on Hortense, bearing all sorts of gifts. Nell arrived with chocolates for
all, and retold the story of those she had given to Moll Davis (which took
away some of the flavour). The French Ambassador, Honoré de Courtin,
was present and reported that the three exchanged frozen compliments.
Hortense congratulated Nell on the publication of her son's patent, and Nell
congratulated her on the restoration of her allowance. Louise smiled coldly
at everyone except Lady Harvey, remembering that it was her brother who
had arranged for Hortense's migration to England. De Courtin observed it
all and not without admiration: 'Everything passed off with great merriment
and with many civilities from one to the other, but I do not suppose that in
all England it would be possible to get together three people more
obnoxious to each other.' Nell complained to him that the King of France
would get more profit by sending her presents than by sending them to
Louise – 'The King is a thousand times fonder of me than her.' He also
reported that Charles had taken to spending his afternoons (from three to
seven) with Hortense again, though in the evenings he was nearly always at
79 Pall Mall.

This was one of de Courtin's last public functions. Louis XIV and
Pomponne began to feel that virtually all his time was spent chronicling the
lives of the royal whores, and not enough in assessing the strength of
Anglo-French relationship, supposedly reinforced by a treaty the previous
year. He was replaced by Paul Barillon d'Amoncourt, Marquis de Branges, a
lawyer and specialist in bribery and corruption. Barillon was urged to
prepare for an upsurge of political activity by the Earl of Shaftesbury, and to
buy as many Members of Parliament as he could; even Sidney, a republican,
became a pensioner (£500 a year) of the French monarch.

Pomponne's intelligence was better than that of most of Charles'
intimates. At the beginning of February 1677 Shaftesbury erupted. When in
pain, which was quite often (a pole of the family coach had pierced his side
when he was a young man), he was at his most contentious. As Dryden
wrote, he was:

> A fiery soul which, working out its way,
> Fretted the pigmy body to decay,
> And o'er informed the tenement of clay.

Shaftesbury's contention was that a statute of Edward III had made of a Parliament prorogued for over a year a Parliament dissolved. Members ought to consider their mandate at an end, and new elections should be held. Danby advised the King to recall both Houses to Westminster and let out of gaol all his friends sent there for public misdemeanours. Among the friends in gaol were Etherege and Rochester, who the previous autumn 'were tossing some fiddlers in a blanket for refusing to play, and a barber, upon ye noise, going to see what ye matter, they seized upon him, and to free himself from them he offered to carry them to ye handsomest woman in Epsom, and directed them to the Constable's house, who, demanding what they came for, they told him a whore, and he, refusing to let them in, they broke open his doores and broke his head and beate him very severely. ... A good man, Mr Downs, tried to save the Constable, but had his head split open with a sprittle staff.' Etherege, Rochester and a crony, Captain Bridges, were released. Rochester to take his place in the House of Lords, and Bridges his as Member for Brentford.

Danby's advice was, as usual, good. Both Houses were full of 'pensioners' who did not want to lose a source of income. There were enough Members of the House of Commons in Danby's pay to mute criticism there, and though some of the King's friends in the House of Lords, notably Buckingham, supported Shaftesbury ('This Statute of Edward III is good. Acts of Parliament are not like women, the worse for being old'), their peers were horrified at what seemed like a Cromwellian attack on the royal prerogative. The rebels were defeated and censured. When they refused to apologize, Shaftesbury and Buckingham were sent to the Tower. Shaftesbury pretended to be in danger of his life and insisted on having his own cook ('You see, my lords, what he thinks of me,' observed the King). Buckingham turned to Nell Gwyn for help.

Nell was very sad to see her old friend down and had long since forgotten the incident in the King's apartments; nearly every man at Court had tried to get his hands under her kerchief at one time or another, and she had recently had to throw Harry Killigrew out of her house, drunk and abusive. Dryden was right to describe Buckingham as 'stiff in his opinions' and 'always in the wrong', but there was no real harm in him. She went to see Laurence Hyde (Clarendon's son and one of her trustees) for advice, and even to her former lover, Charles Buckhurst, now Earl of Dorset. Dorset suggested that she go to see Buckingham in the Tower and gave her a message for the prisoner: 'The best woman in the world brings you this paper, and, at this time, the discreetest. Pray, my Lord, resign your understanding and your interest wholly to her conduct. Mankind is to be redeemed by Eve, with as much honour as the thing will admit of. Separate your concern from your fellow prisoner [Shaftesbury], then an expedient handsome enough, and secret enough to disengage yourself: obey and you are certainly happy.'

Buckingham was moved by his friends' interest and swore he would do anything they asked. Nell assured him that the King was very angry at his political folly, but not inclined to reject him as a friend and companion. Buckingham then wrote to Charles: 'What you have been pleased to say to Mrs Nelly is ten thousand times more than ever I can deserve. What has made this inclination more violent in mee, than perhaps it is in other people, is the honour I had of being bred up with your Majesty from a Childe, for those affections are strongest in men which begin in theyre youngest yeares. And therefore I beseech your Majesty to believe me when I say that I have ever loved you more than all the rest of mankind.'

Charles accepted the apology. Buckingham publicly repudiated Shaftesbury and was freed from the Tower. Montagu was horrified to hear the news and commented: 'I know for certain there is a great cabal to bring in Mr Hyde, and that Nellie and the Duke of Buckingham are in it.' But this was paranoia. The King had defeated his enemies and shown himself to be magnanimous, and on its part the House of Commons was as agreeable, giving him an even larger subsidy than the one for which Danby had asked.

As spring came, the anti-Catholic, pro-Dutch faction in the House was given another startling present. Charles and Danby heard that the Duke of York was trying to arrange a marriage between his daughter Mary and the Dauphin of France, although Mary had remained a Protestant after her father's and late mother's conversion. As Danby said, nothing was more likely to provoke a civil war in England. He suggested instead a marriage between Mary and William of Orange, now permanently promoted from his tiny French principality to be Stadholder of Holland. Mary was not anxious to marry anybody at all, but both James and his daughter were persuaded that it would be a great alliance and that the secret engagements with France could be maintained; it would, in fact, act as a smokescreen and help the Grand Design. The King and Danby were right. Parliament was deceived and delighted and preparations were begun for the wedding.

That autumn of 1677 several attempts were made to persuade Nell to return to the stage. *An Evening's Love* and *The Conquest of Granada* had been played repeatedly, but the pit had made it clear that her replacement, Anne Quin (Ann Quinn) was not her equal. John Dryden had a new play, *All For Love*, which he offered her and said she could have a year to rehearse and learn her lines. Aphra Benn wanted her to take the part of Angelica Bianco in *The Rover* and made her the thinly disguised heroine of *Oroonoko, or The Royal Slave*. Etherege would have overcome his dislike of her (he was down on his luck) and given her *The Man of Mode*. Wycherley was in disgrace for secretly marrying the Countess of Drogheda (he needed the money since the Duchess of Cleveland was no longer supporting him) and would have liked her to do *The Country Wife*. Samuel Pordage offered her the part of Thalestris in *The Siege of Babylon*. *The Dictionary of National Biography* erroneously assumes she accepted some of these offers, as well as the part of Lady Squeamish in Otway's *Friendship in Fashion*, Lady Knowell in Aphra Benn's *Sir Patient Fancy* and Queen Elizabeth in Bank's *The Earl of Essex*.

There is not the slightest scrap of evidence that Nell did take these or any other part on stage, though she often performed prologues and epilogues and sang songs from her great successes, at home and for her guests. She enjoyed going to the theatre and went often with the King and other friends. Her box was always kept empty for her, but she had retired and enjoyed her new status. She hoped that she had not finished increasing it.

At the beginning of September 1677 she told the King that she had turned down all offers to go back to the theatre, so there was now no obstacle to her being created a duchess like Cleveland and Portsmouth, 'whose services had been no greater'. The King temporized and asked Danby what he thought – not, perhaps, a duchess, but a countess? Countess of Greenwich? They had spent many happy hours there, and the title was vacant. Danby was adamant. An orange-wench could not receive a title. Her children were half royal – that was another matter.

Nell soon discovered who had given this advice to the King, and Sir Robert Southwell wrote to the Duke of Ormonde on 22 September: 'Mrs Nelly is at a perfect defiance with him [Danby]. The King looks on with great delight, which has been a fat prognostic unto some.' Sir Robert had been at a party at which Buckingham and Nell, both brilliant mimics, had been doing their imitations of Danby and his half-mad wife. Charles had hinted that Danby would not be his chief minister for much longer, and when he had gone she could have a title. She was to be patient. She did not believe this and said so. Her remarks came to the ears of Danby, who wrote to his wife that same week: 'Remember to send to see my Lord Burford without any message to Nelly, and when Mrs Turner is with you, bid her tell Nelly that you wonder why she should be your Lord's enemy that has always been kind to her, but you wonder more to find her supporting only those who are known to be the King's enemies, for in that you are sure she does very ill.' (Mrs Turner was a spy for Danby, planted in Nell's household as nurse to the boys.)

Nell also failed to get a pension for her old friend Samuel Butler. As Aubrey says: 'He might have had preferments at first; but he would not accept any but very good ones, so at last he had none at all and died in want.' The King had much enjoyed Butler's *Hudibras* just after the Restoration and had sent him a purse but would do no more for him, known as he was for grumbling and gossip. Aubrey commented: 'Satyricall witts disoblige whom they converse with etc and consequently make to themselves many enemies and few friends; and this was his manner and case.'

However, Nell had not done badly recently, and there was always Newmarket. She spent the weeks before the royal wedding there with the King and was clearly a close friend and confidante. The French Ambassador, who had horses of his own, spent much time trying to ingratiate himself with the couple at the Palace or at Nell Gwyn's house. He reported that the King seemed confident that he had won his battle with Parliament, and recommended a payment of £300,000 to remind Charles that the French Treasury always kept its doors open to its friends.

Back in London at the end of October, there were domestic problems to be solved. The Duke of Monmouth's half-sister had had a baby girl and was looking for a godfather. On 1 November the baby's father wrote to a friend that his wife 'thinks the King ought to be kept in reserve for a son, and the Duke of Monmouth does not yet own the alliance enough to hold his niece at the font, and therefore I believe that honour will at last fall upon his Grace of Buckingham. Mrs Nelly, who is his great friend and faithful counsellor, advised him not to lay out all his stock upon the christening, but to reserve a little to buy him new shoes, that he might not dirty her rooms, and a new periwig that she might not smell him stink two storeys high when he knocks at the outward door.'

Then were was the wedding on 4 November, and a new dress. William of Orange did not cut much of a figure and seemed embarrassed when, at the wedding, the King urged him to 'go to for England and St George'. The bridegroom was drunk the following day and accused of trying to break into one of the bedrooms of the maids of honour.

Nell's old friend and colleague Elizabeth Barry was brought to bed of a daughter by Rochester, to whom Savile wrote that Nell, 'the lady's friend and protectrice in the Mall', had complained that she had had to provide the layette and that his Lordship had showed some 'want either of generosity or bowels'. As the Countess of Rochester had died recently, she toyed with the idea of persuading the Earl to marry Elizabeth, but nothing came of it.

There was another theatrical event in mid-December, when a troop of actors was washed ashore at Dover; they had been sent by Louis XIV to Spain but were quickly ordered to London to entertain the King. They presented themselves at 79 Pall Mall and were themselves entertained. After a command performance at Whitehall, Nell was amused to see the King's interest aroused in the young female star of the company. Henry Savile wrote to Rochester that *all* were impressed by the company, 'especially a young wench of fifteen, who had more beauty and sweetness than ever was seen on the stage since a friend of ours left it'.

Rochester was always a good friend and took Nell's part in the War of the

Misses. Since he had been thrown from his horse two years before, he had been less often in Town to defend her but had written some witty verse about Louise Portsmouth (*The Busse, The Royal Kisse, Portsmouth's Looking Glass*). It was knockabout stuff:

> Methinks I see you, newly risen
> From your embroider'd Bed and pissing,
> With studied mien and much grimace,
> Present yourself before your glass,
> To vanish and smooth o'er those graces
> You dubb'd off in your Night Embraces.

The new Venetian Ambassador, in his first *relazione*, commented that Rochester's lampoons were very popular. Once he had had the temerity to write one about the King and had been banished from Court for it, but the hatred of the common people for Louise Portsmouth was so great that he was soon restored to favour. He was said to be the author of *A Pleasant Battle between Two Lapdogs of the Utopian Court*:

> The English lap-dog here does first begin
> The vindication of his lady, Gwynn:
> The other much more Frenchified, alas,
> Shows what his lady is, not what she was.

The dogs fight and are separated by their mistresses.

Portsmouth: Pray Madam, give my dog fair play; I protest you hinder him with your petticoats; he cannot fasten. Madam, fair play is fair play.
Madam Gwynn: Truly, Madam, I thought I knew as well what belonged to dog-fighting as your Ladyship: but since you pretend to instruct me in your French dog-play, pray Madam, stand a little farther, as you respect your own flesh, for my little dog is mettle to the back and smells a Popish Miss at a far greater distance. Pray, Madam, take warning, for you stand on dangerous ground. Haloo, haloo, haloo!! Be brave Tutty. Ha, brave Snap-short. A guinea on Tutty – two to one on Tutty!
Monsieur Done: Tutty it seems beat Snap-short, and the bell Tutty bears home in Victory: farewell!

Begar, begar, me have lost near tousand pound.

The Ambassador, Paolo Sarotti, noted that Rochester was a practical joker and had set himself up as an Italian astrologer for a month, calling himself Alessandro Bendo, with a flowing cloak covered in signs of the zodiac. Nell

Gwyn distributed his advertisements: 'They who will do me the favour to come to me, shall be sure to find me from three o'clock in the afternoon till eight at night, at my lodgings in Tower Street, next door to the sign of the Black Swan, at a goldsmith's house.' Scores of people went to consult the 'famous astrologer', among them Elias Ashmole.

Another of Rochester's recent escapades had been to run naked in Woodstock Park with Lord Lovelace and other friends, after they had been bathing in a river nearby. He was kindhearted as well as highspirited and always came to Nell's assistance when she needed him. Not at all put out by being reminded of his duty to Elizabeth Barry, he tried to intervene with the Earl of Essex, one of Danby's cronies, in an attempt to soften that hard heart.

Nell had lost quite a lot of money gambling, and the King was increasingly reluctant to pay her debts. She needed hard cash that Christmas. Rochester wrote to Essex: 'My part is noe more but to advise her (as I would all I wish well to) by any means to be obliged to Yr Excellence if they can, since there is noe where to bee found a better friend or worthyr patron.' Essex, though he was to regret it, refused to hear the plea, and Nell had to turn to another friend, Sir Robert Howard, author of several plays she had helped to make popular. Sir Robert had come to the end of his creative vein and had decided to 'serve the nation'; he had succeeded Sir George Downing as Secretary to the Treasury, a post which made him indispensable to Danby. He failed to convince Danby that this was a moment to make a generous gesture but on going through the deeds of Nell's Trust discovered that she and her sister had been given pensions to be paid from the revenues of some estates in Ireland. He got in touch with the Duke, who replied that the revenues were blocked, he had been told, by an interminable cause in the Irish Court of Claims. He would do what he could and suggested that, as a temporary expedient, she should be classified as an Irish civil servant – 'let her know all this, and that I am her most obedient ... '.

By Christmas Day and the annual birthday party for Lord James, Nell was on the Irish Civil List. Sir Robert wrote to Ormonde: 'Mrs Nelly has commanded me to present her among your true servants and does think herself to much obliged to Your Excellency, that unless within a little time you command her something that she may serve you in, she swears she will pick a quarrel with you, for she vows she loves you entirely.'

At the party was Thomas Bushell, a famous dabbler in black magic and much else. Aubrey says he was 'the greatest arts master to run into debt in the world. He died £120,000 in debt. He had so delicate a way of making his projects alluring and feazible, profitable, that he drew to his baites not only rich men of no designe, but also the craftiest knaves in the countrey, such who had cosened and undon others. Mr Edmund Wyld says that he tap't the mountaine of Snowdon in Wales, which was like to have drown'd all the country; and they were like to knock him and his men on the head.'

He had made for Rochester a 'Neptune, neatly cutt in wood, holding his trident in his hand, and ayming with it at a duck which perpetually turned round with him, and a spanial swimming after her.' He and 'Alessandro Bendo' greeted the New Year with gloomy horoscopes and predictions of 'frenzies, inflammations and new infirmities proceeding from choleric humours', not to speak of 'troubles from great men and nobles'.

Nell's first troubles came from common burglars, who broke into 79 Pall Mall on the night of 6 January 1678. Optimistically, she offered a reward in *The London Gazette*: 'All goldsmiths and others to whom our silver plate may be sold, marked with the cypher EG., flourished, weighing about eighteen ounces, are desired to apprehend the bearer thereof, till they give notice to Mr Robert Johnson, in Heathcock Alley, Strand, over against Durham Yard, or to Mrs Gwin's porter in the Pell Mell, by whom they shall be rewarded.'

There was a lighter note at the end of the month when Robert Whitcom became the first author to dedicate a book to her, *The Lives and Histories of the Heathen Gods, Goddesses and Demigods*. He wrote of her 'great mind and illustrious troop of sublime thoughts' and of her 'large soul', and, rather more acceptably: 'I knew that curious Nature had extended her endeavours in the formation of your delicate body, and enjoined both it and every limb about you to an exact symmetry and pleasing proportion.'

The spring was a season for complex intrigue, and she was soon in the midst of it. Montagu decided he wanted to return to England for good, but he wanted a post in the Government, ideally the Secretaryship. Coventry was about to resign. Unfortunately for him, Nell's friend Laurence Hyde also wanted Coventry's post and was prepared to offer £10,000 for it and to sell his own place as Master of the Robes to another of Nell's friends, Henry Savile, Coventry's nephew; Buckingham was to get Savile's place as Groom of the Bedchamber. It seems that Barbara Cleveland and Louise Portsmouth both objected to Montagu's proposals for himself, and, indeed, he had nothing to offer in return. He tried to discredit Cleveland by collecting her letters to her latest 'mount', the Marquis de Châtillon and sending them to the King (who was indifferent to her fate), and Louise by revealing that she had told her confessor that, if she got over the pox, she 'would have no commerce with that known enemy to virginity and chastity, the monarch of Great Britain'.

By the beginning of June, the plot had thickened further. Montagu's sister, Lady Elizabeth Harvey, surfaced with an idea for her brother to get Jane Middleton into the King's bed to promote his own interests and those of Shrewsbury and the Green Ribbon Clubs. Jane Middleton was rated the most beautiful young woman in England, and her price was very high. Before he returned to Paris, de Courtin had written to Louvois: 'I would give her all your money if she would listen to my suit, but she once refused a purse of £1,500 offered her by Monsieur de Gramont, so you need not fear for your treasure.' Nell seems to have underrated the attractions of this whore and was certainly taken in by Lady Harvey. Henry Savile wrote to Rochester on 4 June 1678: 'My Lady Hervey who allways loves one civill plott more, is working body and soule to bring Mrs Jenny Middleton into play. How dangerous a new one is to all old ones I need not tell you, but her Ladyship, having little opportunity of seeing Charlemagne upon her owne account, wheadles poor Mrs Nelly into supper twice or thrice a week at W Cs [Chiffinch's] and carrying her with her; so that in good earnest this poor creature is betrayed by her Ladyship to pimp against herselfe; for there her Ladyship whispers and contrives all matters to her owne ends, as the other might easily perceive if she were not too giddy to mistrust a false friend.'

Rochester knew Lady Harvey's husband well (they were both Rangers, Harvey of Richmond Park and Rochester of Woodstock Park) and had also enjoyed Jane Middleton (who seems to have made a special price for him). He told Savile to warn Nell of the danger but added: 'My advice to the lady has ever been this, take your measures just contrary to your rivals, live in peace with the world, and easily with the King: Never be so illnatur'd to stir up his anger against others, but let him forget the use of a passion, which is never to do you good. ... Please him with body, head and heart.'

Shaftesbury, out of the Tower since February, was not optimistic about the success of the Jane Middleton promotion. He was looking for other instruments with which to weaken the Court party. One was the person and religion of James Scott, Duke of Monmouth, the King's favourite child, now a handsome young man and the idol of the mob. Shaftesbury persuaded him to go to his father and ask to be legitimized; this was easy to do, simply by declaring that the King had married his mother, Lucy Walters. If the King complied, the country would have a Protestant heir and the Queen could be sent home to Portugal 'with honour'. Monmouth, who was a friend of Nell, tried to enlist her support and used all his charm in this cause, but the King told her that, rather than put the bastard on the throne by fraud, he would see him hanged at Tyburn.

Far from even giving countenance to Monmouth's ambitions, the King was very busy trying to bring to an end the Franco-Dutch War from which he had withdrawn. The war was a great embarrassment. His own nephew was leading the Dutch armies in person, and he had friends serving with the French. In any event, wars cost money and he needed a steady supply of this from Louis XIV if he were to remain largely independent of Parliaments; his own revenues, though increasing, were always insufficient and his years in poverty in exile had provoked a reaction of extravagance and profligacy which showed no signs of fading after nearly two decades. He charged Laurence Hyde with the delicate negotiations; Laurence's elder brother, Henry, who had succeeded to the title of Earl of Clarendon, had not inherited the old man's shrewdness. Laurence – 'Lory' as the King called him

— was a frequent guest at 79 Pall Mall; he drank heavily and was a violent man but enjoyed a reputation for incorruptibility very rare in those times. In June he went to The Hague with the French terms for peace, and Nell wrote to him there to bring him up to date with all the gossip:

> Pray dear Mr Hide forgive me for not writeing to you before now, for the reasone is I have bin sick thre months and sinse I recovered I have had nothing to intertaine you withall, nor have nothing now worth writing, but that I can holde no longer to let you know I have never ben in any companie wehtout drinking your health, for I love you with all my soule. The pel mel is now to me a dismal place since I have utterly lost Sir Car Scrope, never to be recovered again, for he tould me he could not love alwayes at this rate, and so begune to be a littel uncivil, which I could not suffer from an uglye baux garscon. Mrs Knight's lady mother is dead, and she has put up a scutchin no beiger than my Lady Grin's scunchis. My Lord Rochester is gone in the cuntrei. Mr Savil has got a misfortune, but is upon recovery and is to marry an heiress, who I think wont have an ill time out if he hold up his thumb. My Lord of Dorscitt appears worze in thre months, for he drinkes aile with Shadwell and Mr Haris at the Duke's home all day long. My Lord Bauclaire is goeing into France. We are goeing to sup with the king at Whithall and my lady Harvie. The King remembers his sarvis to you. Now let's talke of state affairs, for we never carried things so cunningly as now, for we don't know whether we shall have peace or war, but I am for war, and for no other reason but that you may come home. I have a thousand merry conseets, but I can't make her write me, and therefore you must take the will for the deed. God bye. Your most loveing obedient, faithfull and humbel servant.
>
>   EG

Hyde and the King, however, were very much against war, and the negotiations were pursued. Pall Mall brightened up a bit, and there was always Newmarket to come. Sir Carr Scrope's incivility got no less, and he called the Duke of York's whore, Catherine Sedley, 'as mad as your mother and as vicious as your father', which made him *persona non grata* everywhere ever after. With Lady Green (Catherine Pegge, a royal whore from the days of exile, mother of two of Charles' children, and a neighbour), she went to the theatre and to the pleasure gardens. Lady Harvey's plot was discovered and the King said he did not find Jane attractive anyway. Louise went to Bath, and Hortense was entertaining poets again in Chelsea. Montagu disgraced himself by seducing the Countess of Sussex and had 'scandalized Paris'. Henry Savile did not get his heiress but did get the Embassy in France.

Nell had the undivided attention of the King at Windsor, and they both rejoiced at the news that Hyde had brought his mission to a successful conclusion: the Treaty of Nimwegen was signed on 10 August, and two days later Hyde was back in England to a hero's welcome.

Everybody said they could now settle down to enjoy the hot summer.

Exits and Entrances, 1678-81

Here lies the Victim of a cruel Fate,
Whom too much Element did ruinate;
'Tis something strange, but yet most wondrous true,
That what we live by, should our Lives undo.
She that so oft had powerful Waters try'd,
At last with silence, in a Fish-pond dy'd.
Fate was unjust, for had he prov'd but kind,
To make it Brandy, he had pleas'd her mind.

Anon., *On the Death of Old Madam Gwinn*

The third personage Shaftesbury was to urge on the political scene could scarcely have been more different from the beautiful, expensive Jane Middleton (who returned to her husband in Ruabon) and the dashing, brave, handsome, if foolish Duke of Monmouth. Like all great actors, he waited a little while lesser performers warmed up the audience.

On 13 August the King gave orders for the Court to move next day to Windsor; Nell Gwyn had gone on ahead to open up her house, and be there to wait on the Queen (as a Lady of the Privy Chamber) if summoned. Charles had given up early morning tennis, but he took a walk every morning in St James's Park, and it was a chance for petitioners to approach him and for friends to converse generally; on this particular morning, he was with a group of Fellows of the Royal Society. At about ten o'clock he was approached by one of the Royal Society's laboratory assistants, Christopher Kirkby, who had a conspiratorial air. The King asked what he had that troubled him.

Kirkby replied: 'Sir, you must take great care. Keep close within this company. Your enemies have a design against your life, and for what I know you may be in danger in this very walk.'

'How may that be?' asked the King.

'You will be shot,' said Kirkby.

The young man was closely interrogated by Lord Thomas Bruce, but in the end this rumour of an attempt on the King's life was relegated to the huge pile of similar unfounded rumours which had accumulated during his reign. In the afternoon the cavalcade set out for Windsor, and that evening 'his Majestie was at supper with Mrs Nelly.'

In London, Kirkby then approached Danby and repeated his warning. When the young laboratory assistant saw that not even the chief minister would take him seriously, he brought on the two principal actors in the discovery of the 'Popish Plot'.

The lesser of the two was known to Danby — Ezreel Tong (or Israel Tonge), a Yorkshireman who had been one of the first professors at the 'Academie for the Benefit of the North' which Cromwell had set up in the bishop's palace at Durham. Aubrey says: 'The Dr had an excellent schoole there, and followed precisely the Jesuites method of teaching; and the boys did profit wonderfully.' He had moved to Islington and founded a private school there, and 'invented the way of teaching the children to write a good hand in twenty days time, by writing over, with black inke, copies printed from copper plates in red ink ... for four howers in a day.' Many children of prominent courtiers sent their children to Dr Tong's school; Nell Gwyn's elder son may have gone there, as did one of Cleveland's sons. Tong's principal occupation in life, however, was not the education of the children of the rich but the unmasking of Jesuits, whom he admired intensely and feared even more. They were about to take over the world, he used to say to anybody who would listen to him.

One man who did listen to him, and who realized that he could be useful, with his unblemished reputation as a pedagogue, was 'Dr' Titus Oates. Little is known about Oates' early life, as he seldom told the truth, least of all about himself and his antecedents. When he was asked where he had been educated and which university had granted him a doctorate, he was vague and contradictory or said merely 'abroad'. He was ordained a clergyman in the Church of England and for a time worked as a naval chaplain; his extra-clerical interest in young sailors lost him that post, and he seems to have had, and lost, innumerable petty offices. Somehow he had managed to get himself into the Jesuits' English College at St-Omer in France, and at that stage, probably about mid-December 1677, he made contact with one of Shaftesbury's agents. Shaftesbury's plan was that Oates should spend six months at St-Omer, pretending conversion to Roman Catholicism; during that time he would procure a list of all the Jesuit fathers in England and the laymen they served and confessed. Jesuits at Court should be urgently identified. Oates did as he was bidden and eventually arrived in England again at the end of August 1678.

On 28 September Oates stood with Tong before Danby and made his 'revelations'. His appearance was revolting. He was short and bandy-legged, and his arms hung limply down at his sides as if they were senseless; his clerical dress was stained with food; he had no neck to speak of and his head seemed to carry on down to his shoulders without interval; his face was huge and round, bisected by a wide, slack mouth, giving him an enormous jaw. But, however unprepossessing, he had a powerful, exciting voice and like many rogues was convincing when he spoke.

Danby listened to the two men all that Saturday and was so impressed that he begged the King to come up from Windsor and hear them the following day. Titus Oates explained 'the Plot' very carefully. It was well known that the Duke of York was a Catholic and had married the Pope's daughter; not content with this, the Pope had decided to have the King assassinated and put his daughter and son-in-law on the thrones of Scotland, England and Ireland. Louis XIV was to pay for an army to be raised in Catholic Ireland, and for militias to be formed by Catholic peers in England and Scotland; prominent among these peers were Arundel, Belasys, Petre, Powis and Stafford. The Archbishop of Dublin would lead the clergy into battle and be made a Cardinal when victory was assured. The City of London would be fired again. The King's person would be attacked either in St James's Park or at Windsor, stabbed or shot with silver bullets (a Jesuit speciality); if all else failed he was to be poisoned by the Queen's physician, who was a Catholic.

Though Danby had wasted two days earlier in the month on the road to Windsor, tipped off by Tong that an assassination attempt was imminent, he was fascinated by the circumstantial detail in Oates' account of the *personae* and mechanics of 'the Plot'. The Duke of York, present with the King at the Sunday hearing, said that as he was supposed to be the principal beneficiary, the 'witnesses' should be heard again by the Privy Council. The King, who had laughed aloud at the thought of the invalid Lord Belasys leading a rebel army, asked a few questions, laughed again and rode back to Windsor and Nell Gwyn. In a few days the racing would start at Newmarket, and they had to get ready for the move.

Unfortunately for those who would dismiss the idea of a plot as nonsense, one of the men Oates named as a spy was found to have compromising letters in his rooms. This man, Edward Coleman, had been a member of the Duke of York's household for years; he was known to be a Catholic, and for this reason the Duke had had to dismiss him from time to time, under pressure, but he was always reinstated as secretary either to the Duke or to the Duchess. Shaftesbury, who disliked Coleman for some reason, ordered a thorough search of his apartments. Danby could not seem to be less preoccupied for the safety of the King, and behind a fireplace the letters were found.

They were extraordinary documents and might have been forged by a rogue like Oates, but they were genuine enough, and there were codes and ciphers, words written in lemon juice between the lines of harmless missives, and so on. The most damning letters were those written to Jesuits at

St-Omer, to Rome and to Brussels, where the Papal Nuncio with the special responsibility for the conversion of England had his seat. To the Nuncio, Monsignor Albani, Coleman had written: ' ... the Duke can show the King the true cause of his misfortunes ... and with the help of money he will without difficulty drive away the Parliament and the Protestants.' there were unfortunate references to the Duke's wedding, and to the choice of the date of that of Princess Mary (4 November, eve of the anniversary of the Gunpowder Plot); there was even more which was never decoded. It was enough to incriminate an innocent man, and there is reason to believe that Coleman was anything but innocent. He was taken to Newgate and interrogated.

On 12 October Oates had another stroke of luck. He had left a full account of 'the Plot' with a London magistrate, Sir Edmund Berry Godfrey, who had promised to make his own inquiries; when he called he was told that the magistrate had disappeared. On 17 October a watchman found Berry Godfrey's body on Primrose Hill; an autopsy revealed that he had been hanged, then pierced with a sword (still in the body). Oates and Tong were received by Shaftesbury, who accused Danby of being very slow to prosecute 'those with a mind to kill His Majesty'. Dr Tong noted that 'Sir Edmund Berry Godfrey' was an anagram of 'Dy'd by Rome's reveng'd fury.' That sword had been wielded by a Jesuit, he was sure. The hanging was the work of Jesuits, too. He knew their style.

By the end of the week, the country was in the grip of hysteria. Omens were seen everywhere. The King had won a race (prize a silver flagon) at Newmarket against the Protestant Duke of Monmouth, Mr Ellyot and Mr Thynne, but his trainer was a Catholic! A contemporary wrote: 'The credulous all over the kingdom were terrified and affrighted with armies landing, of pilgrims, black bills, armies underground and what not.' Ballads and lampoons were on sale at every street corner, exposing the Pope's evil activities. The souvenir industry rose to the occasion. Pewter tankards, silver-hilted knives ('Remember Godfrey' on one side of the blade, 'Remember Religion' on the other), a pack of cards telling the story of 'the Plot'. The houses of well-known Catholics were stoned and relics destroyed; about 30,000 Catholics fled at the worst of the hysteria. The cellars of the Houses of Parliament were searched daily for gunpowder. The prisons began to fill with Catholics and those denounced as plotters and priests by an army of informers. Many of them were obviously innocent, like Samuel Pepys, 'an elderly gentleman who had known the softness and pleasures of life', and his clerk Samuel Atkins. Some, like Nell Gwyn's silversmith, Miles Prance, went off their heads; Prance accused three neighbours, Green, Berry and Hill, of being officers in the secret Catholic militia.

The King realized that he had to do something. Reluctantly, he left Greenwich, to which he had gone from Newmarket to see to the re-rigging of the *Cleveland* (the Duchess had offered to sell it to him) and another yacht named after his sister, *Henrietta*. It was lucky for Pepys and his clerk that Nell could remind Charles that the two men had been on board *Cleveland* the day Sir Edmund Berry Godfrey had been murdered. Returning to London, the King found a long list of persons charged with plotting to take his life, and it says much for his kindness of heart that he took the time to go through the list and strike off those who were to his certain knowledge devoted servants of the Crown. Nell persuaded him to hear Miles Prance, but the silversmith was so demented with fear that he was incoherent; in the end he was released, as being of no possible use as a witness, but the men he had accused were left in gaol. Nor could the Duke of York's secretary, Coleman, be saved, and he was condemned to death. The Duke managed to keep his seat in the House of Lords but all the other Catholic peers were sent away, on suspicion of being somehow involved in the 'damnable and hellish plot for assassinating and murdering of the King and for rooting out and destroying the Protestant religion'.

Neither the Duchess of York nor the Queen, both Catholics, escaped Oates' attention. He even dared to accuse the Queen of complicity in the Plot, in the King's presence, but was silenced when the King drew himself up to his full height and glowered down at the monstrous Oates. The Queen acknowledged 'how completely the King releases me from all trouble. ... Every day he shows more clearly his purpose and goodwill towards me, and thus baffles the hate of my enemies.' The Dukes of York and Monmouth were advised to remove themselves from the capital, the former because his life was in danger, the latter because he was identifying himself too closely with Shaftesbury and his machinations. Even Nell, who was herself becoming identified very closely with the anti-Catholic mob (her two rivals were Catholic, and Sir Edmund Berry Godfrey had been a churchwarden at St Martin-in-the-Fields since she was a child), thought Monmouth was being unnecessarily provocative and upsetting his father at a very dificult moment, and Monmouth heeded her. As Rochester wrote:

> True to the Protestant interest and cause,
> True to the Established Government and Laws;
> The choice delight of the whole mobile,
> Scarce Monmouth's self is more belov'd than she.
> Was this the cause that did their quarrel move
> That both are Rivals in the People's love?

With his brother in Brussels and Monmouth in Scotland, the King had time to try to protect his 'Established Government', and moved to Salisbury to do so; he was advised there by Bishop Burnet, a shrewd politician. An extraordinary plot within a plot came to light, one to rid him of his Protestant chief minister, Danby. It is still not clear how or why it all began,

nor even who was the instigator. Many well-known intriguers were in it —
Louis XIV, Lady Harvey, her brother, Shaftesbury, maybe even
Buckingham, Louise and Nell (the one frightened for her life, the other
anxious for the downfall of a man who had cut her purse). James, Duke of
York, may also have been involved; Louis XIV admired him and was always
telling him how superior he was to his brother.

The man who began it all in London was certainly the French
Ambassador, Barillon. He managed to convince his master that the
Protestant Danby was the real enemy of the Stewarts and of France, and the
greatest obstacle to the Grand Design to restore England and Scotland to the
Church of Rome. If the chief minister could be discredited, Charles could
rule without one and really earn his subsidies from the French Crown. And
the best way to discredit Danby was to let it be known that he had been the
channel down which these subsidies had flowed in the past. In the present
climate of hysteria, almost anything would be believed. Coleman was about
to be hanged and he was virtuous if indiscreet; Danby was neither, and
almost any charge against him would find enthusiastic witnesses and
supporters.

Because so many people were in the conspiracy, the King soon got to hear
of it. Lady Harvey had purloined some compromising letters in the Palace,
during one of her supper parties with Nell — or did Nell give them to her,
convinced as she was that her enemy was her friend? In any event, Lady
Harvey gave the letters to her brother, who, through his former colleagues
at the British Embassy in Paris (he had been replaced by Sunderland, then
Savile), had gathered other compromising material. Louis XIV and
Pomponne had supplied him with even more from the French spy network,
with the promise that if all went well he would be forgiven his
'indiscretions' with Cleveland's daughter. All the material was hidden in
Montague's Town house.

Remembering the discovery of Coleman's letters behind the fireplace, the
King and Danby proposed to the Privy Council on 19 December that they
surround Montagu's house and send men into the adjoining roofs to make
their way down the various chimneys. But the men on the roof made so
much noise that night that Montagu realized what was up, hurried his
papers out of the house under the skirts of a female relative, and next day
appeared before the House of Commons to reveal 'an attempt on a subject's
liberties'. As he said to an attentive assembly, 'I believe that the seizing of
my cabinet and papers was to get into their hands some letters of great
consequence, that I have to produce, revealing the designs of a great
Minister of State.' There was only one great Minister of State, Danby, and
the House assumed, quite rightly, that the papers would damn him — and for
what else, at that time, if not as a participant in the Plot?

Nell saw very little of the King that Christmas, though more than her

Catholic rivals. The party for Lord James Beauclerk had a subdued tone, partly because the boy did not seem well and the physicians did not know what was the matter with him; fortunately, by the middle of January he seemed to have recovered and was seen skating happily.

Danby, too, had a worrying festive season. Montagu's papers had been handed to the Speaker, and a Committee was vetting them. They were, in fact, State papers proving that Danby had received large sums of money from Louis XIV, and though they had been destined for the King, and Parliament knew it, Members did not hesitate to start proceedings for impeachment. Danby was sent to the Tower (where he was to stay for five years). Realizing that the Parliament which had welcomed him in 1661 was no longer 'Cavalier', the King dissolved it, and writs were sent out for the election of a new House of Commons on 24 January.

The election was the first one in which Nell had taken an active part. Lampoons assured her a place on the hustings, as Louise cowered in the country:

> Let Fame that never yet Spoke well of Woman,
> Give out I was a stroling Whore, and Common,
> Yet I have been to him since the first hour,
> As constant as the Needle to the Flower;
> While you to your Eternal Praise and Fame
> To Foreign Scents betray'd the Royal Game.
> My name, thou Jezebel of Pride and Malice,
> Whose father had a hog-stey for his Pallace,
> In my clear Veins but British Bloud does flow,
> Whilst thou like a French Tode-stoul first did grow,
> And from a Birth as poer as they delight,
> Sprang up a Mushroom-Dutchess in a Night.

It was a very theatrical and corrupt contest. To concentrate the minds of voters, Green, Berry and Hill were executed together with six Jesuit priests. Inevitably, the Country Party won and Shaftesbury ordered that bonfires be lit in the City streets, with free beer for all. He celebrated too soon. The King gave no sign that he felt defeated. Very quickly he brought as many of his enemies as possible into the Council, and Shaftesbury was made Lord President. This shrewd and subtle gesture achieved two things: it kept his enemies close to him where he could keep an eye on them, and it discredited them in the new Parliament, where they were accused of just looking for places like anybody else. As Charles said to Lord Thomas Bruce: 'Here is a set of men about me, but they shall know nothing.'

The new House of Commons set to work briskly to debate 'the Plot' and the fact that, 'The Duke of York being a Papist and the hopes his coming soon to the Crown have given the greatest countenance and encouragement to the present conspiracies and designs of Papists against the King and the Protestant religion'. In May a Bill was brought forward to exclude James from the succession. The House debated virtually nothing else, though the Duke did not seem to be alarmed and from Brussels sent to England for his foxhounds and favourite huntsmen.

Shaftesbury, knowing that Danby had been in and out of the Duchess of Portsmouth's bed on many occasions, threatened to prosecute her as a common whore, if she did not use her influence with the King to get him to back the Exclusion Bill. The King refused but made an enthusiastic speech in favour of the Habeas Corpus Bill, which he later signed into Law. Evelyn welcomed the Bill, because it would benefit some of his friends. On 4 June 1679 he recorded in his Diary that he had 'din'd with Mr Pepys in the Tower, whither he was committed by the House of Commons for misdemeanours in the Admiralty where he was Secretary; but I believe unjustly'. The benefit was not immediate, however, because Evelyn on 3 July sent 'a piece of Venison to Mr Pepys, Sec of the Admiralty, still a prisoner. I went and dined with him.'

There was a new campaign to legitimize the Duke of Monmouth and assure him of the succession, but it came to nothing. Nell Gwyn exchanged letters (written by her semi-literate amanuensis) which suggest that she favoured his legitimization, but she was careful not to say so; in June she congratulated him on his victory at Bothwell Brig against a rabble of Covenanters, but she also begged him not to worry his father. Though often surrounded by cheering crowds and exchanging ribald jokes about Louise, she was careful never to be politically indiscreet.

Nell's popularity was immense. Flowers were left outside her house by wellwishers. Tradesmen said it was an honour to serve her. Aphra Benn dedicated a new play to her (*The Feigned Courtesans*) with the words: 'You never appear but you glad the hearts of all that have the happy fortune to see you, as if you were made on purpose to put the whole world in good humour … . When you speak, men crowd to listen with that awful reverence as to holy oracles or divine prophecies, and bear away the precious words to tell at home to all the attentive family the graceful things you uttered, and cry "But, Oh! she speaks with such an air, so gay, that half the beauty's lost in the repetition". ' Duffet tried to match this with: 'She does good as if doing good was not her nature but her business.' There were scores of anonymous and congratulatory odes and ballads:

> So bright your beauty, so sublime your wit,
> None but a prince to wear your chains is fit.
> I could wish something, but all Heaven's store
> Cannot afford one single blessing more;
> Honour nor wealth you want, nor any thing,
> Unless I wish you a perpetual spring

Of youth and blossoming beauties, such as may
Make all your envious rivals pine away.

(*Madam G* by Ephelia)

A skeleton disappeared from her cupboard on 29 July 1679. The *Domestic Intelligence* reported: 'We hear that Madam Ellen Gwyn's mother, sitting lately by the waterside at her house by the Neat-House near Chelsea, fell accidentally into the water and was drowned.' Nicholas (Narcissus) Luttrell in his *Brief Historical Relation of State Affairs* put it more bluntly: 'Mrs Gwyn, mother to Miss Ellen Gwyn, being in drink, was drowned in a ditch near Westminster.' What seems to have happened is that the old woman fell drunk into a stream known as Sandy End (it divided Chelsea from Fulham) and 'so corpulent a mass of flesh would have outvied Neptune's strength to have delivered her straight on shore'; when she heard the news, Nell left Windsor post haste and returned to London. There was a splendid funeral, and the old drunk was buried in St Martin-in-the-Fields in the vicar's vault (the monument was removed when the church was rebuilt in 1721). Rochester came to Town for the ceremony and later wrote:

Nor was her Mother's Funeral less her care,
No cost, no velvet did the Daughter spare:
Five gulded 'Scutcheons did the Herse enrich,
To celebrate this Martyr of the Ditch.
Burnt Brandy did in flaming Brummers flow,
Drank at her Funeral, while her well-leased Shade
Rejoyc'd, even in the sober Fields below,
At all the drunkennes her Death had made.

There were other verses, even less complimentary:

Her Mother griev'd in muddy Ale and Sack
To think her Child should ever prove a Crack;
When she was drunk she always fell asleep,
And when full maudlin, then the whore would weep;
Her tears were brandy, Mundungus her breath,
Bawd was her Life, and Common-shore her Death.
To see her Daughter mourn for such a Beast
Is like her Life, which makes up but one Jest.

(*Satyr Unmuzzled*)

The British Library has preserved a broadsheet entitled:

A True Account of the late most doleful and lamentable tragedy of old Madam Gwinn, mother of Eleanor Gwinn, who was unfortunately drowned in a fish-pond at her own mansion-house, near the

Neat-Houses, with an account how that much deplored accident came to pass and what is expected to be the sequel of the same. With an Epitaph, composed against the solemnity of her pompous funeral, and many other circumstances. ... It is generally believed, that upon so Tragical occasion, the Pallace and the Fish-pond will be forfeited to her most vertuous Daughter Maddam Ellen Gwin, as Lady of the Soil, and chief of all the Bona-Robas that the Suburban Schools of Venus late have fitted for the Game. And now in gratitude to this good Matron's Memory, to be imposed upon her Tomb-stone ... we have composed this Epitaph as followest:

> Here lies the Victim of a cruel Fate [etc]

In the same library is another 'Elegy upon that never to be forgotten Matron, Old Madam Gwinn, who was unfortunately drown'd in her own fishpond':

> I will not say with Typhon's her vast bulk
> O'erspread nine acres, yet her mighty hulk
> Six foot in compass was suppos'd to be,
> Too pondrous for a common destinie. ...
>
> Yet Brandy Merchants sure have cause to grieve
> Because her fate admits of no reprieve.
> Die in their debts she could not, yet they'l find
> Their trade decay'd, for none is left behind;
> That in one day could twenty quarts consume,
> And bravely vaunt, she durst it twice presume. ...
>
> Readers lament! for seldom shall you find
> The weaker sex to bear so strong a mind.
> Strengthened with all the virtues France or th'Rhine,
> England or Spain could infuse from wine.
> But Bacchus, unkind, did tempt her to ingage,
> Where she expired by subtle Neptune's rage.
> The fate was cruel, yet the fame remains;
> For drinking, none like her the world contains.
> So after-ages then, a statue raise,
> That we may eternalize her – praise.

There were worse troubles to come in August. No sooner had Nell buried her mother and returned to Windsor than the King fell ill. He seems to have caught a very bad cold while playing tennis and then sitting fishing by the river without his usual brisk rub-down. His illness frightened both his friends and his enemies. Henry Savile wrote to Rochester that, 'We shall be at war again', and to his brother Sir George, later Marquess of Halifax, that, 'The very thought of Charles' death frights me out of my wits.' For a short time, while the King had a high fever, the fear of death was a real one. What would Monmouth do? As Captain-General of two armies he might emulate Monck and march on London. And James? He would not stand by idly and be usurped. He had already rejected any notion of the monarchy being made elective, or 'joint rule' with William of Orange and Mary.

Fortunately for those who were genuinely afraid of another civil war, Charles recovered. That he did so was partly because Nell, who nursed him with the Queen's permission, managed to keep the physicians away and sent for two women, the wife of Dr Iles, a canon of Christ Church, and a Mrs Holder, who 'haz a great sagacity to curing wounds which she does not doe so much by presedents, as by her own excogitancy'. She had cured the King before, as Aubrey relates: 'His majestie king Charles II had hurt his hand which he intrusted his chirugians to make well; but they ordered him so that they made it much worse, so that it swoll, and pained him up to the shoulder; and pained him so extremely that he could not sleep, and began to be feaverish. Someone told the King what a rare shee-surgeon she was; she was presently sent for at eleven o'clock at night. She presently made a poultisse and applied it, and gave his majesty sudden ease, and he slept well; next day she dressed him and perfectly cured him, to the great griefe of all the surgeons, who envy and hate her.'

By the end of August the King was well, sitting up in bed and eating boiled partridge for breakfast. On 2 September he was well enough to take the Government into his own hands again. He decided that Monmouth was becoming too ambitious, airing again his claim that the King had secretly married his mother, Lucy Walters; Monmouth was sent to Holland. James, who had become rather bored with the hunting in the Low Countries, asked for useful employment and was sent to Scotland; after an uncomfortable journey through the hostile, Protestant north-east of England, he found himself welcomed by a thousand great lords at Berwick and escorted in triumph to Edinburgh. Monmouth hated life at the Hague as much as the astonished Duke of York enjoyed the grouse-shooting and the reverential Scots; Laurence Hyde, now Minister in Holland, reported that the 'boy' was corresponding frantically with Nell Gwyn, hoping for her intervention to end his exile.

The King and Nell went to Newmarket as usual at the end of September, and soon all plots were forgotten at the races. Charles had several promising horses in training – *Woodcock* (on which he had won the previous year), *Shuffler*, *Tankot*, *Corke* and *Roan*. Nell liked to dress up as one of the owners, in a tight-waisted coat, breeches and small periwig, and saunter in the paddocks to see if she were recognized. She amused everybody by day and entertained former colleagues at the King's House who came up in relays to perform for the Court. She was still inexpert at riding and had a bad fall in early October but was consoled on her way back to London by Sir Fleetwood Sheppard, set by the King to put her financial affairs in order; the Vice-Chancellor of Cambridge University, insisted on entertaining her and presented her with an appreciative address in verse. There was just time to order a new dress for the wedding of the Duke of Grafton to Lord Arlington's daughter (on 8 November), and a sailor suit for her elder son, who was to go to Portsmouth to see a new warship launched and given his title, *Burford.*

The Duke of Ormonde and his son the Earl of Arran had been busy about her affairs in Ireland and seem to have brought to a successful conclusion the case in the Irish Court of Claims. The King's estates in Dundalk and Carlingford were made over to Sir Robert Howard as trustee for Nell and her elder son, and a dishonest agent, Mellish, was briskly interrogated, dismissed and imprisoned. In November Sir Robert Howard wrote to the Duke: 'Mrs Nelly presents you with her real acknowledgements for all your favours, and protests that she would write in her own hands, but her wild characters, she says, would distract you.'

The King was in a good humour. Though the Exclusion Bill had passed through the House of Commons, it was defeated in the Lords, largely due to the eloquence of the (now) Lord Halifax. Using the famous charm, Charles had wooed Halifax away from the Country Party (in which he had been uncomfortable anyway) and begged him to become his chief minister (though he still consulted Danby in the Tower). He felt confident enough to face the crowds on 17 November, when Shaftesbury staged a great pageant (nominally to celebrate the accession of Queen Elizabeth I, an anniversary never neglected). A broadsheet described the pageant as 'The Solemn Mock Procession of the Pope, Cardinalls, Jesuits, Fryers etc through ye City of London', and it featured actors playing these worthies, including 'Jesuits' with swords ready to murder another actor playing Sir Edmund Berry Godfrey. There were cheers as the effigy of Queen Elizabeth ('The Saviour of the Protestant Religion') passed by and respectful applause for 'Sir Edmund'.

The King forbade Nell to take part in the procession, as she had been invited to do, but in the evening, when they were burning an effigy of the Pope and carousing, she could not resist the temptation of going out to join in the fun. At one stage her coach was mistaken for that of Louise Portsmouth. Hearing the angry shouts, she stuck her head out of the window and shouted: 'Be still, friends. I am the Protestant whore.'

Nell and the King had another difference of opinion over Monmouth, who was brought over by Shaftesbury at the end of the month. The King was very angry, stripped his son of all his titles and ordered him back to Holland. Monmouth disobeyed his father again and found asylum at 79 Pall

Mall. *The Verney Papers* report that, 'Nelly dus the Duck of Monmouth all the kindness she can, but her interest is nothing. Nell Gwin begg'd hard of his majestie to see him, that he was grown wan, lean and long visaged merely because he was in disfavour; but the King bid her be quiet for he wd not see him.' Barillon, the French Ambassador, was astonished. He wrote to Louis XIV at the beginning of December that, 'The Duke every night sups with Nelly, the courtesan who has borne the King two children, and whom he daily visits.'

Another house guest was the Duke of Buckingham; in a letter to the Duke of Ormonde, Boyle wrote of Buckingham that it was 'his present favour and allowance to have his lodgings in Madame Nelly's house, which doth not a little contribute to the jealousies and dissatisfactions of the people'. The only person who seemed to show (extreme) dissatisfaction that month was Lieutenant Wharton of the Guards: while she was driving in Hyde Park her lead horse bumped Wharton's; he dismounted and ran the carriage horse through. Nell complained and Wharton was banished to Holland.

There was a rumour that she had been murdered by Jesuits, denied in the *Mercurius Domesticus* of 17 December: 'Several false and ridiculous reports have been spread abroad concerning Madam Ellen Gwyn, as to her death or absence from her house, but we are assured that there is no ground for such report and Madam Gwyn is now at her house in good health and has not been absent from it.'

The King was apparently restored to good health, good humour and authority, and presumably Monmouth was not present at the annual Christmas party at 79 Pall Mall. The Duke of Grafton was there with his twelve-year-old bride and so was his sister Charlotte, about to become Countess of Lichfield. The King's Christmas present was particularly generous. He told Nell he intended to giver her a large house just inside the grounds of Windsor Castle, which would take her son's name; the Venetian Ambassador reported that decoration and furnishing had already begun, and the painter Antonio Verrio, having finished work at the castle, was to paint the staircases at Burford House 'with scenes from stories by Ovid'. Edmund Waller and Christopher Wase were at the party, too, full of gossip. There was an exchange between them, Wase offering 'some bitter satyricall verses' on Sir Carr Scroope, Nell's former friend:

> Thy brother murd'd, and this syster whor'd,
> Thy mother, too – and yet thy penne's thy sword.

On this Waller commented that, 'Men write ill things well and good things ill; that satyrically writing was downehill, most easie and natural; that at Billingsgate one might hear good heights of such witt, that the cursed earth naturally produces briars and hawthorns and weeds, but roses and fine flowers require cultivation' (Aubrey). The two men composed their differences.

1680 ought to have been a very happy year for Nell, now the most important political hostess in England, friend of wits, courtiers and statesmen, and as much the idol of the mob as she was of the elite. As Rochester put it:

> She's now the darling Strumpet of the Crowd,
> Forgets her State, and talks to them aloud;
> Lays by her greatness and descends to prate
> With those 'bove whom she's rais'd by wondrous Fate.

On 16 February 1680 she nearly started a riot. She went to the Duke's House with Thomas Herbert, and as she took her seat a drunk in the audience reminded everybody of the incident with Wharton:

> Nelly's horse is dead
> But Nell the whore is here.

Nell shouted something as vulgar at the drunk, but Herbert was enraged, drew his sword and jumped into the pit to avenge the insult; fortunately she was able to restrain him, and the performance was delayed for an hour while the patrons cheered and the drunk was deposited in a horse trough.

The only thing which seems to have distressed her as the year began was the fact that she was still a commoner, and though she made a virtue out of the fact (and Aphra Benn praised her for not having a title), she could not see why she should not be ennobled. Buckingham convinced her that one way of pressing her claim would be to set several titled ladies whoring. There were three likely candidates: Carey, the daughter of Sir Alexander Frazier, the chief of the King's official physicians (who wanted promotion to the peerage for her father), Elizabeth, daughter of the Earl of Ranelagh (who was to promote the interests of the Duke of Ormonde's rivals) and Jane Lawson (who would best advance the claims of Laurence Hyde and his friends). This springtime *divertissement* was the subject of some popular verses:

> Think who they are who would for you procure
> This great preferment to be made a whore:
> Two reverend aunts, renowned in British 'story
> For lust and drunkenness with Nell and Lory.
> These, these are they your fame will sacrifice,
> Your honour sell, and you shall hear the price:
> My Lady Mary [Howard] nothing can design
> But feed her lust with what she gets for thine;
> Old Richmond making thee a glorious punk,
> Shall twice a day with brandy now be drunk;
> Her brother Buckingham shall be restored;
> Nelly a countess, Lory be a lord.

Nothing came of this design, largely because the King had been clapped by a common whore and for the first time in his adult life was losing interest in women. This disappointment was followed by others, 'a year of briars, thornes and weedes'. Nell had to dismiss Sir Fleetwood Sheppard for seducing one of her maids; she was sorry to see him go, because he had been in her household since 1674, first as tutor to her elder son (£200 a year) then as her 'accountant'; he probably stole from her, too, but she recommended him to Dorset and to Henry Savile in Paris, so he avoided poverty and disgrace. To take his place as tutor, she appointed an old colleague, Thomas Otway; he had not been much of an actor, but he wrote some interesting poetry (he managed to get into Samuel Jonson's *Lives of the Poets*), translated Racine and Molière and wrote heroic tragedy in verse. Not all his contemporaries agreed about the quality of his writing:

> Then for that cub, her son and heir,
> Let him remain in Otway's care.
> To make him (if that's possible to be)
> A viler Poet, and more dull than he.

Then, in May, Nell was taken ill. At thirty, it was her first serious illness and there had been much speculation about it, most of it orientated towards a venereal disease picked up from the King, 'his new clap or his old pox'. It seems to have been a debilitating illness, because she was not well enough to attend the spring meeting at Newmarket (the King's horse *Shuffler* beat Mr Griffin's *Ball* over the Beacon course), nor even to go to Windsor to inspect her new house and staircase.

There was worse to come in early June. Her younger son, James, died in Paris.

Nell had not known that he had been taken ill again, and the only explanation of his death was that he had had a 'bad leg'. To the end of her life, she always blamed herself for letting him go abroad, even to friends like Henry Savile, and for not being with him at the end. Later she became convinced that he had been poisoned by Louise, still in ill health and a frequent visitor to France to take the waters at one spa or another. There would be no more Christmas Day birthday parties. She went into deep mourning, shut herself away in Sandford House and spoke to nobody except her servants.

She was not to be left in peace to grieve. On 27 July a messenger forced his way past her porters and brought her a ring and the news that Rochester had died the previous day. Burnet wrote of him: 'Like a Comet, he flashed across the stormy night of the seventeenth century, filling those who knew him with astonishment, leaving behind a memory that faded after many years.' Rochester's own last words were for the Bishop of Salisbury: 'My spirits and body decay so equally together that I shall write a letter as weak as I am in person. I begin to value churchmen above all men in the world and you above all churchmen I know in it.' This was a pious statement, the more suprising since the Countess of Rochester had just poisoned Sir John Denham's second wife with chocolates.

Then Nell's favourite portrait-painter, Sir Peter Lely, died. He had been a frequent and welcome guest at 79 Pall Mall, and she liked him because he always managed to make her look 'vertuose' even in the nude; his portrait of Louise had offered an image of sumptuous sulkiness, and Nell liked that, too.

These two blows seemed to have helped her forget her own loss, and she re-appeared in society again, first in London, then at Windsor. Lady Sunderland wrote to Lord Halifax at the end of the month that, 'There is one place of council I should never have suspected (My Lady Orrery's) till I did know that my Lord Shaftesbury, the Duke of Monmouth and my Lord Cavendish do meet and sup there, and Mrs Nelly, who the King hath forbid letting the Duke of Monmouth come to her house.' It is not quite clear what they were taking council about, other than the general Protestant interest and 'the Plot', and their own desire for advancement, but the hot summer seems to have limited the frequency of their meetings.

Nell did not reappear in London until September, and then only on her own business; on the 14th she witnessed the conveyance of the deeds of Burford House to Dorset, Sir Edward Villiers, Chiffinch and Sir George Hewitt 'in trust for Ellen Gwyn for and during her life, and after her decease for Charles, Earl of Burford, and the heirs male of his body'; two days later she gave power of attorney to a solicitor, Thomas Fraser or Frazier, 'generally to act and agitate all things in and about the receipt of the premises as fully and effectually to all intents and purposes as I myself might or could do the same were I in person present'. There were two bits of building work to be commissioned before Newmarket, a small gate in the back garden wall of 79 Pall Mall and 'a wall for Madam Gwyn's garden on the south side of her house at Windsor'.

At Newmarket the King eventually jollied her out of mourning, as she had so often cheered him up. He was very cheerful, in spite of seeing his *Roan* beaten by Mr Ryder's *Mouse*; he had his revenge when his *Corke* beat Sir Robert Carr's *Small Cole*, and won several hundred pounds. It is said that Charles invited his brother to Newmarket (Nell's dead son had been named after him), and James offered to take her with him to Scotland when he returned there next month. He tried to make it sound exciting. Hunting was no good because of the hills and bogs, but there was good fishing and a game called golf which even women played. There were no Shaftesburys; Lauderdale, whose place he was to take, had suppressed virtually all civil liberties, and peace was the rule even in the Highlands. But somehow he was not convincing, and he would have had to be, because all her life Nell refused to go outside the Home Counties, perhaps because she remembered the discomforts of her childhood, perhaps because she still had a horror of 'rustic humours'. The King did not help. He told her of the agonizing times he had had there thirty years ago, the endless prayers, impossible people like Argyll. Anyway, he needed her in London as his political hostess and channel of information about Shaftesbury's doings. He amused her by telling her the Venetian Ambassador had suggested a Register of Whores; they had one in the Most Serene Republic ('The Catalogue of the Chief and most Honoured Courtesans'). Nell said: 'Sire, you would need Mr Stokes [Aubrey says he "made himselfe mad with Algebra"] to count them.'

There was good news to come on 5 November, Guy Fawkes Day. Shaftesbury, after the success of the pageant the year before, hoped to strengthen his hold on the mob with another, this time re-enacting the Gunpowder Plot. He had lampoons and ballads printed, but the professional actors he had engaged failed to turn up, and the amateur carnival which followed was a flop, too. A new Exclusion Bill was put to the House of Commons on the 11th, but again Halifax had it thrown out of the Lords. On 17 November Shaftesbury tried again to celebrate the anniversay of Elizabeth's accession and the 'salvation of the Protestant religion', but this was drowned by a downpour and the mob were frightened away by new interpretations of the meaning of the comet (Halley's) which was carving its way through the sky like a knife blade.

The King enjoyed a quiet Christmas with Nell – there was some festive ribaldry when a rumour circulated that Sheriff Bethel had been elected in the City because he was secretly married to her – and on 10 January 1681 decided to prorogue and then dissolve Parliament.

After some thought, Halifax and the King decided to call the next meeting of Parliament at Oxford, where the royal standard had been raised by Charles I, and where there were still Cavaliers refighting the Civil War. When the news broke, there was a certain amount of murmuring from Shaftesbury and his friends, but as it was the King's right to call his Lords and Commons together wherever he wanted, there was nothing to be done except to get as many Whigs to Oxford as possible. The Opening was fixed for the third week in March, the Lords in what is now the Bodleian Library and the Commons in Convocation House. The drive to Oxford was a show of strength. The King's Party decorated their houses with portraits of him and showed blue favours; the Country Party fluttered its green ribbons.

The King called both houses to the Bodleian (Geometry School) and warned them not to raise again the matter of the exclusion of his brother from the succession. He said: 'Men ordinarily become more timid as they get older; as for me I shall be, on the contrary, bolder and firmer. ... I do not fear the dangers and calamities which people try to frighten me with. I have the law and reason on my side.' Then he sent them away for the weekend to meditate on their conduct.

It was a merry weekend in Oxford. Nell was there with Lady Kildare, who had kept the King's bed warm during her illness but never became a rival. There was singing and dancing and there were loyal addresses. The only discordant note was struck by the new Vicar of St Martin-in-the-Fields, Thomas Tenison, who came to Oxford to protest that the new lecturer at the church had been appointed without consultation and should be removed; Nell, a parishioner who was to become a friend, pacified Dr Tenison and had the lecturer's appointment cancelled. (Tenison quickly re-appointed him, so honour was satisfied on both sides.)

On 28 March the King turned up at the Bodleian, apparently to receive petitioners and listen to the debate. After ten minutes he withdrew and re-appeared in his robes of State, which had followed him in a closed sedan chair. He summoned the Commons and dissolved Parliament, never to call one again during his reign. 'You are better off,' he told Nell, Lady Kildare and Lord Bruce, 'with one tall king than with five hundred little ones. We shall have peace at last this year.'

This bold stroke revealed the weaknes of the Country Party. The people were tired of plots and executions, and there was no reaction against this action of the King (in the best Cavalier tradition). On 2 July Shaftesbury was arrested and sent to the Tower, where he was to be examined by the Privy Council. He was given the cell next to that of his old enemy Danby; there was never much wrong with the King's sense of humour.

Anti-climax, 1681-5

Imprimis, in Scotland, for converting of Whigs,
In England for Pindaric poems and jigs,.
At Dame Ellen Gwyn's for moving your laughter,
A presage that some good was to follow after.

Haines, *To the King, a Reckoning*

The summer season of 1681 was marked by the publication of the first part of Dryden's *Absalom and Achitopel*, probably written at the behest of Charles II. It is a long satirical poem, attacking Shaftesbury, the City of London, Titus Oates, anybody and everybody who had upset the King. Dryden himself, the Poet Laureate, went to Windsor to read it to Charles and Nell. She had never lost touch with him, and admired his work; she was his favourite actress, and when she had left the stage he had slowly abandoned it himself to concentrate on poetry, translation and criticism. Dryden shared the King's regret that Shaftesbury, a brilliant man, had turned against the Crown:

> Sagacious, bold, and turbulent of wit;
> Restless, unfixed in principles and place;
> In power unpleas'd, impatient of disgrace.
>
> O, had he been content to serve the crown,
> With virtues only proper to the gown.
> Or had the rankness of the soil been freed
> From cockle, that oppress'd the seed;
> David for him his tuneful harp had strung.

The Privy Council shared this regret and freed Shaftesbury from the Tower. It was said that he had been led astray by men like Sheriff Bethel,

> ... whose youth did early promise bring
> Of zeal to God and hatred to his king.

163

Did wisely from expensive sins refrain,
And never broke the sabbath, but for gain ...
During his office, treason was no crime;
The sons of Belial had a glorious time.

A brisk programme of replacement of all disloyal magistrates was begun (as the King put it indelicately, 'We shall see whose arse is blackest'), and Whig mayors were removed from office. Shaftesbury protested in vain. He had no Parliament to support him, and with a rumoured £400,000 having reached the King from Louis XIV there seemed little likelihood that one would be called. In vain he tried to organize demonstrations in the City, and eventually admitted defeat and fled to Holland, complaining, 'the loudest bagpipe in the squeaking train' (Dryden).

It was all good fun. The King was delighted and gave Nell the lease of most of Bestwood Park in Sherwood Forest; it had been first bought by Edward III, who liked hunting there. It is said that the King was teasing Nell about not being able to ride well and only wanting to watch horses run. He said he would give her as much of Sherwood Forest as she could ride round before breakfast, and she chose Bestwood on the advice of the Duke of Buckingham, who knew it well. She is described in the documents which handed over the houses and land as 'Lady Elinor Gwynne of the parish of St Martin-in-the-Fields', which gave rise to a rumour that she had been ennobled *in pectore* and the King was just waiting for the right moment to announce that she had got the coveted title, but there was never any confirmation of the rumour.

Her closeness to the King was remarkable, though she had no rivals on the scene: Barbara Cleveland was permanently in France, Louise Portsmouth came and went to Bourbon there, and Hortense Mazarin led the bohemian life in Chelsea. One of Shaftesbury's Puritan followers, an Alderman Wright, was talking to the King while walking near the racecourse when 'His Majestie met Nell Gwynne and Nell cal'd to him, "Charles, I hope I shall have your company tonight?" ' The Alderman was shocked and complained bitterly about the state of the nation's morals.

There was a little domestic unpleasantness. Her old teacher and lover John Lacy died at his house in Cradle Alley, Drury Lane, where she had first learnt to dance. Then she had to dismiss Otway, who like his predecessor, had got one of her maidservants with child; he was replaced by a Mr Clare, who seems to have been a paragon of virtue.

What started out as a little unpleasantness on her return to Town across Bagshot Heath, turned to comedy. She was stopped by a highwayman, who robbed her cheerfully, then said: 'I hope, madam, you will give me something personal for myself after I have took away the rest.' She is said to have kissed him, at which he gave her back her rings, doffed his hat, bowed and rode away. Louise was also robbed on a return visit, ironically on the Old Portsmouth Road. The highwayman was the same, Old Mobb, who lodged at the Golden Farmer on the Bagshot Road and got his information from the ostlers. The Duchess of Portsmouth was outraged and asked him if he knew who she was.

'Yes,' said Old Mobb, 'you are the richest whore in the kingdom and they say you can do what you like with the King, God Bless Him. But I am the king of this road, so off with your jewels and give me your purse.'

When she protested and said he would be hanged for robbing her, Old Mobb retorted: 'If all sinners were hanged, there would be nobody on the road to rob. Now, come on or I will shoot this fop with you. He looks French to me [it was her nephew]. Remember, I have a whore of my own to keep with contributions from the public, just like Good King Charles.'

When Nell heard of this, it made up for the rhyme which had greeted Louise's return:

> Now Nelly you must be content
> Her Grace begins to reign;
> For all your brat you may be sent
> To Dorset back again.

The eighteenth-century memorialist suggests that it was at some time that year that she had the idea of a 'hospital' where NCOs and men who had served the King could spend the rest of their days in decent comfort and with proper medical attention. He writes: 'Another act of generosity which raised the character of this lady above every other courtesan of these or any other times, was her solicitude to effect the institution of the Chelsea Hospital.' There is some mystery about the genesis of the idea, and some people have cast doubts on Nell's part in the project, but as the old soldiers who moved in there (and their successors) used to toast her formally as their benefactor, these doubts seem churlish. Evelyn recorded in his diary for 30 August 1681 that, 'Sir S. Fox proposed the purchasing of Chelsey College to build an hospital for Souldiers there', but the subject had been raised before.

Nell had been moved to sympathy by a one-legged man who had stopped her coach and asked for alms. Interrogating him, she learned that he had served for years in Tangiers, part of Charles' wife's dowry, and had suffered from every disease known in North Africa before having his leg shot off by a Dutch privateer. It had also occurred to her at her mother's funeral that Civil War veterans must now be in their sixties, and many of them were still indigent. Samuel Pepys, released from the Tower thanks to Nell, and a guest at Burford House during the summer and at 79 Pall Mall in the late autumn, gave her his support and promised that of the Duke of York; in return for his enthusiasm, Nell gave him an engraving of herself as Cupid, dressed in a pair of wings only (he kept it all his life at the Admiralty, to which he had been restored).

It was during the Christmas season that matters were taken a step further. The King appointed Nicholas Johnson treasurer of the *ad hoc* fund established by a 'Committee for the Building of an hospital or infirmary for souldiers'. The Royal Society, which owned Chelsea College, made it over to the King, and Sir Christopher Wren came to 79 Pall Mall (with his sister-in-law Mrs Holder, who had cured the King of his 'fever') and showed the King and Nell some preliminary drawings. The story has it that when Nell saw the drawings, she took her handkerchief, tore it into strips and laid them out to form a hollow square round which a much larger building could be raised. She was also the owner of the land adjoining Chelsea College (the old St James's College site) and made it over to the new Hospital as a gift. At the January 1682 meeting of the Royal Society, Sir Christopher, who was President, recommended the project and its charitable purposes. Sir Stephen Fox at this point certainly contributed £1,300, and from the Secret Service Funds came £6,787. Fox's interest, it has been said unkindly, came from the promptings of his conscience: he had made a lot of money supplying garrisons in Bombay and Tangiers.

While this project was being advanced, January 1682 saw a flurry of diplomatic activity. Foreign rulers, who had been watching to see which of the two adversaries, Charles or Shaftesbury, would win the battle for power in England, sent their ambassadors to present their compliments to the King and assure him of their cousinly devotion. One ambassador with a rather less formal mission was the new emissary from the Sultan of Morocco, an enterprising man who had made himself a fortune by 'taxing' the Sahara trade routes and going into partnership with Berber pirates, offering them safe havens in return for a share of the loot. He felt rich and strong enough to demand the return of Tangiers from the Portuguese, who had taken it from his predecessor by force. However, the Portuguese had given it to King Charles as part of Catherine of Braganza's marriage portion and were not in a position to give it back or sell it to the Sultan. The King of France seems to have been approached to mediate, and he recommended a direct approach to Charles; he had heard that Parliament had been grumbling about the cost of maintaining the garrison now that there were no wars with the Dutch. Louis said he would try to get Louise to use her good offices to ease the negotiations.

On 24 January 1682 Evelyn recorded in his Diary that the Moroccan Ambassador, Nahed Achmet, had arrived and, 'This Evening I was at the Entertainment at the Dut: of Portsmouth's glorious Appartment at W.hall, where was a great banquet of sweetemeates, and Musique etc. but at which both the Ambassador and Retinue behaved themselves with extraordinary Moderation and modestie, though placed about a long Table a Lady between two Moores: viz a Moore, then a Woman, then a Moore etc: and most of these were the King's natural Children viz. the Lady Lichfield, Sussex, DD of Portsmouth, Nelly etc: Concubines and Catell of that sort, as splendid as Jewells and Excesse of bravery could make them. ... '

Evelyn liked the Ambassador and also reported that, 'He liked our Theatres and went sometimes there, where upon any foolish or fantasticall action he could not forbeare laughing, he endeavoured to hide it with extraordinary modesty and gravity: In a word the Russian Ambassador still at Court behaved himselfe like a Clowne, compar'd to this Civil Heathen.'

Louise liked Achmet, too, and he was in her bed within the week, no doubt to pursue his diplomatic activity. She liked coloured men and as long ago as 1679 it had been reported that, 'A blackamore comes between her Quarters.' At the end of his mission, the ambassador paid a respectful as well as an affectionate farewell and wished her son well. Perhaps it was as a result of his services that the King did not oppose the withdrawal of the Tangiers garrison.

The spring of 1682 was taken up with preparations for the laying of the foundation stone for the Royal Hospital, though Newmarket was not neglected. The King was visibly ageing, and no longer rode. He enjoyed a life without fuss, impossible with Louise, so Nell was an ideal companion. As Sir John Reresby wrote: 'The King was much pleased with the country, and so great a lover of the diversions which that place did afford, that he let himself down from majesty to the very degree of a country gentleman. He mixed among the crowd, allowed every man to speak with him that pleased; went a-hawking in the mornings, to cock matches in the afternoons (if there were no horse races), and to plays in the evenings acted by very ordinary Bartholemew Fair comedians.' Politics were left to Halifax, who saw to it that the King was troubled as little as possible after Shaftesbury's defeat. Nell, too, seems to have given up her role as political hostess. As a lampoon put it:

> All matters of state from her soul she does hate
> And leaves to the politic bitches.
> The whore's in the right, for 'tis her delight
> To be scratching just where it itches.

Louise, on the contrary (as the lampoon suggests), had become politically more active. Not content with the Moroccan affair, she managed to ingratiate herself with the Duke of York, who in his brother's absence often functioned as an unofficial regent. Barillon, the French Ambassador, noted Louis XIV's approval: 'The King of England could have taken no resolution more agreeable to his prosperity and reputation than that of re-establishing the Duke of York in all his offices.' The Duke was Lord High Admiral again (the Test Act forgotten) and Pepys probably at the peak of his power from

March 1682 (the return of James to offical life). The Whigs seemed in full flight.

Dryden was at Windsor that summer with the second part of *Absalom and Achitopel*, notable for a portrait of Thomas Shadwell, his rival for the Poet Laureateship (he got it in 1688):

> Round as a glove, and liquor'd every chink,
> Goodly and great he sails behind his link.
> With all his bulk there's nothing lost in Og,
> For every inch that is not fool is rogue;
> A monstrous mass of foul, corrupted matter,
> As all the devils spew'd to make the batter.
> But tho' Heaven made him poor (with rev'rence speaking)
> He never was a poet of God's making.
> The midwife laid her hand on his thick skull,
> With this prophetic blessing: *Be thou dull.*

After Windsor Nell found herself face to face with her unpaid bills and on 4 September 1682 had to write to the Duke of Ormonde:

> This is to beg a favour of Your Grace, which I hope you will stand my friend in. I lately got a friend of mine to advance me on my Irish pension half a year's payment for last Lady Day, which all people have received but me, and I drew bills upon Mr Laurence Steele, my agent, for the payment of the money, not thinking but that before this the bills had been paid; but contrary to my expectation I last night received advice from him that the bills are protested, and he cannot receive any money without Your Grace's positive order to the farmers for it. Your Grace formerly upon the King's letter, which this enclosed is the copy of, was so much mine and Mrs Forster's friend as to give necessary orders for our payments notwithstanding the stop. I hope you will oblige me now upon this request, to give your directions to the farmers, that we may be paid our arrears and what is growing due and you will oblige etc ... .
>
> (Ormonde MSS NS VI 436, Hist. MSS Comm.)

The mills of bureaucracy ground slow but small even in those days, and after a lengthy correspondence the sources of the interference in the payment of her, and her sister's, Irish moneys were found and the flow resumed.

John Wilson suggests that at this time Nell was unfaithful to the King, that there was a sort of musical chairs — Mary Knight courted by Landsdowne but preferring William Colt, Nell pursued by Duncombe but wanting Colt, with the King intervening and awarding Colt to Nell. He quotes some verses of Etherege's, 'Mrs Nellys Complaint':

> To France my baffled, squeaking rival's gone,
> And Colt and all his eyes are now on my own.
> Should he pretend to what's so much my due,
> She might as well take lovely Duncombe too,
> Duncombe by my great sway and power preferred,
> For mounting me well first, now mounts the Guard.

This, however, seems to be another aberration of Etherege's and possibly refers to an old affair (with the City merchant who was said to have kept her and then helped to put her on the stage many years before). Nell's constancy was proverbial, and even at a flirtatious age in flirtatious company she would not have risked what she had gained by it, at a time when she had become virtually 'respectable' in her devotion.

After the autumn meeting at Newmarket, the King and Nell returned to London to a greeting from some law students who had entertained her the previous Christmas. She was presented with a petition to aid those who had been made homeless by the great fire which had destroyed the waterfront at Wapping. It was recorded that the King gave £2,000 and Nell Gwyn £100 to relieve the suffering. She could ill afford to give anything, because she was still having difficulty in getting her revenues from her Irish sources; she wrote to the Earl of Arran begging him to do something about it – 'stand my friend' – and told him that her agent Laurence Steel would do anything he suggested to 'bring the matter to a conclusion'. She also felt herself to be poorer than she was as Christmas approached: when she went to call on Peg Hughes in Hammersmith, she was offered a splendid pearl necklace given to Peg by Prince Rupert on his deathbed that summer, and, wanting to buy it, there was nothing to be done but approach the King and ask him for money. He said she could have either Prince Rupert's Garter for her son (this was, in fact, the Prince's dying wish) or the necklace (fifty large pearls evenly matched). Though she knew the Garter would go to Louise's son, she did not hesitate. She chose the pearls (£4,240).

On 21 January 1683 Shaftesbury died in exile, and the King celebrated, giving more presents to his friends – to Nell he changed the deeds of Burford House so that females could succeed in possession of it (7 February) – but the celebration came too soon. Three weeks after he had gone with Nell to Newmarket in mid-March, the Palace there caught fire and was largely destroyed. Legend has it that Nell said to him: 'Well, Sire, now I can offer you a lodging, as you have done for me.'

The fire may well have saved the King's life ...

Far from having disintegrated on Shaftesbury's death, the Opposition took on a new lease of life. An odd assortment of conspirators, some in Holland (the Earl of Argyll), some in England (including the Earl of Essex, Monmouth, John Locke, the philospher, and sundry survivors of Cromwell's regime), got together a band of mercenaries which was to organize the assassination of both Charles and his brother James as they came back from Newmarket. They had already prepared a haycart which was to block the road at Rye House, near Ware; from inside the reinforced cart and the hedges at the side of the roads (they were high blackthorn, so the Horse Guards could not jump them) forty men would fire on the royal coach and outriders. The Newmarket fire, however, made the King bring forward his return to London by three days, and so the plot failed. Several of the would-be assassins were arrested and tortured and they confessed, naming also the leaders. It was yet another attempt to remove the Catholic natural successor to the throne and proclaim Monmouth king. The Rye House plotters were nearly all arrested; the Earl of Essex, who had been so disobliging to Nell, cut his throat in the Tower; Russell, Sidney the Republican and others were hanged, drawn and quartered and Monmouth went underground (with a modest reward of £500 for his capture).

The King was deeply shocked by the behaviour of his favourite son and for the rest of the year virtually withdrew from public life, leaving the country to his brother to rule. The Queen, Louise and Nell all moved to Windsor for the summer and seem to have been on good terms with each other, sharing out the King between them with little animosity. The reading public for lampoons and ballads did not acknowledge this truth and enjoyed *A Pleasant Dialogue Between Two Wanton Ladies of Pleasure*:

> Quoth Nelly, I prithee, who sent for you here,
>   With a fa la la la fa la la
> 'Tis you with a shame that put in for a share
>   With a fa la la la fa la la
> O do you remember when I was dismay'd
> When you in attire was richly arrayed,
> Alas, I poor Nelly was wronged in my trade
> With a fa la la la la fa la la.
>
>
> I pray now could you not your honour advance
>   With a fa la la la fa la la
> With some noble Peer in the Nation of France
>   With a fa la la la fa la la
> Forsooth you must needs leave your Country dear
> To utter your fine French Commodity here,
> But sorrow and trouble will bring up the rear
>   With a fa la la la la fa la la.
>
>
> No, sweet Madam Nelly, you cannot deny
>   With a fa la la la fa la la
> But you have had the treasure as often as I

With a fa la la la la fa la la
And yet must I only indeed be run down
By you that I value the least in the Town,
If I come in favour upon thee I'll frown
With a fa la la la la fa la la.

And much else in the same vein. In fact, there seem to have been no clashes, and the 'treasure' was there for them all. The King would go hunting or hawking or riding with Nell, still determined to make her a good horsewoman. When he felt less energetic, he would play basset with his wife or crimp with Louise, who was too fat for any sort of violent exercise (but was said to have a charming smile). When he felt scientifically curious, he would work in his laboratory in the castle or look at mechanical marvels he had had built in the grounds (the chief of these was a giant water-engine constructed by Morland).

There was a great coming and going of Fellows of the Royal Society, led by Pepys, President designate, and many of them lodged with Nell at Burford House; she had extended her lands and had so many acres covered with walks and bowling alleys (now part of the Home Park) that for many years it was impossible to complete the Long Walk up to the castle gates. The Fellows held the King in great respect, and Dryden did not exaggerate when he wrote:

Forgiving, humble, bounteous, just and kind:
His conversation, wit and parts,
His knowledge in the noblest useful arts,
Were such dead authors could not give
But habitudes of those who live ...
His apprehension quick, his judgement true;
That the most learn'd, with shame confess
His knowledge more, his reading only less.

Charles' dislike of reading, and preference for being read to, ensured steady employment for many actors and actresses, carefully chosen by Nell. They came in useful for the entertainments at Burford House, which was now completely redecorated and had a cellar as exciting as that in her town house.

On 18 August there was sad news from Stanmore Magna in Middlesex. Charles Hart had died at his home there. Nell sincerely mourned what a broadsheet called 'that worthy and famous actor' (he had retired in 1680). The best obituary was Elkana Settle's: 'But oh, that their oracle [of the Theatre Royal, as the King's House was now often called] should be quite silent ... the best tragedies of the English Stage have received that lustre from Mr Hart's performance ... he has left such an impression behind him, that no less than the interval of an age can make them appear again with half their majesty from any second Hand.' Shortly afterwards, Tom Killigrew died, mourned by both the King and Nell.

Somewhat downhearted by the fire, the assassination plot and the deaths, the King decided that the way to cheer himself up was to have a complete change. For some time he had been discussing with Sir Christopher Wren the idea of building a Palace at Winchester, a modest emulation of Louis XIV's at Versailles. Winchester would become an alternative capital – after all, it had once been the capital of England – and the King could spend less and less time in London, which was obviously not safe and had become duller with the closure of the Duke's House (the two companies merged). The drawings were ready and the King gave orders that the building should be started on the site of the old castle. It was to be in the Classical style, something like a Villa Veneta, with Palladian porticos and colonnades and a tree-lined avenue leading to the cathedral. Courtiers were invited to build their own houses along the avenue, and Nell discussed a project for one while out hawking with Sir Christopher and the King (she was very fond of hawking and knew a great deal about the sport – during that summer the King gave her son the office of Grand Falconer of England on the death of Sir Allen Apsley). In Paris a design has come to light, probably by Vigarani, who built the theatre in the Palace at Versailles, for an 'Opera' at Winchester, and no doubt Nell had a hand in that.

Louise was out of favour in September, and not only because she was tactless enough to pour scorn on an attempt to build a rival to the Sun King's Palace at Versailles. Hortense's nephew, Philippe de Vendôme, Grand Prior of France, arrived in England. He was a handsome twenty-eight-year-old, a bastard grandson of Henry IV (and so a cousin of Charles), and he was glib and greedy. He had heard of Louise's enormous wealth and fading beauty (she was thirty-five and sagging everywhere) and made a set at her. He was in her bed in record time; for the first time in her life she lost her head and heart completely. The French Ambassador reported that she was besotted and showered the young man with gifts. In view of her well-known meanness, it was this which impressed Barillon with the sincerity of her feelings, and he was worried lest she should be dismissed by Charles and lose her position at Court. The King found out about the affaire (or was told) and expelled Vendôme from England, sending an angry note to Louis XIV about this scandalous conduct; Louis replied hoping that the foolish fellow 'would not be allowed to mar the reputation of the dear Duchess'. Lord Bruce recorded in his Diary that this episode marked the beginning of the end for Louise: 'I have good reason to believe that he [Charles] was seeking by degrees to have her to retire.' She was not dismissed, however, and the City of York, which had made her son its High Steward, was pleased to learn that its burgesses would still have access to Court (the boy had great wealth in the North, enjoying a charge on every tone of coal shipped from the Tyne).

Louise did go to France for a holiday, and this was celebrated by the balladeers in *The Duchess of Portsmouth's Garland*:

> When Portsmouth did from England fly, to follow her Vendôme,
> Thus all along the Gally the monarch made his moan,
> O Chantillion, for charity, send me my Cleaveland home!
> Go, Nymph, so foolish and unkind, your wandering Knight pursue
> And leave a love-sick King behind, so faithful and so true,
> You Gods, when you made Love blind, you should have lam'd him too.

She took the opportunity to call on the King of France; Barillon had written praising her recent activities on their behalf: 'The truth about her is, that she has shown great, constant and intelligent zeal for Your Majesty's interests, and given me numberless useful hints and pieces of information.'

While she was gone, Monmouth reappeared and threw himself on the King of England's mercy. Charles pardoned him, as was to be expected, but was furious when the boy retracted his confession, and he was banished 'to Hell or Holland'.

When Hortense lost one of her bohemian lovers in a duel and threatened to become a nun, this was not taken very seriously, but the ludicrous prospect cheered up the King, who even welcomed Buckingham back to Court.

The winter of 1683-4 was the last really happy one in Nell's life. She was sure of the King's devotion, and all her rivals seemed to have faded from the scene (she was called 'the Church of England's Whore' in a new ballad). In December 1883 it was so cold that the Thames froze solid, and she and Charles amused themselves by building a pavilion on the ice and entertaining there; the King, her son and the Duke of Grafton spent hours skating together and would come back with enormous appetites for the meals Nell prepared for them.

With the death of the Earl of St Albans, the title became vacant, and on 5 January Nell's son was made Duke of St Albans (with lodgings in Whitehall and £1,500 a year for himself).

She prepared for her own enjoyment a set of miniatures of all the paintings done of the royal whores by Lely, Verelst, Gascar and Mignard, and copies of her own portraits by Lely and Verelst; she then had made an ingenious 'componable image', a portrait of herself on which she would change her clothes to show the roles she had made famous on the stage (it is now in the Army and Navy Club). Aubrey sent the new Duke of St Albans an account of his discovery of the Avebury stone circles and to Nell a copy of his *The Idea of the Education of a Young Gentleman;* he was in mild disfavour for having been staying with a Catholic friend during 'the Plot' and wanted to remind the King that he had shown him Avebury some years earlier.

Charles also gave Nell the lease of a house and garden, and a stable, in Priest Street, Windsor (she is described as 'Ellenor Gwinn' of St Martin-in-the-Fields, Middlesex) and some land 'in a place there called the Old Hawes between the King's garden there on the north part, and the garden of sundry persons on the west and south parts and the little park of Windsor'. The Dean of Windsor and Provost of Eton College witnessed her initials, EG; it took nearly a year to prepare the documents (she planned to enlarge the house for her son) and she was not pleased.

Nell was short of money again. She had to pawn some jewels; there is a short note, preserved by her bank, asking a Mr Jackson to come to collect them and dispose of them. She had to mortgage Bestwood Park to Sir John Musters for over £3,000, and she was still writing to the Duke of Ormonde about her Irish revenues in February 1684. She seems to have cut down the size of her household, with one public excuse or another, and on 25 February, 1684 wrote to the Duke 'praying Your Grace to give [John Clare] some command in the army of Ireland. I have spoken to the King for him and the King said he would have spoken to your Grace, but least he might forgett it, he bad me do it.' She replaced the tutor with Peter de Launé, no longer needed by the Duke of York, so that the boy could get some glimmerings of the language in preparation for his forthcoming trip to France. But it is typical of her that, 'As she was driving up Ludgate Hill, she saw a poor clergyman in the hands of the sheriff's officers and, struck with compassion, she lighted from her carriage, inquired into the circumstances of his arrest, and paid his debt on the spot; and finding on application to the vouchers he named, that his character was as unexceptionable as his misfortunes were real, she generously befriended him and his family.' This gesture endeared her to her vicar, Dr Tenison, who asked her to intervene with the King on behalf of Huguenot refugees (she helped to settle Dent the watchmaker, Vaillant the bookseller, the Le Beck restaurant in Bedford Square and the Huguenot silk market at Charing Cross); Charles gave her and Tenison some money, but said the vicar's purse was because he 'got curates collecting and cataloguing books to keep them out of the coffee-houses'.

At Easter that year, the King made an unusual gesture, often described as an omen. Evelyn recorded in his Diary for 30 March 1684: 'Hence I went again to Whitehall, where *coram Rege*, preached the B: of Rochester on a text out of Hosea 6.2 touching the subject of the day: After with his Majestie, accompanied with 3 of his natural Sonns (viz. the Dukes of Northumb: Richmond and St Albans, base sonns of Portsmouth, Cleaveland, Nelly – prostitute creatures) went up to the Altar.'

After Easter, Nell paid a visit to one of the Duke of York's former whores, now Lady Williams, who was about to move from St James's Square, and fell in love with some gold ornaments. She had to have them, and because she was still short of money had to petition Pepys to have the Commissioner of Excise, another friend, Ashmole, pay for them. Cunningham records that in a letter to a superior seamstress, 'Madame Jennings, over against the Tub Tavern in Jermyn Street' (mother of Sarah, mother-in-law of John Churchill), she shows the chaos she had to struggle through to put her life into some sort of temporary order:

Madame, I have received your letter and I desire you would speak to my Lady Williams to send me the gold stuff and a note with it, because I must sign it, ye next day, of Mr Trant [the Commissioner]; pray tell her ladyship that I will send her a note of what quantity of things I'll have bought, if her ladyship will put herself to the trouble; when they are bought I will sign a note for her to be paid. Pray, Madame, let my man go with my sedan, and send Potevine [her upholsterer] and Mr Coker down to me for I want them both. The bill to boil the plate is very dear but necessity hath no law. I am afraid, Madame, you have forgot my mantle, which you were to line with musk colour satin, and all my other things, for you send me no patterns or answer. Monsieur Lianey is going away. Please send me word about your son Griffin, for his Majesty is mighty well pleased that he will go along with my Lord Duke [of St Albans]. I am afraid you are so much taken with your own house that you forget my business. My service to Lord Kildare and tell him I love him with all my heart. Pray, Madame, see that Potevine brings now all my things with him, My Lord Duke's bed etc., if he hath not made them up he may do that here [she was writing from Burford House, Windsor], for if I do not get my things out of his hands now, I shall not have them until this time twelvemonth. The Duke brought me down with him my crochet of diamonds; and I love it the better because he brought it. Mr Lumley and everybody else will tell you that it is the finest thing that ever was seen. Good Madame, speak to Mr Beaver [a jeweller] to come down, too, that I may bespeak a ring for the Duke of Grafton before he goes to France. I have continued extreme ill ever since you left me, and I am so still. I believe I shall die. My service to the Duchess of Norfolk, and tell her I am as sick as her Grace, but I do not know what I ail, although she does, which I am overjoyed that she does with her great belly. Pray tell my Lady Williams that the King's mistresses are accounted ill paymasters, but she shall have her money the next day after I have the stuff. Here is a sad slaughter at Windsor, the young men taking their leaves and going to France, and although they are none of my lovers, yet I am loath to

part with the men. Mrs Jennings, I love you will all my heart and so
goodbye! EG.

The migration to France of ambitious young men was to join the armies of
the Holy Roman Empire which, under the Polish King Jan Sobieski, had just
defeated the Turks at Vienna; the Duke of Grafton (his mother, Barbara
Cleveland, regretted it) was a sailor, about to join the Royal Navy, and Nell's
own son was off to enter the French Military Academy.

In May she was at Newmarket with the King, and then with him at
Windsor. In August Charles moved his Court to Winchester for the hawking
and to see how his palace was progressing. There Nell fell foul of the
prebendary of the cathedral, a royal chaplain called Thomas Ken. When Ken
was asked to put her up, because she had no house of her own in
Winchester, and the King liked to have her always close by, he replied: 'A
woman of ill repute ought not to be endured in the house of a clergyman,
least of all in that of the King's Chaplain.' In order to prevent her being
billeted on him against his will, he had the roof taken off his house and slept
in the cathedral. Dr Leggot, the Dean, was more hospitable and built a suite,
with a separate entrance for her, at one end of the Deanery; unfortunately
for him, it was damp, and she had to move to Avington, home of the
Countess of Shrewsbury, where the Duke of Buckingham was also staying.
The King was very amused by the incident and said so to Tenison (after
granting money for his, the first, lending library). Shortly afterwards, when a
bishopric became vacant, Charles called Halifax to him and said: ' 'Odsfish!
Who should have Bath and Wells if not that little black fellow who huffed
Nelly and would not give her a lodging?'

During the autumn, Nell's health seems to have improved and she began
to entertain again. The Duke of York went to one of her soirées at which
Henry Bowman sang, and Pepys went to a dinner in his honour when he
became President of the Royal Society. Another unusual guest was William
Penn, back from founding Pennsylvania (the land was granted to him as a
payment for royal debts to his father, former Lord High Admiral); Penn
brought with him his wife Maria ('Great cures she does, having great skill in
physic and surgery'), so maybe Nell was in her care.

On 23 October Evelyn wrote in his Diary:

I dined at Sir Stephen Foxes with the Duke of Northumberland,
another of his Majestie's natural sonns, by that strumpet Cleaveland:
He seemed to be a Young gent, of good capacity, wellbred, civile and
modest, had been newly come from Travell, and had made his
Campagne at the siege of Luxemburg: Of all his Majestie's children this
seemed the most accomplished, and worth the owning; he is likewise
extraordinary handsome and wellshaped: what the Dukes of

Richmond and St Albans, base sonns of the Dutchesse of Portsmouth a French lasse, and of Nelly, the Comedian and Applewoman's daughter, will prove their youth does not discover, farther than they are both very pretty boys and seeme to have more Witt than the rest.

St Albans was a constant companion of his father, and Nell seems to have given up the idea of sending him to Paris to complete his education. She was worried about the King's health. He was no longer such an early riser, and he had given up playing tennis and pall mall. When he was young, he had taken no notice of the weather, but now he found excuses (it was a cold winter) to take virtually no exercise out of doors, limiting himself to a stroll in St James's Park twice a day. As Christmas approached, he had to give up even the walk in the park because an ulcer opened on his left leg; Bruce had to take him out and about in a carriage. His only consolation was a brief visit from Monmouth, whom he had pardoned yet again and had given permission to return to England in the New Year; he said he wanted all his boys about him. At Nell's Christmas party he seemed a little stronger, but he could not dance.

On Sunday 1 February 1685, the King spent what started out as the usual domestic Sabbath. He began the day with a short drive with Bruce, then listened to Dr Dove preach at Divine Service in his private chapel. He had a good lunch with the Queen, then slept for most of the afternoon, complaining that his leg was hurting him. By the evening, thanks to Mrs Holder, he had recovered sufficiently to go to a party in Louise's apartment. Evelyn, who was there, noted: 'I saw this evening such a scene of profuse gaming ... about twenty of the great courtiers and other dissolute persons were at basset round a large table, a bank of at least £2,000 in gold before them ... and the King in the midst of his concubines ... luxurious dallying and profaneness.' Hortense's page sang, as well as Henry Bowman, and there was other 'Musique'.

The King withdrew early and went to his bedroom with Lord Thomas Bruce. The King was cheerful, as Bruce wrote later: 'As soon as he had put on his nightgown, he went to ease himself, and often more out of custom than necessity, by reason nobody would come in there but the gentleman and groom in waiting; and there he laughed and was most merry and diverting.' It was said that a candle blew out, though there was no wind, and that this was a bad omen, but it did not upset Charles. He talked for over an hour about his new palace at Winchester which was to have its roof leaded that week, and reproved Bruce for not having been to see it. Then he lay down to sleep 'though several circumstances made the lodging very uneasy – the great grate filled with Scotch coal that burnt all night; a dozen dogs came to our bed, and several pendulums that struck at the half and quarter and all not going alike it was a continual chiming. The King being constantly used to it, it was habitual.' However, the King did not have a quiet night and tossed and turned on the high bed. He woke early and dressed, though he was pale and seemed to have difficulty with his speech. He said: 'It is Nelly's birthday today' (it was her thirty-fifth) and asked Bruce what he thought he should give her. Then his barber came in, with a Dr King who was to dress his leg, but as the barber settled the cloth about his neck preparatory to shaving him, he stiffened, stood up, then fell into Bruce's arms 'in a most violent fit of apoplexy'.

Immediately, Bruce sent for more doctors (King was already drawing Charles' blood, though he ought to have had permission from the Privy Council to do so) and for the Duke of York, who slopped in wearing one shoe and one slipper. Bruce and James helped Charles back to bed, and more doctors arrived and began to dose him, bleed him and blister him to keep him conscious. The Queen arrived and stayed at his bedside uninterruptedly for two days, then could stand it no more and asked Bruce to beg the King's pardon for being unable to carry on. Charles commented: 'Alas, poor woman! She beg my pardon! I beg hers with all my heart!' Louise and Hortense were said to be distraught, but were not allowed even into the antechamber, so shut themselves up in their apartments. Nell was excluded, too, and so were Mrs Holder and Mrs Penn (they knew what sort of primitive medicine and surgery would be inflicted on him).

The French Ambassador called on Louise to offer his sympathy and he reported later that, while unwilling to discuss the political consequences of the King's eventual death (rumoured to be imminent), she was worried about his immortal soul. She told Barillon that the King had told her he had been received into the Roman Catholic Church but she could not remember when. He must have a priest, but, of course, none of her Jesuits would be allowed near him. What was to be done? Barillon then hurried to the royal bedchamber to offer his condolences to the Duke of York, and managed to get James on one side and tell him what Louise had said. In view of the chaos and confusion caused by, among others, the new Bishop of Bath and Wells, who kept trying to get the King to receive the Anglican sacraments, James kept his head very well. In a whisper he asked his brother if he wanted a priest; Charles said he did, Father Huddleston if possible. The old priest was quickly found and came in disguise up the backstairs to confess the King and to give him absolution and extreme unction; the man who had saved his life after the battle of Worcester had the satisfaction of saving his soul.

On Thursday the King's condition grew worse. He was still lucid and could joke with his doctors. When they told him not to talk, he said, 'That would have killed Tom Killigrew!' He also made his famous apology for 'being such an unconscionable time dying'. He called to his bedside five of his six bastard dukes, St Albans, Grafton, Northumberland, Southampton and Richmond (Monmouth was still in exile) and they knelt to receive their father's blessing.

On Friday morning he woke at dawn and asked Bruce to have the curtains drawn for the last time so that he could see the daylight. To his brother, according to Evelyn, 'He spoke to be kind to the Dutchesse of Cleaveland and especially Portsmouth, and that Nelly might not starve.' Then he fell into a coma, and shortly afterwards Good King Charles' Golden Days were no more.

Nelly knew he was gone when the passing bell began to sound at St Martin-in-the-Fields. Weeping, she is said to have declaimed the words to one of Charles' favourite songs:

> The glories of our blood and state
> Are shadows, not substantial things.
> There is no armour against fate;
> Death lays his icy hands on kings.

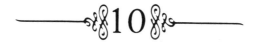

The Last Outrage, 1685-7

Nor would Nelly long be his survivor.
Alas! who was now good enough to drive her?
So she gave way to her consuming grief,
Which brought her past all galley-pot relief.
Howe'er it were, as the old women say,
'Her time was come, and then there's no delay':
So down the Stygian Lake she dropt.

Etherege

Charles II was almost universally mourned, but, paradoxically, there was no great public display of grief, no lying-in-state and no funeral procession through the streets. He was buried at night in Westminster Abbey, in a tomb which was not only undecorated but which for two hundred years bore no inscription, not even his name.

His reign had been a long one, and not without success, but Evelyn gave him little credit for achievement: 'God was incensed to make his reign very troublesome and unprosperous by wars, plagues, fires, loss of reputation by a universal neglect of the public for the love of a voluptuous and sensual life, which a vicious court had brought into credit. I think of it with sorrow and pity when I consider how good and debonair a nature that unhappy prince was; what opportunities he had to make himself the most renowned King that ever swayed the British sceptre.'

Evelyn was less than generous. After an unhappy childhood and early manhood, exile and poverty, Charles had returned to his kingdoms to general acclamation. He had found a country in turmoil, depressed by years of Puritan humbug and hypocrisy, and put a smile back on his subjects' faces. It is certainly true that he spent a lot of time at the races and with women, most of whom were worthless. However, he revived interest in the theatre and encouraged writers of all sorts, tolerating even those like Bunyan and Milton who had views opposed to his own. He brought into being and actively patronized the Royal Society, and could claim to have helped such scientists as Isaac Newton, Robert Boyle, Robert Hooke and Edmund

181

Halley, and to have given a fillip to the systematic study of physics, astronomy, chemistry, agriculture, history and the English language. He was witty and urbane, as those ill-assorted Fellows, Evelyn, Aubrey and Pepys testified in their different ways. Above all he set an example 'to persons of quality who now apply themselves to chemistry, mechanism and mathematics', as Sorbière put it.

Charles also kept more promises than most monarchs, including the one to himself: 'I am weary of travelling and am resolved to go abroad no more. But when I am dead and gone I know not what my brother will do: I am much afraid that when he comes to wear the crown he will be obliged to travel again. And yet I will take care to leave my kingdoms to him in peace, wishing he may keep them so. But this hath all of my fears, little of my hopes and less of my reason.' (Lord Thomas Bruce)

His prophecy was accurate, but James was not at all pessimistic. 'Good King Charles' Golden Days' they may have been, but now the people were anxious for a change of style. James was popular, the Exclusion crisis apparently forgotten; his subjects remembered the hero of Lowestoft and the refurbishing of the Royal Navy after the disasters which followed. He was known to be hardworking, honest and loyal. He was outwardly sober and righteous, though he shared his late brother's weakness for women; fortunately, people said, his whores were cheaper, the chief of them, Catherine Sedley, the daughter of the poet and playwright and a cultivated woman (she said she did not know why James loved her – 'It cannot be my beauty, because I haven't any, and it cannot be my wit because he doesn't have enough to know that I have any').

The only doubt people had in their minds was about James' Catholicism. He reassured them: 'I know the principles of the Church of England are for monarchy and the members of it have shewed themselves good and loyal subjects, therefore I shall always take care to defend and support it.' Anyway, the Queen was no longer young and had been unable to give the nation a Catholic heir; across the waters in Holland waited Protestant William and Mary, who would no doubt step peacefully into James' shoes. The coronation of James and Maria on 23 April 1685 was held to be an occasion for rejoicing; a hundred Tory squires with whom James had hunted overcame their dislike of London and came to cheer.

Nell Gwyn did not attend the coronation. She was deeply distressed by the death of Charles and spoke to nobody for a month after it; swathed in a black cloak, she had stood in a corner of the abbey while he was buried, and when the official mourners had gone was allowed by the guards to put flowers on the tomb. She was rather upset when she was forbidden 'to put her house in mourning, or to use that sort of nails about her coach and chair which it seems is kept as a distinction for the royal family on such occasions', but Louise Portsmouth was likewise forbidden to behave like a member of the royal family.

Now Nell had to shift for herself. Her problem was that, though Sir Charles Lyttleton estimated that she was worth £100,000, only £2,000 a year was income and the rest was in jewels, plate and property. She decided to appeal to the King. She had always got on well with James, had entertained him often and, indeed, had named one of her sons after him with his permission (as she pointed out to the Earl of Tyrconnel). She wrote asking for an audience: 'Had I suferd for my God as I have done for yr brother and you, I should not have needed other of yr kindness or justice to me. I beseech you not to doe anything to the settling of my buisness till I speake with you and apoynt me by Mr Grahams when I may speake with you privetly. God make you as happy as my soule prayes you to be.'

'Mr Grahams' was Colonel Richard Graham, who administered some of the Secret Service Funds she had tapped in the past. Nell need not have worried. James had no intention of letting her starve. He received her in May and gave her £500 to tide her over until her affairs could be put in order. Graham urged James Booth, Nell's secretary, to make a list of all her debts, especially those to tradesmen, and they would be paid as soon as possible; £792. 2s. 3d. was paid out by September, settling most of her accounts, and she was given another £500 'bounty'.

Nell acknowledged James' promptness and kindness: 'This world is not capable of giving me a greater joy and happynes than yr Majesties favour, not as you are King and soe have it in yr poer to do me good, haveing never loved yr brother and yr selfe upon that account, but as to yr persons. Had hee lived, hee told me before he dyed, that the world shud see by what hee did for me that hee had both love and value for me. ... He was my friend and allowed me to tell him all my grifes, and did like a friend advise me and tould me who was my friend and who was not.'

She may have derived some extra satisfaction from the knowledge that she was treated with much more consideration than her rivals. The 'occasional' whores lost everything. Moll Davis had to sell her house in St James's Square. Hortense Mazarin lost her £4,000 a year and had to sell her house in Chelsea and move into a cottage in Fulham; she died, impoverished, on 2 June 1699. Barbara Cleveland was allowed to return to England but lost everything other than her £4,700 from the postal revenues; she went on gamely looking for men to service her (even among her servants) and eventually 'married' a bigamist (Robert Fielding), who stole most of what she had left and left her to die in a cottage in Stanmore on 9 October 1709. Louise Portsmouth lost her £25,000 from Irish estates but kept £5,000 in rents and her postal revenues; she died nearly fifty years later, according to Voltaire, '*une figure encore noble et agréable, que les années n'avaient pas flétrie*' – 'still handsome and agreeable, whom the years had not withered'.

Colonel Graham told Nell that she had been well treated, and tried to explain the difference between the King's attitude to her and to the other 'ladies', but his accent was so thick that she declared she had not understood. She often said she found the Scots incomprehensible, though her Scots acquaintances ranged from Madam Ross, the whore-mistress, to Sir Robert Moray, President of the Royal Society at its inception, and included, of course, two Scots kings. When Sir Robert had tried to explain to her that, if and when he acceded, James would be King James VII of Scotland and II of England, but Charles was Charles II of both countries, she made the famous retort: 'He is my Charles III' – after Hart and Buckhurst. What is certain is that she did appreciate the fact that the King overlooked her friendship with James, Duke of Monmouth. While she was having her first audience of the new King, Monmouth was plotting to overthrow his father's brother.

The Netherlands – Holland in particular – prided themselves on being a place of political asylum for all. They had harboured the Stewarts, and they harboured their enemies. At the accession of James VII and II, Monmouth was keeping company with a rag tag and bobtail of former Cromwellians, Fifth Monarchy Men, Anabaptists and Scottish bigots led by the Earl of Argyll. Somehow, he let himself be convinced that a substantial part of the population of England and Scotland was ready to rise, overthrow the Catholic King and put the Protestant bastard in his place. In 2 May 1685 Argyll sailed for Scotland, with a band of officers hurriedly recruited, declaring that he would raise Clan Campbell and deliver Scotland from the Stewarts and the horrors of Popishness; this was an odd assertion as he was declaring his intent to replace a legitimate Stewart with an illegitimate one. Unfortunately for him, he failed to reach even the Campbell stronghold of Inveraray; he was captured and executed, his followers were branded and transported as slaves to the West Indies. In England, Monmouth was a little more successful, though Argyll's defeat discouraged his friends in Cheshire and the capital. Support was, however, forthcoming in the West Country, especially in Devon and Somerset. He made his way to Taunton, with a rabble carrying muskets, scythes and homemade halberds, and there was proclaimed King.

James was very calm when he heard of the uprising. He put his army under the command of the French Earl of Feversham, who had been trained by Turenne; Churchill and Kirke held subordinate commands. Slowly the loyalist forces closed in on Monmouth, who hesitated before Bristol (which he could have taken) and fell back towards Bridgewater. Though his troops were badly armed, they were more numerous than the King's, and he decided to attack the royal army on Sedgemoor. Typically, he failed to hire a local guide and got himself bogged down. His followers were hacked to pieces and he fled.

Monmouth was found a few days later hiding in a ditch in the New Forest and was taken by Lord Lumley (commanding the Sussex Militia) back to London. On 15 July he was executed – Jack Ketch tried to sever his head five times with the axe, then finished the work with a butcher's knife. As Evelyn said: 'Thus ended this quondam duke, darling of his father and the ladies, debauched by lusts, seduced by crafty knaves.' Those of his followers in the West Country who survived were either shot immediately by Colonel Kirke and his 'Lambs' or later hanged by Judge Jeffreys.

The Monmouth affair caused a great deal of heart-searching among his friends. Many, of course, denied him. It is to Nell Gwyn's great credit that she did not do so, and may even have pleaded for his life, as she had with Charles. Aubrey burned his Life of the traitor. Dryden, who had dedicated *The Indian Emperor* to the Duchess of Monmouth and *Tyrannic Love* to the Duke himself, as Shadwell's friends recalled maliciously, declared himself a Catholic; Evelyn believed that Nell Gwyn had become a Catholic, too, and reported that he had seen them both at Mass – 'Such proselytes were no greate loss to the Church [of England]'. Many ambitious men and frightened friends of the late 'quondam duke' were converted, including James' brother-in-law, the Earl of Sunderland, and the Drummond brothers, James (who became Duke of Perth) and John (Earl of Melfort). It was this sudden rush to Rome which first dimmed the new King's popularity.

Historians have long debated the rapidity with which James dissipated the goodwill and affection which surrounded him that winter of 1685-6. Two years later he was deposed. What did he do wrong? Nell Gwyn always thought him kind but hamfisted in everything he did, and her judgement has much to commend it. He was a despot and told his first Parliament that he wanted his revenues for life; he would not be subjected to inquiry and have his money doled out to him. However, he was not the first despot to surface in English history, and Parliament did not object to his desire for independence; it was the hectoring tone he had inherited from his father which offended and alienated even supporters. James was mean and always tried to avoid paying debts; he owed Pepys £28,000 for work at the Admiralty and as Treasurer of Tangiers and haggled over it to the end of his brief reign. Somehow, his closest servants did not seem to resent this and remained loyal; they defended him by saying he did not believe in buying friends or wasting the country's resources. He was tempted to join in the war against the Turks but resisted the temptation and so pleased the City. And contrary to many people's belief, he had no intention of taking England or Scotland by force back into the Roman Catholic Church: he believed not only in tolerance but also that conversion could be achieved by persuasion.

It was probably his choice of ministers, as much as his policies, which destroyed James and the Stewart dynasty. The Drummond brothers became too powerful too soon (the Duke of Perth Chief Agent in Scotland and the Earl of Melfort Scottish Secretary in London); they also proclaimed their new-found faith too loudly and upset even moderate Protestant opinion. In Ireland the Earl of Tyrconnel, as Lieutenant-General of the Irish Army did not hide his hopes for an independent Catholic Ireland; this was immediately interpreted as a threat of eventual invasion, probably supported by the French. Jeffreys was an able judge, but it was unwise to appoint a man known as a hangman to the office of Lord Chancellor. It was even less wise to appoint Jeffreys and the Catholic convert Earl of Sunderland to head an Ecclesiastical Commission with power to dismiss intolerant bishops; their first act, to deprive the Bishop of London of his living, upset everybody.

In 1686, however, these were only shadows of coming events. Life seemed to go on much as before, and there was certainly no Puritan reaction to the licence personified by Nell, Moll, Barbara and Louise. Nell began to go to the theatre again and was importuned by John German (Germaine), supposedly the bastard son of William of Orange; she refused him, saying she 'would not lay the dog where the deer had lain' and told him to keep himself for Mary Howard, for German was, in fact, cuckolding the Howard Duke of Norfolk at the time.

On one occasion the Duchess and German left London for Windsor quite openly together and, after an evening of cards with Nell and Colonel Henry Cornwall, retired together to bed. Next morning, as a witness said in the eventual divorce trial: 'Mrs Nelly Gwyn came in and asked the Duchess "How did you rest last night?" and asked after Sir John, seeing that she had obviously had a hot night enough to put her hair out of powder and curl, too. The Duchess said she did not know where Sir John was. When Colonel Cornwall came to call, Mrs Nelly said "Well, we will see him come out bye and bye like a drowned rat." ' The cuckolded Duke seldom came to Town, administered three counties for the King and was a great opponent of religious toleration. When James first mooted the repeal of the Test Act and other penal sanctions, he told him he could 'bring all those in favour of repeal up with him in his coach without the least harm to his horses'.

Nell may have emerged again in society but she was very short of money. She wanted to remain faithful to Charles' memory, and James was characteristically careful: though he gave her a new pension on 1 January 1686 (£1,500 a year) and paid off her mortgage on Bestwood Park (£3,774. 2s. 6d.), he handed out money only via her trustees. In December she had to sell her pearls and was in a hurry to have the money; a letter Booth sent from 79 Pall Mall on 10 December urges her banker Mr Child to 'send her the balance of the account I had from Mr Jackson – this note my Lady commanded me to send you last night.' She often tried to break her various trusts but never succeeded.

The problem solved itself. In March 1687 Nell was taken very ill again and this time became partly paralysed.

Some idea of the esteem in which she was held at the time may be had from the fact that she was attended by Dr Richard Lower, one of the leading physicians of the day (Aubrey accuses him of claiming to be the inventor of blood-transfusion, a technique perfected by Aubrey's friend Frances Potter) and a Fellow of the Royal Society. Lower's interests also tends to disprove any suggestion that Nell had become a Catholic, for he was a militant Protestant from Bodmin; Anthony à Wood records that he 'had the Protestant interest much at heart'.

Some biographers have suggested that Nell was brought to her first serious illness by syphilis. As she was not promiscuous and for more than a decade had had sexual relations only with Charles II, this would mean that she had caught it from him. But Aubrey makes no mention of this, and he was always quick to record a pox or a clap caught by a notable, like some precursor of a Department of Health zealot. The King's venereal diseases were quickly cured and the general assumption has been that he gave it only to Louise Portsmouth. The notes left by Dr Lower do not make it clear what Nell died of, except 'apoplexy' (*Ellis Correspondence*); in Bax's biography, a surgeon offers it as his opinion that the apoplexy 'was almost certainly due to syphilis'. Whatever the truth, she remained lucid for most of the time, and Richard Lower enjoyed her reminiscences of Court life; he had been one of the favourite doctors (with Scarborough) of Charles II and had been in attendance at the last.

Dr Tenison, Vicar of St Martin-in-the-Fields, was a frequent visitor to the sickroom and brought with him on several occasions the former French Ambassador, the Marquis de Ruvigny. Evelyn records that de Ruvigny was in London at the head of a congregation 'of about 100 French Protestants refugies from the Persecution' and they seemed to have used St Martin's; this was courageous of Tenison, of whom Evelyn says: 'The pains he takes and care of his parish will, I feare, weare him out, which would be an inexpressible loss.' He was known to be the best preacher in England and an uncompromising Christian; he had agreed to the Duke of Monmouth's request that he attend him on the scaffold, and Nell also respected him for that. She gave de Ruvigny a purse for his refugees and said that England was the better for having them than the departed Louise.

By the end of June, Nell had been told by Lower that she was dying. Like any mother, she was worried about her son: he had left her to go to fight in the Imperial Army, then driving the Turks down the Danube (he may have been present at the sack of Buda and certainly distinguished himself at the siege of Belgrade). He was not very bright, but courageous. Would he survive when she had gone? He would have a considerable estate, and before she returned to Portugal, Catherine of Braganza had made him an allowance of £2,000 a year. Would he waste it all, perhaps gamble away the money as she would have done?

She need not have worried. The young Duke of St Albans might not have inherited his father's intelligence or intellect, but he was just as affable. He managed to be all things to all men and seems to have had no enemies; unlike Waller, Davenant, Churchill and Halifax, he was never accused of trimming nor, like his half-brother the Duke of Grafton (who, with Churchill, deserted his King and uncle in 1688), of being a traitor. He was tactfully absent when his uncle was dethroned, and on his return to England became a favourite of William III, the Dutchman who had done the dethroning. Under William and Mary, the Duke was Captain of the Gentleman Pensioners and Lord of the Bedchamber, among other stewardships and lieutenancies. He also served Anne Stewart well (in spite of the emnity of Sarah Churchill), but when the choice had to be made in 1714 between the legitimate successor, his Catholic cousin James VIII and III, and the Protestant Hanoverians in the person of George I, he chose the Whig candidate. He was installed a Knight of the Garter by George I and died full of age and honours in 1726 while taking the waters at Bath. His father had found an heiress for him, Lady Diana de Vere, daughter of the Earl of Oxford (grandson of the Earl who farted in Queen Elizabeth's face and banished himself from Court for five years), and they had five children.

The prospects for other friends and relatives were dimmer. Her old friend Rochester was dead and his title gone to another friend, Lory Hyde. Buckingham had died shortly after she had taken to her sick bed; he 'yielded up the ghost at Helmesley in Yorkshire in a little ale house were these eight months he hath been without meat or money, deserted of all his servants almost'. He had caught a cold after a day in the hunting field, and his body, weakened by other excesses, could not fight back. Nell was sorry to be unable to attend the funeral in Westminster Abbey. Henry Savile was dying. Peg Hughes was back on the stage but not doing too well. The Duchess of Norfolk was in a French nunnery, and Arabella Churchill was now respectably married (Mrs Godfrey). Town was certainly not what it had been.

At the beginning of July Dr Lower's place was taken by Dr Christian Harel. He had also been one of Charles II's physicians; they had met at The Hague, where Harel was born, while Charles was still in exile. The new doctor's task was to make Nell's last few months as comfortable as possible, and he apparently enjoyed a certain reputation in the therapy of pain. He had no personal relationship with his patient and, indeed, presented his bill for £109 'for all remedies and medicins delivrd to Mrs Ellin Gwyn deceased' three days after her death.

She made her will that month and chose her executors well. Lory Hyde, now Earl of Rochester, was chief of these, with Sir Robert Sawyer ('a dull fat man and forward to serve all the designs of the Court'), Henry Sidney and Thomas, eighth Earl of Pembroke, a mathematician who was soon to become President of the Royal Society. The will was witnessed by her secretary James Booth, Lady Hamilton Sandys, Edward Wybourne, Bishop John Warner and William Scarborough. This first testament was a very simple one, leaving everything to 'my dear natural son, His Grace the Duke of St Albans and the heirs of his body', with the exception of a payment to the executors of 'one hundred pounds of lawful money apiece, in consideration of their care and trouble herein, and furthermore all there severall and respective expenses'.

During the months of August and September Dr Tenison was again a frequent visitor. He was sad to know that his unusual parishioner was dying. He knew that Nell enjoyed his visits and what Evelyn called 'his holy conversation, very learned and ingeniose', and he enjoyed her company. She was interested, he said later, in the reason for 'her' Charles' late conversion. Was it a 'real sentiment'? There could be nothing to gain on earth. Was it gratitude to Father Huddleston, miraculously at hand during the sudden, brief terminal illness? She had heard the story of Huddleston's part in the King's escape after Worcester many time from Charles. She asked him to explain what the new King was up to, taking on the Anglican Establishment and probably making some more 'travelling' inevitable? What would the Archbishop of Canterbury (William Sancroft) do about the suspension of the Bishop of London? What would the other bishops do? (Ely, St Asaph, Bath and Wells, Chichester, Bristol and Peterborough joined Canterbury in the rebellion which marked the beginning of the end of the reign.) What did he think about religious toleration? About sin? Would she, a whore, be saved?

Tenison was a Broad Church Anglican, disinclined to favour a return to Rome but totally loyal to the Head of the Church of England, even if that Head were a Roman Catholic. It was a position of great subtlety which she may or may not have appreciated. What is known is that on 18 October 1687 she added some new provisions to her will:

that I may be buried in the Church of St Martin-in-the-Fields;
that Dr Tenison may preach my funeral sermon;
that there may be a decent pulpit cloth and cushion given to St Martin-in-the-Fields;
that [the Duke of St Albans] would give £100 for the use of the poor of the said St Martin-in-the-Fields and St James Westminster, to be given into the hands of the said Dr Tenison for taking any poor debtors of the said parish out of prison, and for cloaths this winter, and other necessaries as he shall find most fit:
that for showing my charity to those who differ from me in religion, I desire that £50 may be put into the hands of any two persons of the Roman religion, may dispose of it for the use of the poor of that religion inhabiting the parish of St James aforesaid;

that Mrs Rose Forster [newly widowed again] may have £200 given to
her, any time within a year after my decease;
that Jo my porter may have £10 given to him;
that my present nurses may have £10 and mourning, besides the wages
due to each;
that £20 each year may be given for the release of poor debtors each
Christmas Day.

These provisions are a testament in themselves to Nell's charitable nature, as
well as her involvement, like that of all her fellow subjects, in the debate on
the freedom to worship as conscience dictates.

She died on 14 November 1687, and on 17 December (as Dr Harel was
getting paid in cash for his medicines) Tenison preached her funeral sermon
to a crowded church.

Just before she died, Nell Gwyn confided in James Booth that maybe she
had asked too much of the thirty-four-year-old, ambitious vicar. Maybe she
had compromised his elevation to a bishopric? Maybe 'certain persons'
would take it ill that he had spoken so eloquently of a whore? She was right
about the 'certain persons', among them Evelyn, but wrong about Tenison's
prospects. When there was a protest, some years later, about his elevation to
the See of Lincoln, Queen Mary observed: 'If I can read a man's heart
through his looks, had she not made a truly pious end the Doctor could
never have been induced to speak well of her.' Tenison went farther than
Lincoln on the Anglican road to ecclesiastical preferment. He became
Archbishop of Canterbury, lived to see the coming-in of the Hanoverians
and died in 1715.

What is left of Pretty Witty Nell now, other than her mortal remains
somewhere in the rebuilt crypt of St Martin-in-the-Fields, home of the
English down-and-out.

Until quite recently, she was remembered at the Savoy Chapel, where she
sometimes attended Divine Service. On the Sunday in the Octave of
Christmas, it was the custom to put a chair near the door of the chapel
(where she sat, a discreet distance from the King) and on the chair a cloth,
on that a plate with an orange on it. It was a way of remembering the
orange-girl, who perhaps more than anybody other than her master typifies
the Restoration.

Colley Cibber, the Hanoverian hack who did so much to give Grub Street
a bad name, is unusually generous to Nell Gwyn. He writes: ' ... if we
consider her in all the disadvantages of her rank and education, she does not
appear to have had any criminal errors more remarkable than her sex's frailty
to answer for ... she had less to be laid to her charge than any other of those
Ladies who were in the same state of preferment ... was as visibly

distinguished by her particular personal inclination to the King, as her rivals were by their titles and grandeur.'

For the millions who neither preach, write nor legislate, Nell Gwyn has become part of the sort of history sometimes classified as folklore. She was a folk heroine in her day, and all her causes seemed to have triumphed: the Protestant succession is so assured that even a present-day Prince could not take a Catholic bride without renouncing his claim to the throne; the Entente Cordiale is the right mixture of political rivalry and the triumph of French perfumes and cuisine; the Royal Hospital Chelsea is a secure home for old soldiers, who still drink her health; even her notion of constitutional monarchy, with the King at the racecourse and Parliament stalemating itself, seems to have prevailed.

What she would have thought of her name being used by a block of 'luxury flats' and a nursery school is difficult to say. She would enjoy the pubs which bear her name, even enjoy the fact that they still cannot agree on how it should be spelt.

Bibliography

Bibliography

Archivio di Stato (Gran Ducato di Toscana [Ingh. 1669]), Florence
Archivio di Stato (Rep. Serenissima [Relaz. Ingh. 1671-81]), Venice
Archives, Ministère des Relations Extérieures, Corr. Anglt., Vols. 72-76, 119-123, 130, 131, 154
Archives of Childs Bank (Glyn Mills), 1 Fleet Street, London
Biblioteca Nazionale Marciana (Relaz. Ingh. 1671-73), Venice
Bodleian Library, Oxford, All Souls MSS 171
British Museum Library, Harleian MSS 6914, 6913, 7319, 7317; Stowe MSS; Le Fleming MSS; State Papers Dom.; Add. MSS folio 59B 26683; State Trials, Vol. 12; Ballads on the Death of Madam Gwynne
Calendar of Treasury Books: Secret Service accounts of Charles II and James II, 1851
Camden Society Miscellany, Vol. 5
Greater London Council Record Office (St Martin-in-the-Fields Title Deeds)
Historical Manuscripts Commission Reports (esp. 2, 7, 9)
National Library of Dublin (Ormonde MSS)
Westminster City Public Library (St Martin-in-the-Fields Rate Books 1670-72)
Windsor, St George's Chapel MSS, Vols. X-XI

Aubrey, J., *Brief Lives*, ed. Powell (1959)
Bax, C., *Pretty Witty Nelly* (1932)
Bevan, B., *Nell Gwyn* (1969)
Boswell, E., *The Restoration Court Stage* (1932)
Browning, A., *The Earl of Danby* (1944)
Bryant, A., *King Charles II* (1933)
Burghclere, W., *Buckingham* (1903)
Burnet, G., *History of his own Time* (1723) (History of the Reign of Charles II Vol. 1); *Life of Rochester* (1681)
Cartwright, J., *Madame* (1900)
Chapman, H., *Privileged Persons, Four 17th-Century Studies* (1966)
Chesterton, C., *The Story of Nell Gwyn* (1911)

Chetwood, W.R.A., *General History of the English Stage* (1749)

Cibber, Colley, *Apology of his Life*, Vols. 1-2 (1740)

Cunningham, P., *Story of Nell Gwynne* (1852); ed. H.B. Wheatley (1892); ed. G. Goodwin (1908)

Dasent, A.I., *Nell Gwynne* (1924); *Private Life of Charles II* (1927); *History of St James Square* (1895)

Descriptive Catalogue of Naval MSS (1926)

Dryden, J., *Works*, ed. Sir W. Scott (1808); *Dryden's Mind and Art* ed. B. King (Edinburgh, 1969); *Essential Articles for the Study of John Dryden*, ed. H.T. Swedenborg (Hamden, Conn., 1966)

Ellis, J., *The Correspondence, 1686-88*

Etherege, G., *Letter Book* (1928)

Evelyn, J., *Memoirs*, Vols. 1-111 (OUP, 1959)

Fairburn, J. (ed. plus comment), *Life, Amours and Exploits of Nell Gwin* (1820)

Firpo, L., *Ambasciatori Veneti in Inghilterra* (UTET, Milan, 1978)

Forneron, J., *Louise de Keroualle* (Paris, 1887)

Genest, J., *Account of the English Stage, 1660-1830* (1832)

Grignan, Comtesse de, *Letters from Marquise de Devigné* (1927)

Granger, J., *A Biographical History of England* (1775)

Halifax, Marquis of, *A Character of Charles II; Character of a Trimmer* (1688)

Hamilton, A., *Memoirs of the Comte de Grammont*, ed. G. Goodwin (1903)

Hartmann, C.H., *A Vagabond Duchess* (1927); *Charles II and Madame*, (1934)

Hatton, Viscount, *Correspondence of the Hatton Family, 1601-1704*

Hibbert, C., *The Court at Windsor* (1964)

Home, G., *Epsom* (1901)

Hotson, J., *Commonwealth and Restoration Stage* (1928)

Jameson, A., *Memoirs of the Beauties of the Court of Charles II* (1851)

Jusserand, J.J.A., *French Ambassador at the Court of Charles II* (1892)

Kent, W., *London Worthies* (1949)

Luttrell, N., *Brief Relation of State Affairs* (1857)

MacQueen Pope, W.J., *Theatre Royal, Drury Lane*

Marvell, A., ed. H.M. Margoliouth, *The Poems and Letters* (1927)

Melville, L., *Nell Gwyn* (1923)

Memoirs of the Life of E. Gwinn, anon. see Fairburn (1752)

Morah, P., *The Year of the Restoration* (1960)

Ogg, D., *The Rochester Savile Letters* (1940)

Oldys, W., *Short History of the English Stage* (1741)

Oliver, J.H., *Sir Robert Howard, 1626-98* (1963)

Pelican Guide to English Literature, ed. B. Ford, Vol. IV (1982)

Pepys, S., *Diary* (1962)

Plumptre, E.H., *Life of Thomas Ken* (1885)

Powell, R.H.A., *Medical Topography of Tunbridge Wells* (1846)

Smith, A., *The Lives of the Court Beauties* (1715); *The Court of Venus* (1716)

Soulié, J., *Nell Gwyn* (Paris, 1955)

Steinman, G.S.A., *Memoir of Mrs Myddleton* (1864)

Summers, M., *The Restoration Theatre* (1934); *The Playhouse of Pepys* (1935)

Tighe and Davis, *Annals of Windsor*, Vol. 2

Verney, M.M., *Memoirs of the Verney Family* (1907)

Ward, N., *The London Spy* (1703)

Warbuton, E., *Prince Rupert* (1849)

Williams, H., *Rival Sultanas* (1915)

Wilson, J.H., *Nell Gwyn, Royal Mistress* (1952); *The Court Wits of the Restoration* (1948)

Index